Trail Map: How to Read This Report

- As with *The Internet Report*, we have prepared this report with many audiences in mind. The universes of media, advertising, and technology are merging with the Internet — this report should provide a lexicon for individuals from all areas to understand the dynamics of this new market. It should be used as a reference for identifying risks, rewards, market opportunities, investment ideas, competitive strategies, products, and how advertising on the Internet really works. Since this report was published during the ski season (and in the spirit of extending the analogy we used at the beginning of *The Internet Report*), we offer some trail identifiers to help the reader navigate through it.

Novice — You think *Yahoo!* is something you say at a dude ranch and a browser is someone who window-shops:

Read the Overview and Chapters 1 through 14.

Intermediate — For those familiar with the media and advertising biz (you speak in CPM), but want some more in-depth information on technology and the Internet (you think bandwidth is a measurement for boxer shorts):

Read the Overview, Chapters 1, 2, 4, 5, 6, 8, 10, and 14, and browse 3, 7, 9, and 12.

Expert — For those who are savvy about the Internet and high technology (you can write your own HTML), but need some background on media (you think "effective reach" is a metric for Mike Tyson):

Read the Overview, Chapters 1, 2, 3, 5, 6, 8, 9, 10, 13 and 14, and browse 5, 7, 11, and 12.

Double Diamond — If Bill Gates and Ted Turner call you for strategic advice, but you want to understand the underlying strategies of this new market:

Read the Overview, Chapters 1 and 2, and browse 3, 5, and 8.

Note: For industry-specific terms and phrases, it may be helpful to refer to the Glossary we have provided in Chapter 11.

the Internet Advertising Report

the Internet Advertising Report

Mary Meeker

HarperBusiness

A Division of HarperCollinsPublishers

HarperCollins books may be purchased for educational, business, or sales promotional use. For information please write: Special Markets Department, HarperCollins Publishers, Inc., 10 East 53rd Street, New York, NY 10022.

FIRST EDITION

ISBN 0-88730-882-1

97 98 99 00 01 ❖/CWO 10 9 8 7 6 5 4 3 2 1

The Internet Advertising Report — Table of Contents

Acknowledgments

A report of this scope would not have been possible without a lot of hard work and support from many people.

Just one year ago, HarperCollins took a flyer and published Morgan Stanley's "The Internet Report," one of the first Wall Street research reports ever published as a book. It was a success, appearing on a few best-seller lists, including one compiled by Internet-commerce pioneer Amazon.com. My co-authors on that report, Chris DePuy and Samantha McCuen, and I dubbed ourselves "accidental authors." We never considered that there might be a sequel.

The impetus for writing "The Internet Report" came from our sense that the Internet was evolving faster than any other new technology we know of, and that normal beings and investors (along with Wall Street analysts) were having a tough time coping with the pace of change. Quite frankly, we were compelled to put most of what we knew about the Internet on paper (and in digital format) by our desire to slow the volume of Internet-related phone calls and e-mail we were receiving.

If anything, the volume of phone calls and e-mail only surged since "The Internet Report" was published. So has the pace of change in the Internet arena. In fact, the problems and issues surrounding the Internet have grown like kudzu. One of the biggest could be put this way: "It's easy to lose money on the Internet, but how does one make money on the Internet?"

Many pioneers believe that the Internet will evolve as other media have (newspapers, magazines, radio, and television), and that advertising will play a major role in the development of this new medium. We concur. However, we discovered some deep misperceptions among technologists, media people, and everyone else about how the Internet and advertising work together. We wrote "The Internet Advertising Report" to define the terminology, shed light on the subject of the Internet and advertising, and even to figure out some stuff ourselves!

In writing this book, I've relied on various media reports and sources. But I've also been able to tap some great sources closer to home, including Morgan Stanley analysts Doug Arthur (Publishing), Rich Bilotti (Cable Television), Frank Bodenchak (Broadcasting), Michael Russell (Advertising), and Chris DePuy (Data Networking and Internet Infrastructure). Doug was particularly helpful in augmenting the report. Gillian Munson, Ramsay Gayner, and Leo Bernstein provided invaluable assistance and feedback. Mayree Clark, Phil Friedman, George Kelly, Joe Perella, and Terry Meguid were key advocates in committing the resources needed for this project.

Morgan Stanley's Technology and Media investment banking teams have been critical in helping to uncover emerging companies in all areas of technology, most recently those related to the Internet. Drew Guevara, Rex Golding, Mike Grimes, Jeff Sine, Francis Barker, Ruth Porat, Jim Liang, Chris Pasko, Mark Menell, and Derek Harrar were particularly helpful with their contributions to "The Internet Advertising Report."

Once again, our crack technology-loving editorial team of Fred Miller and Andy McCann operated in the zone to whip this report into shape. And our graphics/publishing and printing teams, including Claudette Bell (along with Giovanna Marcone, Dana Salley, and Mariella Talleyrand) and Jeff Pellet, wrapped it all up.

I would like particularly to acknowledge the contributions of Russ Grandinetti, who did a major chunk of the core work for this project. Without him, this report couldn't have been published. Russ was "Mr. All Night and Mr. All Day."

Finally, there is a large cast of non-Morgan Stanley characters, including technology/media/Internet pioneers, experts, advisers, and friends, who shared loads of invaluable insights that made their way into this report. To all of them, again, thanks, and I hope this book does you justice.

Mary Meeker
New York City
February 1997

The Internet Advertising Report

Overview

Background Thoughts

By our math, one Internet year equals three PC years (imagine going from the 386 chip to the Pentium Pro in 12 months!). Just one year ago, we spent a lot of hours describing exactly what an Internet browser did and why it was, well, *cool*. Now, a little over a year later, more than 50 million people are using Netscape's Web browsers. Clearly, we can move from great unknowns to mass consumption very quickly these days. It took the world 15 years to go from fewer than 1 million PC users to 150 million (1980–95) — we estimate that in no more than five years, the number of Internet users will jump from less than 1 million to about 150 million (1995–2000). Since 15 years divided by five years equals three years, one could say that it's kind of a dog's life to live at the Internet's pace.

Following our report of one year ago — Morgan Stanley's "The Internet Report" — we think that enough visibility has developed that we can now more closely examine one of the biggest unknowns in the Internet arena — advertising. In this report, we will try to answer a number of key questions: Will Internet-based advertising work? How big can it be? How much money will companies spend to deliver advertising messages to potential customers? Is there lots of excitement over a lot, or very little? Is the Internet spawning the next mass medium? And, as demand for Internet services continues to surge, what's the likelihood of an Internet bandwidth meltdown, anyway? Based on our review of the development of new media in the past, we conclude that, in time, the opportunity for advertising and direct marketing on the Web will be significant. Even so, there will be fits and starts along the way.

Public Market Proxies for Internet Advertising Trends

In our opinion, there are currently three good public-market proxies for the growth trends in Internet-related advertising: CNET, Yahoo! (which we do not cover), and America Online. Watching these three companies should give investors a good feel for the health and direction of the Internet.

CNET, which went public in July 1996, is the first public company that is a pure play on Internet content. The company generates revenue largely from selling advertising for its Web sites, which focus on technology-related news and information. CNET supported $4.4 million in December-quarter revenue from Internet advertising (up from $393 thousand in the previous year and up 60% on a quarter-to-quarter basis). Traffic (based on average daily page views) grew 55% quarter-to-quarter, to 2.3 million page views per day from 1.5 million in 3Q. CNET had 101 advertisers, up from 75 in 3Q, taking up 65% of available inventory in the period. The CPM (cost per thousand impressions) for CNET.COM remained constant at $75 from 3Q to 4Q.

Yahoo!, a leading search engine and content aggregation site on the Web, went public in April 1996. The company supported $8.6 million in 4Q revenue, all from advertising (up 695% from a year ago and 55% from 3Q). Traffic grew 33% quarter-to-quarter, to 20 million daily page views from 15 million in 3Q. Yahoo! had 550 advertisers, up 62% from 340 in 3Q. We estimate that, based upon its revenues, page views, and CPMs, Yahoo! was able to sell about 25% of available inventory in the quarter. We estimate that the average CPM for Yahoo! in 4Q was $23, about the same as in 3Q.

America Online, a public company since March 1992, is the largest Internet online service, with more than 8 million subscribers. In 4Q the company supported $11.4 million in revenue related to advertising (up 637% year-over-year and 154% quarter-to-quarter). Traffic grew 71% quarter-to-quarter (spurred by AOL's move to unlimited-usage pricing in December) to 158 million page views per day, including content, Internet, main menu, and member services. If we included AOL's People Connection (chat) and mail usage, average 4Q daily page views would have been nearly 284 million. AOL had 157 advertisers, up from 50 in 3Q, taking up 70% of available inventory in the quarter. Average CPM, across various AOL channels/pages, is currently around $45.

As a potential proxy, on an annualized run-rate basis, AOL's advertising business is at a higher run rate than MTV's advertising business was in 1983, and is close to the advertising revenue run rate for the entire cable network industry in 1980. In 1983, MTV generated $25 million in advertising revenue; in 1996, MTV (plus VH-1) garnered over $430 million in ad revenue. We think it's important, as well as symbolic, that AOL recently hired Bob Pittman, an early pioneer in the cable industry (and founder of MTV and Nickelodeon), to run AOL Networks.

For now, we are using advertising trends for CNET, Yahoo!, and America Online to gauge market growth. We like these as proxy companies for several reasons: 1) Based on usage, they are leaders in their spaces — content, search, and online, respectively; 2) they have "skin in the game" — if these companies don't generate revenue from advertising they will have big problems; and 3) general market data in emerging or fragmented markets can be suspect; in other words, we'll take Intel as a proxy for PC unit growth, thank you, and for now we like such companies as CNET and America Online for online/Internet advertising. (In this report, we use the terms "online," "Internet," and "Web" interchangeably, as do most people nowadays, although there are technical differences.)

In aggregate, these three so-called Internet advertising "leaders" generated a puny total of $24 million in Internet-

related advertising revenue in 4Q. Neither AOL nor CNET is running at a profit, although, impressively, Yahoo! did post a very modest profit in 4Q — cash burn for almost all companies in this industry is expected to last for a while — and many advertising-supported Web sites are expected to fail. Heretofore, the advertising model on the Web simply has not worked. Nonetheless, these are early days, and we believe that some big winners in this space will emerge, in time.

An Internet Portfolio

For investors, Morgan Stanley's Internet investment approach continues to focus on a portfolio of companies (Table 1): *Internet infrastructure* companies, such as Cisco (followed by George Kelly and Chris DePuy); *Internet software* companies, such as Netscape and Microsoft; and *Internet content/aggregation* companies, such as America Online (Microsoft also fits here). We believe that rounding out an Internet portfolio with certain emerging companies that rely on *Internet advertising,* such as CNET, makes sense.

We have some observations about this portfolio approach. First, these stocks, in general, have performed well, and we believe any investment in the current stock market is a market call as much as a stock call. Second, Internet advertising is still in the very early stages and, in our opinion, business-model viability (for relevant companies, America Online and CNET) will become clearer in mid-1997. Third, investors in the rapidly emerging, and rapidly changing, Internet space must have a high-risk profile, must be selective, and must be nimble.

Internet Advertising — Small but Mighty

Advertising revenue in the Internet space has been small (Figure 1) but growing rapidly (Figure 2). According to 3Q data from Jupiter Communications' AdSpend report, the annual revenue run-rate for Web advertising is $264 million (in comparison, cable industry ad revenue in 1982 was $230 million and is expected to top $6 billion in 1996). Further, Jupiter estimates that 1996 Internet-based advertising (including online services like America Online and Web-based "push" services) should be over $300 million, up from $55 million in 1995.

While small, the Internet's revenue ramp is fast. It was only about a year and a half ago that crazy little Netscape

Table 1
Morgan Stanley Technology Research Recommended Internet Stock Portfolio

	Price 3/13/97	1997 YTD Return	1996 Return	Mkt. Cap. ($B)	Mkt. Cap./ C1997E Rev.	C1997E P/E
America Online	$44	32%	(11%)	$5.0	2.4	NM
Cisco Systems	52	(18)	71	35.9	4.7	22
CNET	22	(24)	81	0.3	8.0	NM
Microsoft	100	21	88	129.9	106.7	39
Netscape	27	(52)	(18)	2.5	4.5	50
Unweighted Mean		**(15)**	**44**			

America Online, CNET, Microsoft, and Netscape are covered by Mary Meeker. Cisco is covered by George Kelly and Chris DePuy.
E = Morgan Stanley Technology Research Estimate.

supported $14 million in quarterly revenue — the company just printed $115 million in revenue for 4Q96. So, things move quickly in the Internet world. If advertising on the Web works, then it makes sense that it will lag core Internet growth but should, on a relative basis, ramp just as rapidly.

By its very nature, advertising is an inexact science. Companies spend millions of dollars on advertising and advertising research and, when push comes to shove, have a difficult time proving the benefit of the effort. As retailer John Wannamaker once said, "Half the money I spend on advertising is wasted, and the trouble is, I don't know which half." Anyway, ads should be for TVs, radios, newspapers, magazines, envelopes, or towed by planes at the beach, right? Did the Fairchild Eight or Steve Jobs ever envision banner ads floating on PCs in the workplace? Probably not.

So we were a little suspicious about this ad stuff, initially. But our spreadsheets, Internet companies' "forward looking" statements, our Web-weary eyeballs, and our growing number of new media contacts in advertising and corporations have been telling us that the momentum is strong. We like momentum! If past is prologue, when a new medium emerges, advertising opportunities become significant — especially when a new *mass* medium is created.

We define a mass-communications medium as communication from one person or group of persons through a transmitting device (a medium) to a large audience or market. And, in looking at the evolution of other mass media, one can draw corollaries with the early stages of the Internet's development.

We have taken a pass at potential growth rates for Internet advertising (Figure 3). Extrapolating current advertising spending rates per Web user (of $9) to the year 2000 with an estimated 157 million Internet users) implies that Web-related advertising could become a $1.4 billion business in 2000. If we tweak the spending rate per user to $25, we get to $3.9 billion in annual revenue, and it's easy to ramp up the per-user spending. In our opinion, these assumptions may prove to be conservative. For example, the average amount spent in four of the top five mass media is $281 per user annually, so it seems like there could be lots of upside to our Internet estimate. The bottom line, though, is that it's still too early to tell which scenario will play out — although, for now, things are looking good, feeling good, and we are bullish about the growth of advertising on the Web.

Figure 1
1996E Advertising Revenue for Various Media
($ Millions)

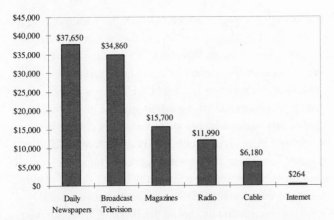

Source: Veronis, Suhler Associates, Paul Kagan Associates, Jupiter Communications. (Internet revenue estimate based on annualized run-rate of industry's 3Q96 revenue of $66 million).

Figure 2
Internet Advertising Revenue Growth by Quarter
($ Millions)

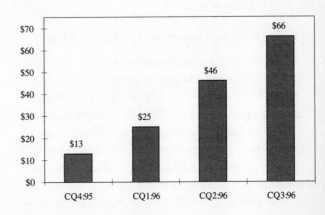

Source: Jupiter Communications.

Figure 3

Estimated Web Users vs. Advertising Revenue, Using Various Steady-State Assumptions, 1995–2000E

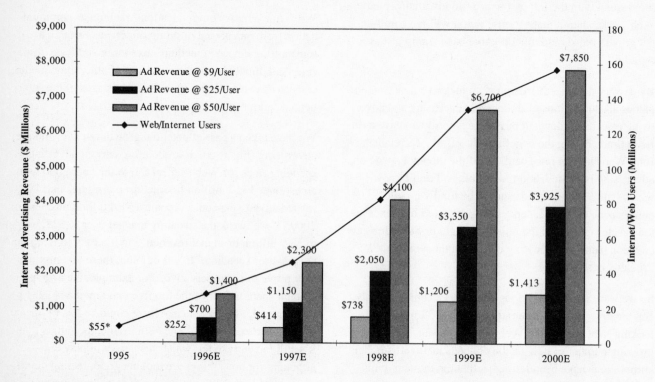

Source: Morgan Stanley Technology Research.
* 1995 contains actual revenue, as reported by Jupiter Communications.
E = Morgan Stanley Technology Research Estimate.

Details of our analysis follow — see pages 2-3 and 2-4. As a sanity check, we have compiled similar historical data for other media (newspapers, magazines, radio, broadcast, and cable TV) in Chapter 9.

Just Give Those Ad-Types Some Eyeballs and Ears

To us, the Internet potentially represents the creation of the greatest, most efficient distribution vehicle in the history of the planet. In time, an e-mail address will be as common as phone numbers are today. History has taught us that changes in the distribution of goods and services create substantial business opportunities for deft companies. With the Internet, which offers ubiquitous points-of-sale, advertising in time will become, in effect, transactions, thus making the total business opportunity created by the Web quite substantial.

Advertisers will buy eyeballs and ears through any conduit or distribution vehicle that delivers a desirable audience — the opportunity to market goods and ideas gets advertisers

stoked. And the direct, interactive marketing capability of the Web is very intriguing to advertisers, compared with the hit-or-miss nature of broadcast marketing.

For example, a master marketer would get a lot more jazzed about putting up a billboard for the hot BMW Z3 roadster convertible in Woodside, Calif., than in Anchorage. However, that same marketer should get even more interested if a Web site (such as CNET, at www.cnet.com) can route advertisements to a demographic group that includes only males who are at least 35 years old, have household incomes in excess of $100,000, live in California, and use Pentium PCs with Netscape Navigator — and then provide that demographic sample with a click-of-the-mouse option to visit BMW's site (www.bmwusa.com), view color animated images of the BMW Z3 roadster, take a virtual test drive (complete with roaring engine), view color options and price packages, and then click to the local dealer's site or to Auto-by-Tel (www.autobytel.com) to inquire about or buy the car at the best price (taking care of any hassles via e-mail). Further, that same marketer could get pretty excited about using agenting technology to find Web users who have expressed interest in BMWs in the past, and sending them HTML-rich e-mail about BMWs.

Here's a great Web marketing story: Cisco, the internet-working company, established a business-to-business commerce area (Cisco Connection Online) on its Web site five months ago and recently indicated that it has generated $75 million in sales to date. These are huge numbers, and the company's products sell at prices ranging from hundreds to hundreds-of-thousands of dollars! Cisco believes its Web-related sales could reach a $1 billion run-rate by July 1997 (upwards of 30% of its total sales). The efficiencies and gross margins that Cisco can achieve through selling on the Web can be pretty sweet — and, yes, it's keeping its customers happy and providing fast response time and round-the-clock service and support.

Advertising on the Web is not just about advertising and distributing messages. It's also about building customer relationships, building "cyber"-brands, providing customer services, generating electronic sales of goods and services, efficiently delivering marketing messages to appropriate audiences, and creating mass customization and interactive/direct marketing.

At the same time, the onus is on the creators of Web sites to deliver audiences (eyeballs and ears) with compelling demographics to advertisers. Web publishers have to create information or content for their sites that will not only add new users but also keep the old ones coming back. Again, advertisers are simply buying space and time to nab eyeballs and ears, just as soap operas were created to sell detergent to housewives doing the ironing in the afternoon, while Monday Night Football was created to sell beer to couch potatoes in the evening. On the Web, one finds ads for Cisco routers on CNET, while the NFL has ads on ESPN SportsZone. Been there, done that? Yep.

In the history of the Web (which generally is said to have been born in March 1993 with the debut of the Mosaic browser), advertising usually has taken the form of banner ads, which emerged in late 1994. Since then, a Web advertising infrastructure has evolved; it includes companies that create ads, buy ads, sell ads, measure ads, and manage ads. Late 1996 marked the time when many advertisers

shifted their Web advertising budgets from experimental status to advertising budget line items, along with magazines, radio, and TV.

Recently, *Advertising Age* indicated that 46 of the 100 top domestic advertising spenders have purchased Web advertising in 1996 and nearly all have corporate Web sites. The biggest issue for advertisers continues to be market size (while 28 million users is a big number, the user "traffic" is very scattered), followed by the compiling of statistics for measurement. Frankly, though, the measurement of advertising efficiency has always been weird science. In our view, the good news/bad news about the Web is that, in time, efficiency tracking and the measurement of computer-generated ads to users will become precise — and this may add to the confusion about the accuracy of "soft" advertising data in other media.

Internet Breakage and Changing Business Models

One of the biggest issues facing the Internet as a whole this year and next is *breakage*. The Internet is overcrowded and capacity-constrained, and it can be trying, even impossible, sometimes to visit one's favorite Web site. Even a "brief" technology meltdown (of Metcalfe-ian proportions), which cannot be ruled out, would likely cause dislocations in the growth for Internet-based advertising. In addition, FCC changes to local access charges could also have a negative impact. However, despite these worries, we believe that the organic demand for Internet services is so significant that the industry will just power through the problems, and what appear to be major dislocations of the moment will, over time, barely appear as blips on the growth charts.

Another issue for the Internet is the impact of *changing business models*. We call many of the first round of Internet firms the Kamikaze companies. The most extreme companies, in our view, are Netscape and America Online. In late 1994, Netscape decided to throw a Hail Mary pass — in a quite unorthodox move, it began to give away its Netscape Navigator browser program for *free* via Web downloads. Within 24 months, Netscape had become the fastest-growing software company in history (based on first-year revenue), garnering in excess of 50 million customers. America Online has burned hundreds of millions in cash in its quest to nab online subscribers — it now has more than

On the Horizon

As Internet advertising ebbs and flows over the next 12–18 months, the key events to look for, in our opinion, include:

- The launch of major Web-site sponsorships by corporate advertisers. Expect some excellent examples on AOL. The likes of Procter & Gamble and General Motors debut innovative Web advertising.

- A rise in the cross-promotion of Web sites in TV, print, and radio.

- An increase in cross-media events, like big TV ad campaigns launched simultaneously with Web events (recent examples are the Olympics, the NCAA College Basketball Tournament, and the Super Bowl).

- Appreciation of the emergence of cyberbrands (such as AOL, MSNBC, CNET, Yahoo!, and Motley Fool) becomes more pronounced.

- Web content continues to improve — more users get hooked and usage rises, with the best sites getting better.

- Improvements in Web-advertising creative — ads become more entertaining and useful. The competitive juices on Madison Avenue start flowing.

- An increase in advertising budgets devoted to online advertising — Web ad spending continues to support strong sequential growth.

- Several major Web publishers go out of business (or are acquired at low prices) due to high cash burn. Business models that work on the Web remain minorities, and Web publishers continue to scramble for new types of Internet revenue streams.

- The best Web sites remain inventory-constrained, subsequently limiting their revenue growth. CPMs rise for the best sites, but fall for the also-ran sites.

- Nielsen ratings continue to indicate that TV viewership, especially for the 18- to 34-year-old demographic, is falling due to rising online usage.

- Concerns about the reliability of Web ad-measurement tools continue to rise. Several major advertisers complain about poor response rates on the Web. Management tools/metrics improve.

- The impact of ad "filtering" software on ad delivery becomes a growing issue for Web publishers and advertisers.

- Complaints about Internet/online system breakage (slow response time and disconnects) continue to nag the industry.

- Online evolution analogies with cable become clearer (like the emergence of brands, channels, and networks), and the opportunity for direct marketing on the Web is supported by strong revenue growth from related companies.

- Web commerce companies, like Amazon.com and Cisco Connection Online, continue to show strong revenue growth.

- Mid-1997 (2Q–3Q) becomes a critical juncture for Internet advertisers — what is working and what is not working will be clearer.

- Post-Christmas Web-shopping data from the likes of www.llbean.com provide useful insights into consumer Internet buying patterns.

- Audio and chat begin to play an important role in Internet advertising and marketing.

8 million customers, who pay on average $17 per month for an annual revenue run rate of $1.6 billion. Not bad, although the company's still burning cash.

The good news and bad news here is that being reckless or aggressive can be great for Internet companies, or awful! Changing business models, driven by Web-related trends, have caused companies to commit unnatural acts — like giving away products and sucking up increasing costs to fortify user bases — in the hope that, ultimately, customers will pay for the products or advertisers will support ongoing business efforts.

By Macromedia's own estimates, it has had 20 million downloads of its Shockwave product but no direct revenue to show for it. Despite having an awesome brand and a hugely successful magazine, investors balked at *Wired* magazine's online-related cash burn. Intuit has reorganized and increased operating expenses in an attempt to tap the opportunity for Web-based financial services — a business that the company believes may not turn a profit for three years.

Our point here is simple: If advertising and transaction revenues on the Web don't ramp nicely, then lots more cash will be burned than generated — for lots of companies that appear to be strategically well positioned. It's noteworthy that in the magazine business, start-ups typically burn cash for three years and make-or-break in year three. In summary, the jury is still out on whether lots of Web sites can become financially viable through advertising support, but we believe that a select few will benefit from impressive traffic and eventually become quite successful.

Onward with the Report

In this report, we attempt to describe the trends, the terminology, and the outlook for Internet-based advertising. To update what we said in *The Internet Report*, in December 1995: "Two things are certain: Growth will be significant (in fits and starts) and investors will vacillate between riding the growth wave and worrying about risk/reward and valuations; and companies, strategies, and the very structure of the market will change rapidly. When we first set out to write this report, we wanted it to answer all the questions about [advertising on] the Internet. The goal was impossible to achieve; by its very nature the Internet is chaotic and can only be described clearly in hindsight. Consider this report our puck on the ice at the beginning of a very long game."

For the purposes of our discussion, we have limited our analysis almost exclusively to the U.S. However, since about 40% of Web usage is outside the U.S., the worldwide business opportunity should be significant. For now, though, all of the highest-traffic sites are U.S.-based, as are most Internet advertisers.

Note: All Web page addresses in this report are simplified. For example, Microsoft's site would be listed as www.microsoft.com (which will work just fine with the latest versions of Netscape Navigator and Internet Explorer), rather than the more technically correct http://www.microsoft.com/.

Our outline for this report is as follows:

1) Assess the potential of the Internet as an advertising medium.
2) Who buys and sells Internet advertising?
3) Where are advertising dollars spent in traditional media? What's the value of an eye? Of an ear?
4) An update on Internet usage trends/forecasts.
5) The latest and greatest from some of the hottest Web sites.
6) Buzzword mania — the nuts and bolts of Internet advertising.
7) The whys and hows of advertising measurement.
8) How companies can succeed in Internet advertising.
9) A look at the histories of traditional media.
10) Emerging companies in the Internet advertising space.
11) A glossary of Internet advertising terms.
12) A time line history of Internet advertising.
13) Advertising data.
14) Rate card data.

Chapter Summaries

Like *The Internet Report*, this document is a beast to read, so for the tired, the weary, and the sane, we offer the summary points from each chapter in the following pages:

Chapter 1: Assessing The Potential of the Internet as an Advertising Medium

♦ We believe that **Internet usage will continue to ramp** (it's a secular thing) and that **Internet-based advertising/marketing spending will continue to rise from a very low, early stage base.** This ramp in usage and ad support will not likely be smooth, as concerns related to bandwidth constraints, still relatively high PC costs, market-size confusion (consumer versus corporate users), and effective advertising asset allocation and measurement will ebb and flow.

♦ However, we posit that, in time, the **Internet could prove to be the next mass medium** and that users will embrace it, on a relative basis, faster than prior media (newspapers, magazines, radio, broadcast television, and cable television). So far, they already have. For now, though, the Internet's user base of an estimated 20–35 million pales in size compared with the "mass" media, which have hundreds of millions of users. But the base of PC users (nearly 165 million) bodes well for a rapid Internet ramp.

♦ **Advertising on the Web is not just about advertising and distributing messages. It's also about building customer relationships, building "cyber" brands, providing customer services, generating electronic sales of goods and services, efficiently delivering marketing messages to appropriate audiences, and creating mass customization and interactive/direct marketing.** The advertising opportunity on the Web is very different than it is for other media. Internet advertising is more robust than radio or television advertising. Through the Internet, users can receive very specialized information, offered in an intriguing way, with new and rich measurement opportunities (as good as direct mail, but without waiting for the post office).

♦ The **benefits of obtaining information and entertainment via the Internet** (such as interactive information when you want it, where you want it) **are just too compelling** (especially for the well-trained Generation X audience) **when compared with traditional media.** And if past is prologue, advertisers will find it tough to resist the opportunity to nab new eyeballs — that's what they exist to do.

♦ The trends in the evolution of traditional media indicate that there may be **similarities between the evolution of cable television programming and the Internet.** Successful media companies on the Internet will likely be those that build the best brands, "channel" expertise, and drive revenue from advertising and premium pricing models — America Online appears to be very well positioned here (the near-term trick will be for AOL to figure out how to generate positive cash flow, given its recent price changes). But it's important to note that many companies that attempt to use this model will likely fail, and consolidation will likely ensue.

♦ As new media have evolved, there have been several pervasive themes in their development: 1) **New technologies/changes** create new media opportunities and secular media changes; 2) **young visionaries** who understand all dynamics of the media (market, technology, and business) take huge bets and drive the new industries forward; 3) content drivers in new media can vary, but in time focus on the same themes; 4) as new media develop, **massive new franchises/brands and wealth are created;** 5) **advertising pays for a large chunk of the operating costs** for mass media; 6) **new talent/celebrities/brands** drive the success of new media acceptance; and 7) over time, **media properties are consolidated** and the best operations survive.

Chapter 2: Internet Advertising — Where the Money Is Today, Where It Might Be Tomorrow

◆ **The biggest advertisers on the Internet were also the biggest recipients of advertising revenue.** And in 3Q96, the **ten highest-grossing revenue sites accounted for 56% of total Web ad revenue.** As one might expect, the most trafficked sites on the Internet generate the highest advertising revenue.

◆ **As online media become more established, and more "eyeballs" start moving online, we look for the time spent per person online to also rise significantly.**

◆ Jupiter Communications estimates that **$13 million in Web-based ad revenue was generated in 4Q95, $24 million in 1Q96, $43 million in 2Q96, and $66 million in 3Q96.** That's an average of 72% **sequential growth.**

◆ **Extrapolating the current advertising spending rate per Web user (of $9) out to the year 2000** (with an estimated 157 million Internet users) implies that **Web-related advertising spending/revenue could be a $1.4 billion business in 2000,** up from a current estimated run-rate of $264 million (implying compounded annual revenue growth of 52%). But, it's reasonable to assume that ad spending on a per user basis will rise as the medium grows and becomes better understood, so that **$1.4 billion number could prove to be quite conservative.** We present other, more aggressive, assumptions in this chapter.

◆ **There is an inventory paradox on the Web.** While there is an enormous amount of available inventory on the Web in aggregate, the highest traffic sites have a limited amount of high-traffic inventory. This paradox can govern revenue growth for the Web in aggregate by keeping CPMs low and for the highest traffic sites in particular by keeping CPMs high, but with limited space.

◆ This chapter also takes a look at some of the hot online channels.

Chapter 3: Where Are Advertising Dollars Spent in Traditional Media? What's the Value of an Eyeball or an Ear?

◆ **Media usage is staggeringly high, and advertising support of media has been, and should continue to be, the major component of media company revenue streams.**

◆ In 1995, the average American watched TV for 1,575 hours, read newspapers for 165 hours, and used consumer online and Internet services for 7 hours (average use for an America Online user is 100 hours per year and rising — this is active use, as opposed to the passive use of other media). And the number of Internet users (estimated at 7% of the U.S. population and 0.4% of the worldwide population) is still quite small compared with the audiences for mass media.

◆ **Domestic annual measured media advertising spending (including television, radio, daily newspapers, and magazines) was $100 billion in 1995** (broadcast television accounted for 32% of the total; cable television, 5%; daily newspapers, 37%; magazines, 15%; and radio, 11%).

◆ **Broadcast television and broadcast radio are 100% funded by advertising,** while 80% of newspaper revenue, 50% of cable network revenue, and 63% of magazine industry revenue are derived from advertising.

◆ **To date, advertising revenue in the Internet space has been small (but growing rapidly), and, according to Jupiter/AdSpend's 3Q results, the annual revenue run-rate for Web advertising revenue is $264 million.** Jupiter/AdSpend also notes that 1996 Internet-based advertising should be nearly $311 million, up from $55 million in 1995. Our bet is that, in time, successful Internet sites will support significant advertising revenue, and that the interactive nature of the Web could assist the rollout of transaction-based revenue and point-of-purchase sales for Web sites.

◆ **Traditional media buying has been based on CPMs (cost-per-thousand impressions).** So far, this model has been the standard advertising rate card pricing tool for Web sites. **While CPMs on the Web vary widely, on average they have been at higher levels than they are in most other media** due to: 1) the lack of accurate measurement of a potentially desirable Web audience; 2) the focused nature of Web advertisers (for now, mostly Internet, technology, and telecommunications companies); 3) the small supply of highly trafficked Web sites; and, to some degree, 4) the experimental nature (and relatively small size) of Internet ad budgets to date, which may be less price-sensitive at this stage. It is possible that direct-marketing nature of the Web could continue to put upward pressure on CPMs for the hottest Web sites.

One of the biggest problems that hot Web sites deal with is the creation of high-quality inventory — while millions of Internet users may come to the "front door" (a great place for ads and high CPMs), once users go through the door, they have sometimes thousands of different potential routes — subsequently, user traffic levels spread and diminish quickly, thus limiting high-traffic inventory on even the highest traffic sites.

◆ **Growth in Internet advertising may affect advertising growth in other media.**

Chapter 4: An Update on Internet Usage Trends/Forecasts

◆ **The Internet is growing at an unprecedented pace**, and, for now, most market data are suspect. There are numbers that seem solid, like the 8 million-plus America Online users (largely consumers) and the 50 million users of Netscape Navigator (although Netscape believes that 80% of those users are Intranet users, and frequency of usage "beyond the firewall" is tough to predict).

◆ We believe there **are currently 20–35 million Internet users (our point estimate for the end of 1996 is 28 million).** That's a huge range, but big at both ends, nonetheless, and it's especially compelling since we believe there were only about 8 million users one year ago. These users are a mix of both business people and consumers.

◆ We project **compounded annual growth in Internet users for the next four years of 54%,** and we believe that **more than 150 million people will use the Internet by the year 2000** — in fact, this assumption may be conservative, since there are already 150–200 million PC users worldwide.

◆ **Web demographics are compelling for marketers.**

Chapter 5: The Latest and Greatest from Some of the Hottest Web Sites

◆ In this section, we show **examples of how various content providers are approaching their online content offerings, in the hopes of gaining traffic/users, luring advertisers, and generating revenue in other ways.**

Chapter 6: Buzzword Mania — The Nuts and Bolts of Internet Advertising

◆ In this section we describe **the current offerings of the ever-changing array of Internet advertising products/methods,** including banner ads (the "billboards of the information superhighway"), buttons, key words, portals, hot corners, "offline" ads, sponsored content, targeted direct mail, and pay-per lead.

◆ We also discuss **the current state of, and potential for, other revenue models for the Web related to transactions and subscriptions.**

◆ In a new medium, there is a natural tendency initially to adopt the business models of those media that have preceded it (i.e., the traditional CPM model). **No doubt, Internet advertising dynamics/methods will change — Netizens are already calling for the "death of the banner" ad. The bottom line is that we think advertisers will shift spending to where they can find the best advertising/marketing value and get the most bang for the buck; agencies will strive to change or improve their**

offerings to make advertisers happy; and Web content providers will scramble to provide relevant demographics to advertisers. As technologies improve, the very nature of Internet advertising should change, too. We believe that America Online, thanks to its current features of the service (plus upcoming rollouts for members like streaming media, new offline technology, and AOL Phone), will be a hotbed for innovation in online advertising.

Chapter 7: The Whys and Hows of Advertising Measurement

◆ **The principal element that drives advertising in all media is ratings.** And each medium uses a different unit to judge viewership.

◆ **Advertisers will not be totally comfortable advertising on the Web until confidence builds that Web advertising measurement is accurate and auditable by a reliable third party in a "Nielsen-like" way.** This relates to accurate information and tracking of site traffic and activity, advertisement delivery accuracy, and user response. Scores of new companies are emerging to create solutions for these problems.

◆ **The power of ratings was evident in the recent skirmish between TV broadcasters and Nielsen Media Research. Nielsen claims that TV lost viewers this fall, especially those in the 18-to-34-year-old demographic, to, yes, other pursuits, like online services and the Web.** The TV networks claim that the Nielsen ratings, which they have relied on for years to gauge viewership and revenue, are now unreliable and suspect — NBC and Fox are considering lawsuits against Nielsen, and the six commercial-broadcast networks could end up owing advertisers something like $100 million for lost airtime. Meanwhile, the FCC has launched an investigation of the issue. We don't have all the facts here, but we do know that America Online alone has seven million-plus subscribers (93% of whom are in the U.S., or 3% of U.S. households), who pay AOL an average of $17 or more per month and, on average, use the service for eight hours per month. So, our instincts tell us that Nielsen is on to something. Coopers & Lybrand recently reported that 58% of Internet users indicate that their online time comes at the expense of watching television.

Chapter 8: How Companies Can Succeed in Internet Advertising

◆ Given the potential size of the opportunity for advertising on the Web, we think **companies that want to be successful in the Internet ad game need to prove there is a business model that works, determine growth factors, provide good feedback to advertisers, and make the right friends.**

Chapter 9: A Look at the Histories of Traditional Media. Yes, Been There ... Done That ...

◆ In a sentence: Been there, done that. **There have been five major media that have developed in the U.S. since the Pilgrims landed at Plymouth Rock. And while we haven't spent a lot of time trying to figure out if Steve Case was separated at intellectual birth from Ben Franklin or William Paley, we think a few key points (articulated in Chapter 3) can be gleaned from a little journey through time to look at the evolutions of newspapers, magazines, radio, broadcast TV, and cable TV. And, yes, we conclude: Been there, done that.** In this chapter, we devote snippets of air time to five media time capsules.

◆ Our conclusions and analogies? In **Newspapers,** it's easy to say that Will Hearst (of @Home Networks) was "separated at birth" from William Randolph Hearst (of The Hearst Corporation); in **Magazines,** Steve Case (America Online) was separated at birth from Henry Luce (*Time* magazine); in **Broadcast TV,** Marc Andreessen (Netscape) was separated at birth from David Sarnoff (American Marconi/RCA/NBC), while Halsey Minor (CNET) was separated at birth from William Paley (CBS), David and Tom Gardner (The Motley Fool) were separated at birth from Chet Huntley and David Brinkley (NBC's "The Huntley-Brinkley Report"), and Ted Leonsis (AOL) was separated at birth from Brandon Tartikoff (NBC); in **Cable TV,** Steve Case was again separated at birth from a unique combination of John Malone (TCI) and Ted Turner (Turner Broadcasting), and, in the easiest call, Bob Pittman (AOL) was separated at birth from himself, Bob Pittman (MTV). Finally, Bill Gates (Microsoft) may end up being separated at birth from all of the above.

◆ The good news? We don't yet know who was separated at birth from Elsie the Cow, Captain Kangaroo, Mister Magoo, and Doris Day (much to our surprise, Martha Stewart doesn't have a Web site yet). And we can't wait to figure out who was separated at birth from George Burns and Gracie Allen.

Chapter 10: Emerging Companies in the Internet Ad Space

◆ There are **many existing and emerging companies, both public and private, capitalizing on the rapid growth of advertising on the Web.**

◆ We have identified four unique Internet market subsegments, comprising four major categories (besides the companies that create and operate Internet sites that are funded, in whole or in part, by advertising dollars):

1. **Advertising Agencies and Web Site Developers** — Companies involved in the generation of Internet advertising campaigns, from campaign planning to media buying, as well as developers of sites that allow companies to promote their brands and develop an online consumer presence. Since advertising is essentially the promotion of the company and its products and services, on the Web this is achieved either through buying advertising space at other sites or through simply designing a site that serves the same purpose.

2. **Market Research Providers** — In such a new field, advertisers, publishers, investors, and other interested parties are all looking for real data about what's happening, how big it is, and where it's going. These are companies that are tracking the evolution of Internet technology with a focus on its impact on business and certain industries, including the Web advertising arena.

3. **Traffic Measurement and Analysis Companies** — To validate advertising media buys on the Internet, advertisers need to be able to justify and verify the investments they make. These companies fill that need by offering software and services to aid publishers in tracking traffic and executing advertising delivery on their Web sites.

4. **Networks/Rep Firms** — These companies provide value-added services for Web advertisers and publishers alike, by brokering the distribution of advertisements and overseeing their delivery.

5. **Order Processing and Support** — Companies that provide outsourcing services to Internet publishers and service providers.

Table 2
Public Internet Companies

	Ticker	Offer Date	Split Adjusted IPO Price	Price 3/13/97	Discount/ Premium % to IPO	52 Week High	52 Week Low	Discount/ Premium % to the 52-Wk High	Low	Current S/O(MM)	Current Mkt. Cap. ($ MM)
Infrastructure											
Data Networking/Telecommunication Equipment											
Ascend	ASND	5/12/94	2	57	2,756	80	38	(29)	49	128	7,296
Cascade	CSCC	7/28/94	3	29	1,050	91	25	(68)	17	99	2,871
Cisco	CSCO	2/1/90	1	52	5,100	76	41	(31)	28	676	35,152
US Robotics	USRX	10/1/91	4	59	1,593	106	46	(44)	29	96	5,664
							Avg	*(43)*	*31*	*Total*	*50,983*
Internet Security Equipment and Software											
Axent Technologies	AXNT	4/24/96	14	14	0	24	9	(42)	49	10	140
Check Point Software	CHKPF	6/28/96	14	20	42	36	13	(45)	50	33	660
CyberGuard (1)(2)(3)	CYBG	10/7/94	3	11	254	25	7	(58)	52	7	77
Cylink	CYLK	2/15/96	15	10	(34)	25	9	(60)	13	25	250
Dr. Solomon's	SOLLY	11/26/96	17	25	48	28	17	(9)	52	18	450
Milkyway (CN)	MKY-T	7/2/96	10	4	(63)	14	3	(74)	9	9	36
Raptor	RAPT	2/6/96	15	14	(4)	39	13	(63)	13	13	182
Secure Computing	SCUR	11/17/95	16	7	(57)	38	6	(82)	22	15	105
Security Dynamics	SDTI	12/13/94	4	23	484	55	23	(57)	3	34	782
Trusted Info Sys.	TISX	10/9/96	13	15	15	18	10	(18)	52	11	165
V-One	VONE	10/23/96	5	6	23	9	4	(34)	44	13	78
Vasco Data Security	VASC-U	8/10/90	0	5	8,547	11	3	(51)	69	16	80
							Avg	*(49)*	*36*	*Total*	*3,005*
Internet Service Providers											
BBN Planet/BBN Corp. (4)	BBN	1970s	N/M	20	-	31	16	(36)	29	21	420
Digex	DIGX	10/17/96	10	11	4	13	10	(18)	5	11	121
Earthlink	ELNK	1/22/97	13	11	(17)	23	10	(52)	5	9	99
Hookup Communications (CN) *	HU-T	3/25/96	8	1	(91)	7	1	(91)	1	7	7
ID Internet Direct (CN) (5)(6) *	IDX-V	2/28/92	0	0	98	2	0	(84)	13	8	0
IDT	IDTC	3/15/96	10	6	(43)	18	5	(67)	7	21	126
iStar Internet Inc.(CN) (7) *	WWW-T	11/27/95	12	3	(77)	9	2	(69)	36	24	72
Metricom	MCOM	5/1/92	6	12	98	20	11	(40)	10	13	156
WorldCom (9)*	WCOM	(10)	N/M	24	-	29	18	(16)	33	866	20,784
MindSpring	MSPG	3/14/96	8	8	3	13	5	(37)	57	7	56
Netcom	NETC	12/15/94	13	9	(32)	45	9	(80)	0	12	108
OzEmail	OZEMY	5/28/96	14	8	(43)	17	6	(53)	33	10	80
PSINet	PSIX	5/1/95	12	7	(42)	19	7	(64)	3	40	280
Rocky Mountain Internet	RMII	9/5/96	4	2	(39)	3	1	(32)	113	4	8
Startronix	STNX	7/7/86	5	0	(92)	2	0	(82)	177	15	0
							Avg (9)	*(57)*	*35*	*Total (9)*	*1,355*
Total for Infrastructure (9)							*Avg*	*(51)*	*35*	*Total*	*55,343*
Software and Services											
Application Software											
Accent Software	ACNTF	7/21/95	5	3	(39)	35	3	(92)	7	12	36
ForeFront	FFGI	12/20/95	8	4	(45)	22	4	(80)	17	6	24
FTP Software	FTPS	12/16/93	5	7	50	14	5	(53)	38	34	238
MetaTools	MTLS	12/12/95	18	13	(26)	41	11	(67)	24	12	156
Microsoft (9)*	MSFT	3/13/86	1	100	16,504	104	49	(4)	104	1,304	130,400
NetManage	NETM	9/20/93	4	4	(2)	19	4	(79)	4	43	172
Netscape	NSCP	8/8/95	14	27	96	75	26	(64)	7	91	2,457
Spyglass	SPYG	6/27/95	9	9	(6)	35	8	(76)	3	12	108
VocalTec	VOCLF	2/6/96	19	7	(64)	14	4	(52)	77	9	63
Voxware	VOXW	10/30/96	8	5	(33)	9	2	(43)	150	12	60
							Avg (9)	*(67)*	*36*	*Total (9)*	*3,314*
Enterprise and Related Software											
Business Objects	BOBJY	9/23/94	18	9	(46)	56	9	(83)	9	16	144
Verity	VRTY	10/6/95	12	8	(32)	41	7	(80)	10	11	88
Open Text	OTEXF	1/23/96	15	9	(42)	17	4	(47)	112	17	153
Versant	VSNT	7/18/96	8	10	25	28	8	(65)	25	9	90
Visigenic	VSGN	8/8/96	8	10	27	18	8	(48)	23	14	140
							Avg	*(65)*	*36*	*Total*	*615*

Sources: Bloomberg, Securities Data Corp., NASDAQ Stock Market, FactSet Data, latest quarterly report, prospectus, and Morgan Stanley

Table 2 *(continued)*

Public Internet Companies

	Ticker	Offer Date	Split Adjusted IPO Price	Price 3/13/97	Discount/ Premium % to IPO	52 Week High	52 Week Low	Discount/ Premium % to the 52-Wk High	Discount/ Premium % to the 52-Wk Low	Current S/O(MM)	Current Mkt. Cap. ($ MM)
Commerce Enablers											
Broadvision	BVSN	6/20/96	7	9	27	10	5	(14)	69	20	180
Connect	CNKT	8/14/96	6	4	(31)	10	4	(59)	0	19	76
Cybercash	CYCH	2/15/96	17	15	(11)	65	12	(77)	23	11	165
Edify	EDFY	5/2/96	15	11	(28)	56	10	(81)	6	16	176
OneWave	OWAV	7/1/96	16	2	(86)	22	2	(89)	9	15	30
Open Market	OMKT	5/22/96	18	10	(43)	42	10	(76)	6	28	280
Premenos	PRMO	9/19/95	18	7	(56)	26	7	(73)	6	11	77
							Avg	(67)	17	*Total*	984
Internet/Online Consulting and Development											
CKS Group	CKSG	12/14/95	17	29	70	45	18	(36)	60	13	377
Eagle River Interactive	ERIV	3/21/96	13	10	(22)	23	5	(55)	103	13	130
The Leap Group	LEAP	9/27/96	10	7	(29)	11	5	(32)	36	14	98
							Avg	(123)	199	*Total*	605
Total for Software and Services (9)							*Avg*	*(63)*	*34*	*Total*	*5,518*

Content/Aggregation

	Ticker	Offer Date	Split Adjusted IPO Price	Price 3/13/97	Discount/ Premium % to IPO	52 Week High	52 Week Low	Discount/ Premium % to the 52-Wk High	Discount/ Premium % to the 52-Wk Low	Current S/O(MM)	Current Mkt. Cap. ($ MM)
Organization/Aggregation											
Excite	XCIT	4/3/96	17	15	(15)	22	5	(33)	190	16	240
Infoseek	SEEK	6/11/96	12	7	(39)	17	5	(55)	40	26	182
Lycos	LCOS	4/1/96	16	13	(19)	29	6	(56)	126	14	182
Yahoo!	YHOO	4/14/96	13	23	75	43	16	(47)	47	27	621
							Avg	(48)	101	*Total*	1,225
Online Services/Information Services											
America Online	AOL	3/92	1	44	4,300	71	22	(38)	97	110	4,840
Compuserve	CSRV	4/18/96	30	10	(66)	36	9	(72)	17	93	930
Individual	INDV	3/15/96	14	7	(54)	25	4	(73)	68	14	98
Infonautics	INFO	4/29/96	14	2	(84)	15	2	(85)	0	9	18
M.A.I.D.	MAIDY	11/24/95	15	11	(26)	21	9	(47)	20	23	253
Online Systems	WEBB	5/22/96	7	4	(37)	11	3	(62)	36	3	12
							Avg	(63)	40	*Total*	6,151
Publication/Static											
CMG Information Services	CMGI	1/25/94	8	13	64	43	9	(69)	44	9	117
Mecklermedia	MECK	2/11/94	3	26	767	30	10	(13)	157	8	208
							Avg	(41)	100	*Total*	325
Publication/Interactive											
CNET	CNWK	7/1/96	16	22	38	36	12	(38)	87	13	286
							Avg	(38)	87	*Total*	286
Transaction Processing and Financial Services											
CheckFree	CKFR	9/27/95	18	14	(24)	25	11	(46)	30	54	756
CUC International	CU	11/5/84	1	25	1,668	28	18	(10)	35	397	9,925
CyberCash	CYCH	2/15/96	17	15	(11)	65	12	(77)	23	11	165
E-Trade	EGRP	8/15/96	11	22	106	27	8	(19)	162	30	660
First Virtual	FVHI	12/13/96	9	8	(17)	10	7	(21)	3	10	80
iMall, Inc. (8)	IIML	1/24/96	3	3	2	16	2	(82)	75	57	171
Security First Network Bank	SFNB	5/23/96	20	9	(55)	45	9	(80)	3	8	72
							Avg	(48)	47	*Total*	11,829
Total for Content/Aggregation							*Avg*	*(56)*	*54*	*Total*	*19,816*

	Ticker			Price 3/13/97		52 Week High	52 Week Low	Disc/Prem High	Disc/Prem Low		Mkt. Cap.
Total for all Internet Companies (9)							*Avg*	**(56)**	**42**	**Total**	**80,677**
Amex Internet Index	IIX	--	--	209		279	190	(25)	10		
MS Tech 35	MSH	--	--	371		427	266	(13)	39		

Note: Share data are taken from FactSet, prospectus or latest quarterly report   * Indicates data not included in market cap. figures
(1) On 10/7/94 Harris Computer Systems Corp. was spun off from Harris Corp. and began trading publicly under (NASDAQ: NHWK) on 10/10/94.
(2) The spin-off was in the form of a tax-free stock dividend to holders of Harris Corp.on the basis of one share in the new company for every 20 Harris shares.
(3) On 6/27/96 Harris Computer Systems changed its name to Cyberguard (NASDAQ: CYBG).
(4) BBN Corp. was founded in the 1940s. Its internet business began in 1995   (5) Changed name to ID Internet Direct from Arling, effective December 7, 1995
(6) ID Internet Direct agreed to merge with Montreal based Totalnet Inc. to trade publicy under TotalNet name.
(7) Created by merger of NSTN Incorporated and i*internet Inc. in August 1995
(8) Began trading after merger with Nature's Gift, a previously publicly traded company
(9) Microsoft and WorldCom not included in average discount/premium to 52-week high/low or in market cap. figures   (CN) = Canadian company
(10) WorldCom, formerly LDDS Communications, was a private company until it merger with publicly traded IDB Communications in 1989
Sources: Bloomberg, Securities Data Corp., NASDAQ Stock Market, FactSet Data, latest quarterly report, prospectus, and Morgan Stanley

Chapter 1: Assessing the Potential of the Internet as an Advertising Medium

Summary

◆ We believe that **Internet usage will continue to ramp** (it's a secular thing) and that **Internet-based advertising/marketing spending will continue to rise from a very low, early stage base.** This ramp in usage and ad support will not likely be smooth, as concerns related to bandwidth constraints, still relatively high PC costs, market-size confusion (consumer versus corporate users), and effective advertising asset allocation and measurement will ebb and flow.

◆ However, we posit that, in time, the **Internet could prove to be the next mass medium** and that users will embrace it, on a relative basis, faster than prior media (newspapers, magazines, radio, broadcast television, and cable television). So far, they already have. For now, though, the Internet's user base of an estimated 20–35 million pales in size compared with the "mass" media, which have hundreds of millions of users. But the base of PC users (more than 165 million) bodes well for a rapid Internet ramp.

◆ **Advertising on the Web is not just about advertising and distributing messages. It's also about building customer relationships, building "cyber" brands, providing customer services, generating electronic sales of goods and services, efficiently delivering marketing messages to appropriate audiences, and creating mass customization and interactive/direct marketing.** The advertising opportunity on the Web is very different than it is for other media. Internet advertising is more robust than radio or television advertising. Through the Internet, users can receive very specialized information, offered in an intriguing way, with new and rich measurement opportunities (as good as direct mail, but without waiting for the post office).

◆ The **benefits of obtaining information and entertainment via the Internet** (such as interactive information when you want it, where you want it) **are just too compelling** (especially for the well-trained Generation X audience) **when compared with traditional media.** And if past is prologue, advertisers will find it tough to resist the opportunity to nab new eyeballs — that's what they exist to do.

◆ The trends in the evolution of traditional media indicate that there may be **similarities between the evolution of cable television programming and the Internet.** Successful media companies on the Internet will likely be those that build the best brands, "channel" expertise, and drive revenue from advertising and premium pricing models — America Online appears to be very well positioned here (the near-term trick will be for AOL to figure out how to generate positive cash flow, given its recent price changes). But it's important to note that many companies that attempt to use this model will likely fail, and consolidation will likely ensue.

◆ As new media have evolved, there have been several pervasive themes in their development: 1) **New technologies/changes** create new media opportunities and secular media changes; 2) **young visionaries** who understand all dynamics of the media (market, technology, and business) take huge bets and drive the new industries forward; 3) content drivers in new media can vary, but in time focus on the same themes; 4) as new media develop, **massive new franchises/brands and wealth are created;** 5) **advertising pays for a large chunk of the operating costs** for mass media; 6) **new talent/celebrities/brands** drive the success of new media acceptance; and 7) over time, **media properties are consolidated** and the best operations survive.

A Quick Backgrounder on Ad-Supported Media

New media tend to emerge in patterns. First, early adopters and experimenters try the new stuff; then, if acceptance ensues, thousands of business people flock to join in, creating a gold-rush mentality. Business failures and successes follow, and over time a few powerful franchises develop, such as *The New York Times*, *The Los Angeles Times*, and *The Washington Post* in newspapers; Time Warner and Meredith in magazines; Westinghouse/CBS/Infinity, Clear Channel Communications, and Evergreen Media in radio; ABC, CBS, NBC, and Fox in broadcast television; Cox, Tele-Communications, Inc., and Time Warner in cable-TV; and America Online in online services. Often, many of these companies are key players in multiple media, and major cross-selling/promotion also occurs.

We have studied the past to help us anticipate the future — and project who the winning media companies on the Internet will be — by tracing the evolution of mass media that are largely advertising supported. In the next few pages we quickly discuss the history of various media; a more extensive discussion can be found in Chapter 9.

Advertising Rules

Most of the $175 billion in annual revenue (according to Veronis, Suhler & Associates) received by American mass media companies is advertising-based. Newspapers, television, and radio are supported by advertising. Magazines and some cable television networks receive more than 50% of revenue from ads, while revenue for companies in the movie, recording, and book businesses is related to direct sales. We note that advertising spending in the U.S. accounts for about 50% of the world's advertising market.

Advertising, in one form or another, has been around for countless years, but its style and delivery mechanisms change over time. Vendors have proven time and again that when a new medium that has the potential to reach the masses develops, they will try to quickly get in the game to find more eyeballs/ears to receive marketing messages — advertising has been essential to the development and proliferation of newspapers, magazines, broadcast radio, broadcast television, and cable television.

The value of advertising is summed up nicely by Agee, Ault, and Emery in their book *Mass Communications:* "Advertising is indelibly woven into the fabric of our soci-

ety. It is credited with raising our standard of living, lowering unit costs of mass-produced goods, providing information, and helping new firms enter the marketplace. Without advertising we would pay far more for most of the mass media that we enjoy."

History Says the 'Next' Medium Always Must Offer Advantages Over the 'Last' Medium

Typically, new media have done some key things "better" than older media. For example, newspapers were better than town criers because the information was recorded; magazines were better than newspapers because they focused on national issues (and had cool pictures); radio was better than magazines because it was live and timely; television was better than radio because it was live, timely, and had cool pictures; and we contend that the Internet is better than television because it provides live, timely, viewable, and often storable information and entertainment when users want it, with the powerful addition of interactivity. While Internet video and images aren't nearly as nice as those on TV, if Andy Grove and Intel have their way, they will be soon: At the recent Comdex convention, Mr. Grove demo'ed a full-screen playback of the film "Twister" on a PC with a P6 using MMX technology. But it wasn't so many years ago that we were standing in a small room in San Jose marveling at jerky, postage-stamp-size video-in-a-window on a computer. Oh, that Moore's Law....

Usually, new media evolutions have initially been gaited by the deployment of appropriate "receivers." The evolution of newspapers was gaited by low literacy levels and high product cost; magazine usage growth was gaited by the same issues, plus high distribution costs; radio and television usage growth was gaited by widespread deployment of high-cost radio and television receivers; cable television usage growth was gaited by the deployment of high-cost coaxial cable; and Internet growth is governed by the high-cost of PCs and the high-cost of high-speed Internet access (although low-speed access is reasonably priced).

Note, however, that one key difference regarding the Internet is that there are something like over 165 million PC users worldwide, and many are lacking only a modem and a Web connection. In effect, the receivers (PCs) and infrastructure (phone lines) already exist — they simply need low-cost upgrades and, in time, increased low-cost bandwidth. And if network computers and Web TVs are successful (with lower relative prices than PCs), these products could also help expand the Internet user base.

For advertisers, each new medium has offered new opportunities — newspapers offered local markets and audiences who were focused on making purchases; magazines offered both a narrower market focus (and thus a more segmented, targeted audience) and larger (even national) audiences; radio delivered real-time information (locally and nationally), replete with the ability to generate powerful creative (the art/design within an advertisement) through sound; and TV added pictures to the sound.

The Internet adds the element of interactivity and the ability to make purchases "in band." It's the only medium where a user can see an ad, inquire about the product/service quickly or in detail, make an immediate purchase, and even save time and money.

Common Themes in the Creation of New Media

As new media have evolved, several pervasive themes in their development have been seen:

1) *New technologies/changes create new media opportunities and secular media changes.* For example, the success of newspapers was assisted by the creation of, and improvements to, the printing press; magazines were aided by improvements in transportation and a reduction in postage costs; and radio and television were created by technological inventions. For the Internet, the fundamental technology change was the introduction of the Web's graphical user interface, Mosaic, to a large base of PC users.

2) *Young visionaries who understand all dynamics of the new media (market, technology, and business) take great leaps and drive the new industries forward.* These visionaries include: Ben Franklin and John Pulitzer in newspapers; Henry Luce in magazines; David Sarnoff in radio; and David Sarnoff, William Paley, and Ted Turner in television. In the online world, early leaders that come to mind include Steve Case of America Online, Marc Andreessen of Netscape, Halsey Minor of CNET, and Jerry Yang and Dave Filo of Yahoo!.

3) *Content drivers in new media can vary, but, in time, they focus on the same themes.* News drove newspapers; education drove magazines; entertainment drove radio and television; movies (HBO) drove cable television; pornography

drove home video; and chat drove online. In time, media offerings cover the gamut: news, weather, sports, entertainment, and so on.

4) *As new media develop, major franchises/brands and wealth are created.* The five largest media companies in the world, Bertelsmann AG (with 1995 annual revenues of $14 billion), The Walt Disney Co. ($12 billion), Viacom Inc. ($12 billion), News Corp. ($9 billion), and Time Warner Inc. ($8 billion), have all benefited significantly from the evolution of new media in the past.

5) *Advertising pays for a large chunk of the operating costs for mass media.* But broad-based skepticism about the benefits of advertising have been prevalent in the early days of every mass medium — and there is a lag between the time a medium reaches mass consumption and the point at which advertising revenue ramps dramatically (Figures 1-1 through 1-13). Low costs for consumers are key to the broad acceptance of a new medium — and advertising helps drive down costs.

6) *New talent, celebrities, and brands drive the success of new media acceptance.* For example, in the U.S.: Edgar Allan Poe, Nathaniel Hawthorne, and Margaret Bourke-White helped popularize magazines; Edward R. Murrow and Jack Benny helped radio; and Milton Berle and Ed Sullivan bolstered television viewership. In our view, early Internet talent is prevalent on sites such as Motley Fool, HotWired, CNET, Slate, and NetGuide.

7) *Over time, media properties are consolidated and the best operations survive.* Media tend to be ruled by oligopolies. Scale is important, and being No. 1 in a market is far more lucrative than being No. 2. In newspapers there is typically one leading paper in each major city. Time Inc. magazines receive about one-third of all magazine advertising. In each of the top 50 radio markets, the top three operators control an average 65% of revenues. Further, the top five radio operators in the U.S. control 20% of the $12 billion-plus industry revenue, and the top 15 control over one-third (34%). In broadcast TV, ABC, CBS, NBC, and Fox rule. In cable television, there is usually one leading brand per category; for example, MTV owns music, ESPN owns sports, and CNN owns news. In the online world, AOL has most of the customers.

In media, a few brands typically lead each category, but a few companies tend to own leading brands across media. We believe that low barriers to entry for generating Internet content initially will allow for many more players to produce content in the same genre. However, given the efficiencies that media buyers derive from purchasing through larger players, the additional power that a strong brand affords them, and the prohibitive cash burn of many of the Internet content providers to date, we expect eventual consolidation of properties and brands for Internet companies as well.

In our view, for now, the companies in the best position to be media consolidators on the Web are America Online and Microsoft — thanks to AOL and Windows, respectively. These companies are in the unique position of being

---

The Historical Precedent for Media Consolidation

"Media coagulates; it doesn't disaggregate."

- Top 25 newspapers account for 88% of all circulation.

- Only 31 magazines generate more than $200 million; Time Inc. represents 30% of advertising market.

- Only four TV networks; two are upstarts.

- Only 20 real cable network brands; only two are generating in excess of $1 billion in revenues.

- Five MSOs with 3 million or more cable customers.

- All cable original-content brands share common characteristics:
  - Associated/owned by distributors/MSOs
  - Own multiple networks for cross-promotion
  - Offer national and local ad buys
  - Rely on multiple revenue streams; no cable network would be profitable relying solely on advertising
  - Even when circulation slows, advertising spending increases
  - Entrepreneurial talent with access to cash

Source: America Online.

"dashboards" and offering simplicity and branding to the Web. And they have the opportunity to generate revenue from multiple sources, including advertising, royalties, merchandising, transactions, and access fees.

High and to the Right:
Growth in Advertising Revenue in Media

McCann-Erickson has a wonderful database of info on the growth of advertising revenue in various media. The following charts, which are based on those data, look like stocks we wish we had owned! What can be learned from these charts? Well, advertising can be a very good thing, and it has grown rapidly with media user growth. Indeed, if Internet usage does scale to the masses, McCann-Erickson may need to add a new ad chart to its collection (see our hypothetical pass at this on pages 4 and 29). It is worth noting that, while these charts don't seem to display growth bumps along the way, such bumps certainly existed! (The data contained in these charts are actual revenue and have not been adjusted for inflation.)In addition, with the exception of cable, advertising growth tended to lag subscriber growth by a wide margin in the early days of evolution of new media. Content came first, followed by subscribers, and only then followed by advertising revenue. Arguably, cable experienced less lag because, by the time it rolled out, advertisers were savvier about the evolution of new media (a positive note for Internet companies). In addition, the measurements and standards for the medium (TV) had already been established and simply had to be applied to the new form. On the flip side, though, the early cable pioneers attest that generating advertising revenue was not nearly as easy as the graphs imply (a sobering note for Internet companies).

Finally, high operating expenses were required to build the infrastructure for radio and television — these builds occurred well before the advertising revenue was generated — not dissimilar to what we see with the Internet today. The good news for the Internet is that the basic infrastructure is in place: PCs, modems, data networking, phone networks, satellites, CATV networks, cash networks, and paging/cellular networks.

Figure 1-1

Adoption Curves for Various Media — The Web Is Ramping Fast

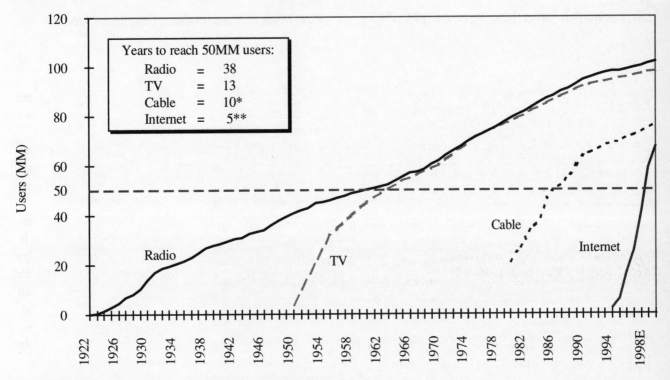

Years to reach 50MM users:		
Radio	=	38
TV	=	13
Cable	=	10*
Internet	=	5**

Source: Morgan Stanley Technology Research. E = Morgan Stanley Research Estimate.
* We use the launch of HBO in 1976 as our estimate for the beginning of cable as an entertainment/advertising medium. Though cable technology was developed in the late 1940's, its initial use was primarily for the improvement of reception in remote areas. It was not until HBO began to distribute its pay-TV movie service via satellite in 1976 that the medium became a distinct content and advertising alternative to broadcast television.
** Morgan Stanley Technology Research Estimate.

Figure 1-1 shows the adoption curves for several key media (radio, TV, cable, and the Internet). Although these numbers are not adjusted for population growth, it is clear to us that the adoption rates for new media have accelerated over time — TV was faster than radio, cable came on even faster (despite the new infrastructure it required that previous broadcast media did not), and we believe that the Internet has surpassed all of these in its rate of adoption. And when adoption of a new medium has been faster, the flow of advertising revenues has increased more quickly.

U.S. Newspapers

Figure 1-1

U.S. Newspaper Advertising Revenue, 1935–95*

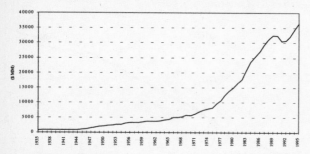

Source: McCann-Erickson.
* Data not adjusted for inflation.

Figure 1-2

U.S. Sunday Newspaper Circulation
Vs. Advertising Revenue, 1946–95*

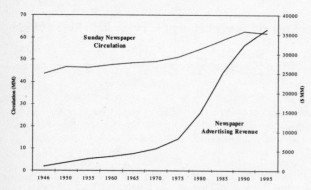

Source: McCann-Erickson, Newspaper Association of America.
* Data not adjusted for inflation.

Figure 1-3

U.S. Newspaper Advertising Revenue
Per Sunday Newspaper Circulated, 1946–95*

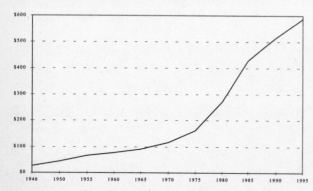

Source: McCann-Erickson, Newspaper Association of America.
* Data not adjusted for inflation.

U.S. Magazines

Figure 1-4

U.S. Magazine Advertising Revenue, 1935–95*

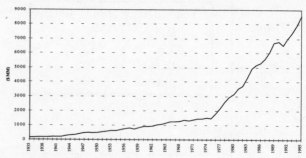

Source: McCann-Erickson.
* Data not adjusted for inflation.

U.S. Radio

Figure 1-5
U.S. Radio Advertising Revenue, 1935–95*

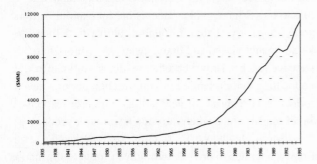

Source: McCann-Erickson.
* Data not adjusted for inflation.

Figure 1-6
U.S. Radio Households (1921–95)
Vs. Advertising Revenue (1935–95)*

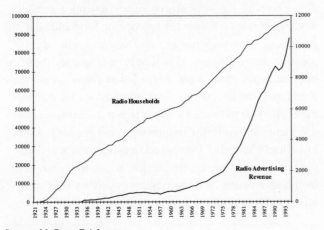

Source: McCann-Erickson.
* Data not adjusted for inflation.

Figure 1-7
U.S. Radio Advertising Revenue
Per Household, 1935–95*

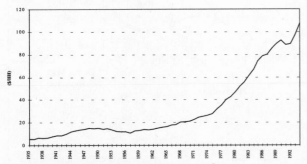

Source: McCann-Erickson, TV Dimensions '96.
* Data not adjusted for inflation.

U.S. Broadcast Television

Figure 1-8
U.S. Broadcast Television Advertising Revenue, 1949–95*

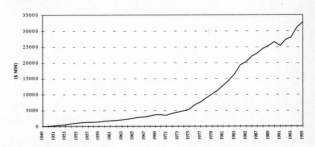

Source: McCann-Erickson.
* Data not adjusted for inflation.

Figure 1-9
U.S. Broadcast Television Households
Vs. Advertising Revenue, 1950–95*

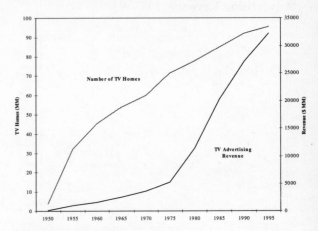

Source: McCann-Erickson, TV Dimensions '96.
* Data not adjusted for inflation.

Figure 1-10
U.S. Broadcast Television Advertising Revenue
Per Household, 1950–95*

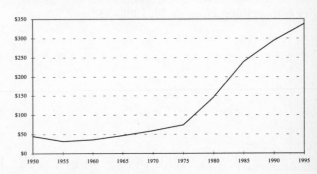

Source: McCann-Erickson, TV Dimensions '96.
* Data not adjusted for inflation.

U.S. Cable Television

Figure 1-11

U.S. Cable Television Advertising Revenue, 1980–95*

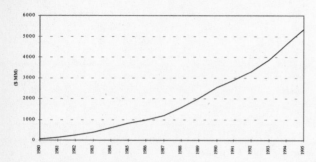

Source: Paul Kagan Associates.
* Data not adjusted for inflation.

Figure 1-12

U.S. Cable Television Households Vs. Advertising Revenue, 1985–95*

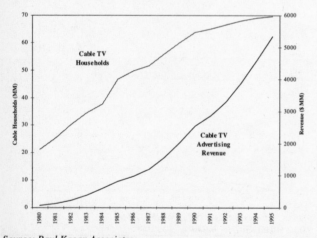

Source: Paul Kagan Associates.
* Data not adjusted for inflation.

Figure 1-13

U.S. Cable Advertising Revenue Per Subscribing Household, 1980–95*

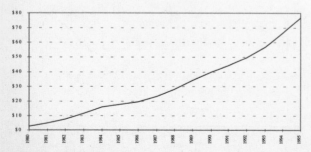

Source: Paul Kagan Associates.
* Data not adjusted for inflation.

Each Medium has Pros and Cons for Advertisers

Advertisers define objectives for their campaigns and then overlay the particular strengths and weaknesses of each medium in deciding which, and how much of each, medium to buy (Figure 1-14). Television, for example, offers strong image advertising (through its ability to deliver life-like audio and video) and brand awareness (through its extensive reach). However, other media are more effective in educating and disseminating information about a new product (such as print) or generating direct user response (direct mail). Thus, when introducing a major product, an advertiser might choose TV to build awareness and a series of newspaper ads to provide additional product information, details on where and how to purchase the product, any promotions or discounts, and the like. Other media can be used to supplement and reinforce these messages, such as outdoor billboard ads or radio.

To accomplish the particular objectives of each campaign, advertisers must consider the appropriate level of reach (the percentage of an audience exposed to at least one ad impression over a give period of time) and frequency (how often each person or home is exposed to a message). Figure 1-15 charts the effectiveness of traditional media in delivering each. Due to limited Internet penetration (relative to TV, radio, and so forth) and the large and growing number of online "channels," Internet advertising cannot yet provide the reach of these other media. It can, however, deliver a high degree of frequency, especially on sites with repeat/habitual users.

Figure 1-14

Advertising Objectives of Various Media

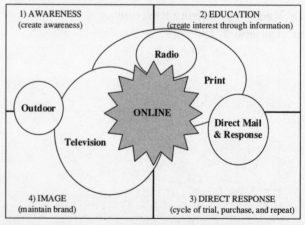

Source: Steve Goldberg, Microsoft Advertising Business Unit.

Although Internet advertising is still new, the medium has several qualities that make it an attractive vehicle for advertisers in achieving their objectives (Figure 1-14 and Table 1-1). It integrates many of the positive advertising elements of major media: visual impact (like TV), with a higher degree of attention from the active (versus passive) viewer with each impression; selectivity and segmentation (like radio and magazines, and it enhances these features with interactive capabilities); quick and accurate measurement; and users can be captured at the most opportune moments (when they are ready to purchase goods or services).

Other advantages for advertisers include: parallel delivery of an ad with the content a user is searching for, like a billboard for a restaurant along a highway (in TV, advertisements are delivered serially with content); continuous and global user access (at no extra cost); the ability to change creative almost immediately; and the opportunity to leverage continuous improvement in Web technology and tools to create compelling, interactive, and tailored ads to increasingly well-defined demographics.

The downside for Internet advertisers relates primarily to the unproven nature of the medium. Everything is in a state of flux. Additionally, the tools, measurements, and standards for the medium have not evolved enough to give advertisers the type of feedback they need to judge the return on their investments. The size of the market is subject to debate, and the means of understanding the reach and frequency of ad delivery are not yet available.

As these tools, methods, and standards mature, and as major advertisers start making sizable commitments to interactive campaigns, the role of advertising agencies, networks, and auditors as intermediaries should also grow. We have already seen the rise of several major players in this area (see our list of the players in the advertising space). We believe these interactive agencies must begin to

Figure 1-15

Reach and Frequency of Traditional Media

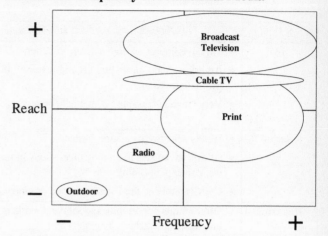

Source: Steve Goldberg, Microsoft Advertising Business Unit.

develop and drive real business models for pricing and delivery.

As the Internet grows, there should be ample room for many companies to grow. However, if, and when, we hit a soft patch in either spending or traffic (or both), companies in this young medium may get crunched. Pricing and total dollars spent may be squeezed, significantly affecting companies with business plans that depend on a continued steep ramp in ad spending. This sector is also vulnerable to a downturn in the economy, as such a cycle would cause advertisers to cut back first in secondary media in their ad budgets, including "experiments," such as Web campaigns.

For now though, all signs look extremely positive for a continued growth in spending. Increasingly, advertisers are coming to realize that Web advertising offers higher awareness of their company, easy methods of information distribution (including speech and video presentations), improved ability to craft company image and brand, an immediate direct line between customers and staff, and reduced costs of performing all of these marketing tasks.

Table 1-1

Selected Advertiser Pros and Cons for the Major Media and the Internet

Medium	Pros for Generating Advertising Revenue	Cons for Generating Advertising Revenue
TV	• Intrusive impact — high awareness getter. • Ability to demonstrate product and feature "slice of life" situations. • Very "merchandisable" with media buyers.	• Ratings fragmenting, rising costs, "clutter." • Heavy "downscale" audience skew. • Time is sold in multi-program packages. Networks often require major up-front commitments. Both limit the advertiser's flexibility.
Radio	• Highly selective by station format. • Allows advertisers to employ time-of-day or time-of-week to exploit timing factors. • Copy can rely on the listener's mood or imagination.	• Audience surveys are limited in scope, do not provide socio-economic demographics. • Difficult to buy with so many stations to consider. • Copy testing is difficult, few statistical guidelines.
Magazines	• Offer unique opportunities to segment markets, demographically and psychographically. • Ads can be studied, reviewed at leisure. High impact can be attained with good graphics and literate, informative copy.	• Reader controls ad exposure, can ignore campaign, especially for new products. • Difficult to exploit "timing" aspects.
Newspapers	• High single-day reach opportunity to exploit immediacy, especially on key shopping days. • Reader often shops for specific information when ready to buy. • Portable format.	• Lack of demographic selectivity, despite increased zoning — many markets have only one paper. • High cost for large-size units. • Presumes lack of creative opportunities for "emotional" selling campaigns. • Low-quality reproduction, lack of color.
Internet	• Internet advertisements are accessed on demand 24 hours a day, 365 days a year, and costs are the same regardless of audience location. • Accessed primarily because of interest in the content, so market segmentation opportunity is large. • Opportunity to create one-to-one direct marketing relationship with consumer. • Multimedia will increasingly make creative more attractive and compelling. • Distribution costs are low (just technology costs), so the millions of consumers reached cost the same as one. • Advertising and content can be updated, supplemented, or changed at any time, and are therefore always up-to-date. Response (click-through rate) and results (page views) of advertising are immediately measurable. • Ease of logical navigation — you click when and where you want, and spend as much time as desired there.	• No clear standard or language of measurement. • Immature measurement tools and metrics. • Although the variety of ad content format and style that the Internet allows can be considered a positive in some respects, it also makes apples-to-apples comparisons difficult for media buyers. • Difficult to measure size of market, therefore difficult to estimate rating, share, or reach and frequency. • Audience is still small.

Source: TV Dimensions '96, Morgan Stanley Technology Research.

Chapter 2: Internet Advertising —
Where the Money Is Today, Where It Might Be Tomorrow

Summary

◆ **The biggest advertisers on the Internet were also the biggest recipients of advertising revenue.** And in 3Q96, the **ten highest-grossing revenue sites accounted for 56% of total Web ad revenue.** As one might expect, the most trafficked sites on the Internet generate the highest advertising revenue.

◆ **As online media become more established, and more "eyeballs" start moving online, we look for the time spent per person online to also rise significantly.**

◆ Jupiter Communications estimates that **$13 million in Web-based ad revenue was generated in 4Q95, $24 million in 1Q96, $43 million in 2Q96, and $66 million in 3Q96.** That's an average of 72% **sequential growth.**

◆ **Extrapolating the current advertising spending rate per Web user (of $9) out to the year 2000** (with an estimated 157 million Internet users) implies that **Web-related advertising spending/revenue could be a $1.4 billion business in 2000,** up from a current estimated run-rate of $264 million (implying compounded annual revenue growth of 52%). But, it's reasonable to assume that ad spending on a per user basis will rise as the medium grows and becomes better understood, so **that $1.4 billion number could prove to be quite conservative.** We present other, more aggressive, assumptions in this chapter.

◆ **There is an inventory paradox on the Web.** While there is an enormous amount of available inventory on the Web in aggregate, the highest traffic sites have a limited amount of high-traffic inventory. This paradox can govern revenue growth for the Web in aggregate by keeping CPMs low and for the highest traffic sites in particular by keeping CPMs high, but with limited space.

◆ This chapter also takes a look at some of the hot online channels.

Advertising — The Big Spenders Spend the Big Bucks

The biggest advertisers in the U.S. are dominated by consumer products companies (Table 2-1). While several of these companies (such as Toyota and General Motors) have begun to dabble in advertising spending on the Internet, most Internet-based spending is generated by technology-oriented companies (such as Microsoft, Netscape, and AT&T).

Internet Advertising Spending —
Oh, We Would Love to Extrapolate the Current Trends!

In 1995, the time spent using consumer online or Internet access services averaged about seven hours per person per year, according to Veronis, Suhler and Associates. Looking ahead, as online media become more established and as more "eyeballs" start moving online, we look for the time

Table 2-1

U.S. Advertising Spending Leaders, 1995

Rank	Advertiser	Total U.S. Ad Spending ($MM)
1	Procter & Gamble	$2,777
2	Phillip Morris	2,577
3	General Motors	2,047
4	Time Warner	1,307
5	Walt Disney	1,296
6	Sears, Roebuck	1,226
7	Chrysler	1,222
8	PepsiCo	1,197
9	Johnson & Johnson	1,173
10	Ford Motor	1,149
11	AT&T Corp.	1,064
12	Warner-Lambert	979
13	Grand Metropolitan	951
14	McDonald's	880
15	Unilever NV	858
16	Kellogg	740
17	Toyota	733
18	Sony	674
19	Viacom	647
20	American Home Products	634

Source: Advertising Age.

Figure 2-1

Internet Advertising Revenue Growth by Quarter

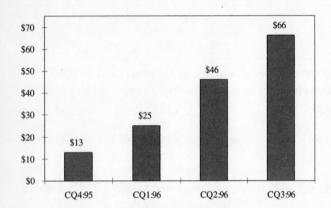

Source: Jupiter Communications.

It took years for measuring techniques and standards to mature or evolve in other media, and although it may not take quite as long in the case of the Internet (nothing does), these techniques and standards are nonetheless still in the larval stages. One thing, however, seems certain — the Internet as a medium and an advertising vehicle is growing in significance. Though the number of eyeballs required to make it a profitable, viable medium for ad-based companies has not yet reached critical mass, it is getting there quickly. Jupiter Communications estimates that $13 million in Web-based ad revenue was generated in 4Q95, $25 million in 1Q96, $46 million in 2Q96, and $66 million in 3Q96 (Figure 2-1). That's an average of 72% sequential growth. (Though Jupiter's absolute estimates are inflated by 10% or more in comparison with the actual reported revenues of some companies, its methodology has been consistent over time and we believe it offers the best estimates of market size and growth currently available).

Internet advertising should experience seasonality similar to that observed in traditional media (as discussed in Chapter 3), where 1Q and 3Q are typically weaker quarters. The Jupiter results for 3Q96 showed a sequential increase of 43%, down from the 84% increase from 1Q to 2Q. We believe that this is in part due to the sluggishness of summer media buying, and that revenue growth will pick up again in the seasonally strong 4Q.

Anecdotally, Internet advertisers are confirming strong results. We believe that by mid-1997 (2Q and 3Q), appreciation of the potential size of the Internet advertising market opportunity will become more clear and will hit the mainstream.

Interestingly, in 4Q96, "sold out" became a common comment among the hottest Web publishers. As in all media, there is a finite amount of available/good inventory to sell to advertisers. And like the real-estate mantra of "location, location, location," advertisers want to be where the traffic is.

While the Internet appears to be the land of unlimited advertising space, as the hundreds of thousands of Web sites out there mean there are hundreds of thousands of pages, the traffic/eyeballs tends to fall off quickly as one clicks deeper into a Web site.

So, the hottest sites find themselves running out of "hot," highly trafficked inventory to sell. And they are moving quickly to create more areas or sites that they hope will also become high-traffic areas.

The good news? CPMs (or cost-per-thousand impressions delivered — the industry defines an impression as simply one "media exposure" to an ad) for the hot areas are stable, and even rising in some instances. Due to rising traffic at hot Web sites, advertiser buying patterns, and business seasonality, inventory is becoming more difficult for Web publishers to manage. In general, we believe that, over time (thanks in part to the ability to provide targeted delivery of ads), CPMs at the best sites will continue to experience upward price pressure.

Advertising Growth Variables/Metrics for Web Publishers

- Traffic growth (site visits and page views)
- Available inventory
- Advertising sell-through of inventory
- CPM (cost-per-impression)
- Number of new advertisers
- Market share (and loyalty of customer base)
- Migration of total advertising spending to new media

Web Ad Growth Forecasting — Fun with Numbers

Estimates of Web ad revenue in the year 2000 range from $1.7 billion to as high as $5 billion. In any case, the point is simple: Web ad revenue is likely to become a big number, and quickly. Using the high end of these estimates ($5 billion), along with our estimate of about 150 million Internet users by the turn of the century, implies an average amount of advertising spent per online user of $33 — this compares with 1995 domestic annual advertising spending of about $340 per broadcast TV household, $83 per cable TV household, $116 per radio household, and $586 per level of Sunday newspaper circulation (Table 2-2).

So… if the past levels of advertising spending per eyeball for other media are prologue, then advertising on the Internet could be one big honkin' business opportunity!

Note the following data points: As we have mentioned, the current annual advertising revenue run rate on the Web is $264 million, and our average estimate for the current number of Web users is 28 million — this implies that, on average, $9 in advertising spending is targeted at each user on an annual basis. The same math for AOL (a $28 million advertising run rate, divided by 8 million users) implies that, on average, AOL generates $4 in annual advertising revenue per customer.

If we extrapolate the current advertising spending rate per Web user (of $9) out to the year 2000 (with 157 million Internet users), Web-related advertising spending/revenue could be a $1.4 billion business in 2000, up from a current estimated revenue run rate of $264 million (implying compounded annual revenue growth of 52%). But it's reasonable to assume that advertising spending on a per user basis will rise as the medium grows and becomes better understood, so this $1.4 billion estimate could prove to be quite conservative. If, indeed, the Internet becomes a mass medium, these powerful advertising-related revenue growth assumptions are very reasonable and beatable, in our opinion.

Let's tweak the numbers a bit (Figure 2-2 and Table 2-3). If we assume there are 157 million Internet users in 2000, and we ramp our advertising-spending-per-user estimate to $25, this implies a $3.9 billion business opportunity; and if we ramp to $50, it implies $7.9 billion. Clearly time will tell which scenario plays out, but our spreadsheet speaks clearly — Internet advertising spending should ramp fast!

Table 2-2
1995 U.S. Spending per Household For Various Media

Medium	1995 Advertising Spending ($MM)	No. of Households (MM)	Advertising Spending/ Household ($)
Broadcast TV	$32,270	95	$340
Radio	11,338	98	116
Cable	5,324	64	83
Newspapers	36,317	62*	586
Total	**$85,249**	**319**	**$1,125**
Average	**21,312**	**80**	**281**

Newspaper Households are actually Sunday circulation.
Sources: 1995 Advertising Revenue - McCann-Erickson, Households - TV Dimensions '96, Newspaper Association of America, Paul Kagan Associates, Morgan Stanley Technology Research

Figure 2-2

Estimated Web Users vs. Advertising Revenue Using Various Steady-State Assumptions, 1995–2000E

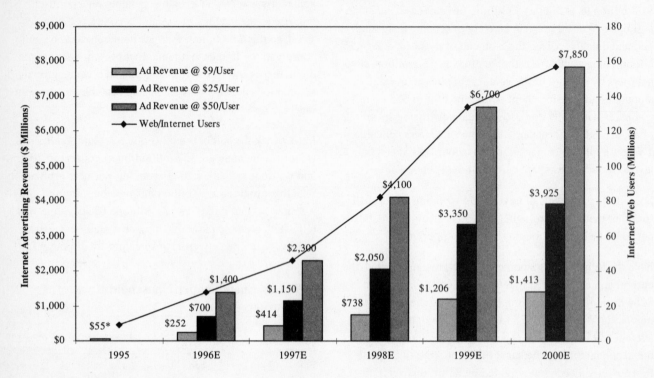

Source: Morgan Stanley Technology Research.
* 1995 contains actual revenue, as reported by Jupiter Communications.
E = Morgan Stanley Research Estimate.

Table 2-3

Estimated Web Users vs. Advertising Revenue, Using Various Steady-State Assumptions, 1995–2000E

($ Million)	1995	1996E	1997E	1998E	1999E	2000E
Estimated Worldwide Web Users (MM)	9	28	46	82	134	157
Annual Advertising Spending per User Assumption ($)						
$50	–	$1,400	$2,300	$4,100	$6,700	$7,850
25	–	700	1,150	2,050	3,350	3,825
9	55*	252	414	738	1,206	1,413

Source: Morgan Stanley Technology Research. Note: Steady-state assumptions are used for directional purposes only — it's likely that if Web advertising is well accepted, spending will likely rise steadily over time.
* 1995 contains actual revenue, as reported by Jupiter Communications.
E = Morgan Stanley Research Estimate.

Table 2-4

Top 20 Web Advertisers and Publishers by Estimated 3Q96 Spending/Revenue

Rank	Web Advertisers	3Q96 Spending (000's$)	YTD Spending (000's$)	YTD Rank	Rank	Web Publishers	3Q96 Revenue (000's$)	YTD Revenue (000's$)	YTD Rank
1	Microsoft	$2,901	$5,819	1	1	Netscape	$8,203	$17,867	1
2	AT&T	2,088	3,823	3	2	Yahoo!	5,561	11,251	2
3	Netscape	1,879	4,052	2	3	Infoseek	4,909	10,694	3
4	Excite	1,539	3,390	5	4	Excite*	3,630	7,271	5
5	Infoseek	1,512	3,285	6	5	Lycos	3,425	7,548	4
6	IBM	1,484	3,571	4	6	CNET	3,045	6,221	6
7	McKinley Group	1,381	2,849	7	7	WebCrawler*	2,908	5,068	8
8	Lycos	1,300	2,595	9	8	ZD Net	2,235	5,418	7
9	Yahoo!	1,250	2,590	10	9	Magellan*	1,823	2,936	13
10	Nynex	1,241	2,790	8	10	ESPNET SportsZone	1,705	4,148	9
11	SportsLine USA	793	1,463	14	11	Pathfinder	1,548	3,613	10
12	Amazon.com	643	986	18	12	CMP TechWeb	1,532	3,381	12
13	Toyota	602	1,471	13	13	Wall Street Journal Interactive	1,387	2,121	17
14	CNET	592	2,146	11	14	USA TODAY	1,354	2,238	16
15	NewsPage (Individual)	579	1,332	15	15	NewsPage (Individual)	1,347	3,492	11
16	Sprint	541	1,162	16	16	CNN Interactive	1,238	2,713	14
17	Travelocity	540	941	20	17	HotWired	795	2,261	15
18	Digital Equipment Corp.	491	1,636	12	18	Jumbo!	668	1,287	18
19	Ziff-Davis	488	877	23	19	Playboy	588	1,246	19
20	Procter & Gamble	480	969	19	20	HomeArts Network	473	797	23

Source: Jupiter Communications.
* Excite acquired Magellan in 3Q96, making the combined 3Q revenue estimate for both sites $5.5 million, effectively ranking the combined company third. On November 25, 1996, Excite became AOL's exclusive Internet search service and acquired WebCrawler.
(Note: Jupiter's estimates are calculated using the rate cards supplied by each site and extrapolating with an estimate of the number of banners each delivered. This does not take into account discounts, barter, and other factors, which are fairly prevalent, and can overestimate true revenue. For example, CNET reported Internet advertising revenue of $2.7 million in 3Q96, 10% lower than Jupiter's $3.0 million estimate, and Excite reported Internet advertising revenue, including Magellan, of $4.0 million, 38% below Jupiter's combined estimate of $5.5 million).

The State of Web Advertising

A handful of companies are winning with advertising revenue on the Web, but these same companies tend to also spend lots of money to advertise on the Web.

Currently, as with other media, Web advertising is rather top-heavy (Figure 2-3). According to Jupiter Communications, more than 900 sites were selling advertising on the Web in 3Q96 and thousands of companies were displaying ad banners (the rise of ad networks, a phenomenon discussed later, allows many more sites to "trade" ad space without actually selling to advertisers). However, the majority of ad spending and revenue is concentrated among a few advertisers and the top sites (Table 2-4). In 3Q96, the ten highest-grossing revenue sites accounted for 57% of total Web ad revenue. In addition, many of the biggest Web advertisers are also the biggest recipients of Web advertising revenue.

Jupiter used published rate-card rates to arrive at its revenue estimates and compared its data with publicly available information and the ad-supported sites themselves to arrive

at its estimates. Skeptics argue that it's not uncommon (in fact, it's often typical) for rate card prices to be discounted. Jupiter's revenue estimates may thus be high, but they do have directional significance.

Of the top ten revenue-generating sites (shown with estimated 1Q, 2Q, and 3Q revenue data in Figure 2-4 and Table 2-5), five are search engines (Infoseek, Lycos, Yahoo!,

Figure 2-3

Concentration of Ad Revenue on the Web, 3Q96

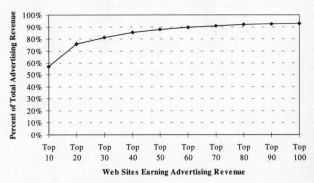

Source: Jupiter Communications.

Excite, and Magellan) and one, Netscape, is an aggregator of these search engines as well as the home page of the browser that holds an estimated 70%-plus market share in that space.

As we have noted, there is some discrepancy between the estimates reported by Jupiter Communications and the actual advertising revenue realized. 1996 reported online advertising revenue and average daily page views for the four search engines are shown in Figures 2-5 and 2-6 and Tables 2-6 and 2-7. Though slightly different, these metrics echo the directional significance of the Jupiter estimates — online advertising revenue and its key drivers have continued to display rapid growth.

Table 2-5

1996 Year-to-Date Quarterly Web Advertising Revenue for the Top 10 Sites
(Ranked by Estimated 3Q96 Revenue)

($ Million)	1Q	2Q	3Q
Netscape	$1.9	$7.8	$8.2
Yahoo!	2.0	3.7	5.6
Infoseek	2.0	3.8	4.9
Excite*	1.2	2.4	3.6
Lycos	1.6	2.3	3.4
CNET	1.1	2.1	3.0
WebCrawler*	0.9	1.2	2.9
ZD Net	1.1	2.1	2.2
Magellan*	0.3	0.8	1.8
ESPNET SportsZone	1.1	1.3	1.7

*Source: Jupiter Communications. * Excite acquired Magellan in 3Q96, making the combined 3Q revenue estimate for both sites $5.5 million, effectively ranking the combined company third. On November 25, 1996, Excite became AOL's exclusive Internet search service and acquired WebCrawler.*

Figure 2-4

1996 Year-to-Date Quarterly Web Advertising Revenue for the Top 10 Sites
(Ranked by Estimated 3Q96 Revenue)

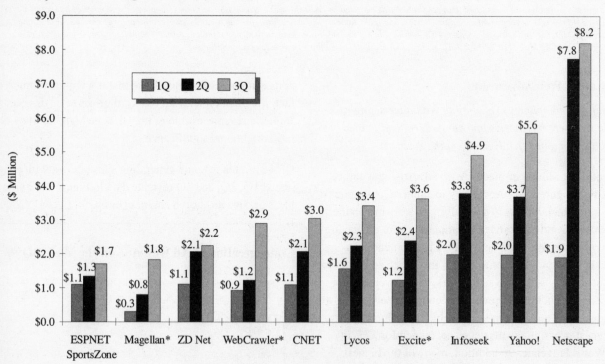

Top 10 Web Sites by 3Q96 Web Advertising Revenue

Source: Jupiter Communications.
* Excite acquired Magellan in 3Q96, making the combined 3Q revenue estimate for both sites $5.5 million, effectively ranking the combined company third. On November 25, 1996, Excite became AOL's exclusive Internet search service and acquired WebCrawler.
(Note: Jupiter's estimates are calculated using the rate cards supplied by each site and extrapolating with an estimate of the number of banners each delivered. This does not take into account discounts, barter, and other factors, which are fairly prevalent, and can overestimate true revenue. For example, CNET reported Internet advertising revenue of $2.7 million in 3Q96, 10% lower than Jupiter's $3.0 million estimate, and Excite reported Internet advertising revenue, including Magellan, of $4.0 million, 38% below Jupiter's combined estimate of $5.5 million).

Figure 2-5

1996 Quarterly Online Advertising Revenue for Four Leading Search Engines

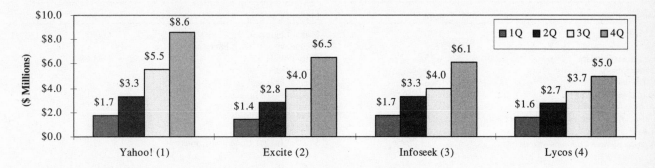

Source: Morgan Stanley Technology Research.

Figure 2-6

1996 End of Quarter Average Daily Page Views for Four Leading Search Engines

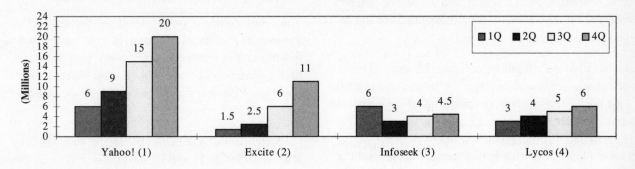

Source: Morgan Stanley Technology Research.

Table 2-6

1996 Quarterly Online Advertising Revenue for Four Leading Search Engines

($ Millions)	1Q	2Q	3Q	4Q
Yahoo! (1)	$1.7	$3.3	$5.5	$8.6
Excite (2)	1.4	2.8	4.0	6.5
Infoseek (3)	1.7	3.3	4.0	6.1
Lycos (4)	1.6	2.7	3.7	5.0

Source: Morgan Stanley Technology Research.

Table 2-7

1996 End of Quarter Average Daily Page Views for Four Leading Search Engines

(Millions)	1Q	2Q	3Q	4Q
Yahoo! (1)	6	9	15	20
Excite (2)	1.5	2.5	6	11
Infoseek (3)	6	3	4	4.5
Lycos (4)	3	4	5	6

Source: Morgan Stanley Technology Research.

(1) Yahoo! owns a minority interest in Yahoo! Japan and there is therefore no contribution from this site to these revenue figures. The company did, however, report Yahoo! Japan's daily page view increased from about 1 million pages per day in September to about 1.4 million per day in December, and these figures are included in these 3Q and 4Q page view estimates.

(2) On November 25, 1996, Excite became AOL's exclusive Internet search service and acquired WebCrawler. In addition, Excite acquired Magellan in 3Q96. The combined sites in the new Excite Group had an unduplicated reach of 45.6 in December, according to PC Meter. Magellan is included in Excite's 3Q revenue estimate and in its reporting of 3Q page views. For 4Q, the company reported a range of 10-12 million pages per day. We have used 11 million, the midpoint of that range, as our estimate.

(3) Infoseek was the only search engine on the Netscape search page until April 11, 1996.

(4) Fiscal year-end for Lycos is in July, so 1Q figures end in April, 2Q in July, 3Q in October, and 4Q in January.

Table 2-8
Web Ad Spending by Industry Category, 3Q96

Industry Category	Share
Web Related	32%
Computer Related	22
Consumer Goods	13
Telecommunications	9
Other Services	6
Publishing & Media	6
Auto & Accessories	5
Financial Services Insurance & Real Estate	5
Travel	2

Source: Jupiter Communications.

Table 2-9
Web Publishing Revenue by Industry Category, 3Q96

Industry Category	Share
Search Engines & Directories	40%
Computers & Related Interests	18
Entry Portals	14
News Media	12
General Interests	8
7Sports/Men's Interests	4
Other Content Sites	30
Other Listings	10

Source: Jupiter Communications.

The current concentration of advertising revenue among a small group of sites could diminish a bit with the creation of additional quality sites and an improved Internet advertising infrastructure (which includes ad networks, measurement/tracking software and tools, well-defined standards, advertising sales channels, and the host of elements that comprise the traditional advertising purchase and delivery infrastructure).

Traditional media advertising revenue also tends to be somewhat concentrated, but there are several characteristics of the Internet that we believe could erode the oligopolistic nature of traditional media, such as the low barriers to entry, the reduced cost of publishing or broadcasting (no print, paper, or other distribution costs), and the resulting proliferation of many targeted special-interest and segmented sites. Advertisers may be able to gain greater reach by spreading their buying across a large number of sites.

Conversely, we believe that the mega-cyber channels will begin to emerge in 1997 and that Web site consolidation will ensue. So the strong will become stronger and the weaker will fail, while the super low-cost niche players that can provide advertisers with very good targeted marketing will also do well.

So Far, Web Advertisers Tend to Be Technology Firms

The Internet has yet to make inroads with lots of the big traditional advertisers. In 3Q, 54% of Web advertising spending came from Web- and computer-related companies (Table 2-8). The list of top advertisers is lacking in the major ad spenders one finds in traditional media. In fact, using *Advertising Age's* list of top 100 advertisers, Jupiter's study ranked only 11 of the top traditional media buyers among the top 50 Web advertisers. Cracking the top 50 list didn't take much, either — a company would only need to have spent $72,000.

The Higher the Traffic, the Higher the Revenue

Since most companies with advertising-bearing Web sites generate ad revenue as a function of page views (each page downloaded by a user is counted as one page view), the high-revenue sites are some of the most highly visited on the Web. Plain and simple, more eyeballs mean more dollars.

PC Meter tracks consumer traffic on the Web, via software it has installed on PCs in 10,000 homes, and ranks the top sites based on reach. The reach of a Web site is defined as the percentage of the total available audience in a given time period that makes a request at that site.

According to PC Meter's December survey, the most popular Web sites based on reach (Table 2-10) were the Excite Group (with a reach of 45.6), AOL (45.0), Yahoo! (36.6), Netscape (35.8), and Microsoft (21.6). The Excite Group is composed of Excite (www.excite.com), WebCrawler (www.webcrawler.com), and Magellan (www.mckinley.com).

In addition, PC Meter tracks the popularity of various Web sites on a category-by-category basis (Tables 2-11 through 2-27). Though PC Meter's data are among the best proxies for site popularity in these early stages of Internet development and measurement, keep in mind that these data are strictly a consumer, and not a business, measurement.

Table 2-10

Top 25 Web Sites Based on Reach, December 1996

Rank	Site	URL(s)	Reach
1	Excite Group	(1)	45.6
2	AOL	www.aol.com	45.0
3	Yahoo!	www.yahoo.com	36.6
4	Netscape	www.netscape.com	35.8
5	Microsoft	www.microsoft.com	21.6
6	Geocities	www.geocities.com	16.7
7	Infoseek	www.infoseek.com	16.5
8	Lycos	www.lycos.com	16.3
9	Microsoft Network	www.msn.com	14.9
10	Digital	www.digital.com	13.7
11	CNET	(2)	11.8
12	Prodigy	www.prodigy.com	11.3
13	Ziff-Davis	(3)	11.0
14	Compuserve	www.compuserve.com	10.5
15	Four11 Network	www.four11.com, www.lookup.com, www.wp.com	9.8
16	Switchboard	www.switchboard.com	7.5
17	Earthlink	www.earthlink.com	7.1
18	Netcom	www.netcom.com	7.0
19	RealAudio	www.realaudio.com	7.0
20	Pathfinder	www.pathfinder.com	6.8
21	GNN	www.gnn.com	6.5
22	Amateurs	www.amateurs.com	6.3
23	AT&T	www.att.net	6.3
24	Angelfire	www.angelfire.com	5.7
25	Tripod	www.tripod.com	5.6

(1) The Excite Group consists of www.excite.com, www.webcrawler.com, www.mckinley.com, and www.city.net.
(2) CNET sample includes www.cnet.com, www.gamecenter.com, www.search.com, www.shareware.com, www.download.com, www.news.com, www.activex.com, and www.mediadome.com.
(3) Ziff-Davis sample includes www.anchordesk.com, www.cdrom.com, www.cieurope.com, www.cobb.com, www.compint.com, www.complife.com, www.computerlife.com, www.cshopper.com, www.downloadnow.com, www.egm2.com, www.egmmag.com, egr www.cdrom.com, www.familypc.com, www.gamespot.com, www.hotfiles.com, www.interactive-week.com, www.macuser.com, www.macweek.com, www.netbuyer.com, www.nuke.com, www.pccomp.com, www.pccomputing.com, www.pcmag.com, www.pcmagazine.com, www.pcmagcd.com, www.pcweek.com, www.pview.com, www.techlocator.com, www.thesite.com, www.topfive.com, www.transfusion.com, www.underground-online.com, www.videogamespot.com, www.wsources.com, www.yahoocomputing.com, www.yil.com, www.zd.com, www.zdbop.com, www.zdil.com, www.zdimag.com, www.zdlabs.com, www.zdnet.com, www.zdtv.com, www.zdu.com, www.ziff-davis.com, www.ziff.com.

Source: PC Meter.

Table 2-11

Top Site Categories Based on Reach, December 1996

Rank	Category	Reach
1	Unclassified*	84.3
2	Search Engine	70.6
3	Marketing/Corporate	63.8
4	Commercial Online	63.0
5	News/Information/Entertainment	58.8
6	Internet Service Provider	58.1
7	Web Services	53.2
8	Education	44.9
9	Shopping	28.4
10	Adult Content	26.8
11	Directories	19.1
12	Government	18.5
13	Travel/Tourism	11.6

* PC Meter codes approximately 2,000 sites. Any other site visited would fall in the Unclassified category.

Source: PC Meter.

Table 2-12

Top 5 Search Engines Based on Reach, December 1996

Rank	Site	URL(s)	Reach
1	Excite Group	(1)	45.6
2	Yahoo!	www.yahoo.com	36.6
3	Infoseek	www.infoseek.com	16.5
4	Lycos	www.lycos.com	16.3
5	AltaVista	www.digital.com	13.7

(1) The Excite Group consists of www.excite.com, www.webcrawler.com, www.mckinley.com, and www.city.net.

Source: PC Meter.

Table 2-13

Top 5 Marketing/Corporate Sites Based on Reach, December 1996

Rank	Site	URL	Reach
1	Netscape	www.netscape.com	35.8
2	Microsoft	www.microsoft.com	21.2
3	AT&T	www.att.com	4.1
4	Sony	www.sony.com	3.8
5	Macromedia	www.macromedia.com	3.5

Source: PC Meter.

Table 2-14

Top 5 Commercial Online Service Sites Based on Reach, December 1996

Rank	Site	URL	Reach
1	America Online	www.aol.com	45.0
2	Microsoft Network	www.msn.com	14.9
3	Prodigy	www.prodigy.com	11.3
4	CompuServe	www.compuserve.com	10.5
5	WOW*	www.wow.com	1.0

*Source: PC Meter. * CompuServe announced in November 1996 that it would discontinue Wow! on January 31, 1997.*

Table 2-15

Top 5 Web Services Sites Based on Reach, December 1996

Rank	Site	URL	Reach
1	GeoCities	www.geocities.com	16.7
2	RealAudio	www.realaudio.com	7.0
3	Angelfire	www.angelfire.com	5.7
4	Tripod	www.tripod.com	5.6
5	Educational Information Network	www.einet.net	5.3

Source: PC Meter.

Table 2-16

Top 5 Web Technology/Software Shopping Sites Based on Reach, December 1996

Rank	Site	URL	Reach
1	Shareware.com	www.shareware.com	4.6
2	Download.com	www.download.com	3.4
3	ZDNet Software Library	www.hotfiles.com	2.4
4	Jumbo	www.jumbo.com	1.5
5	Walnut Creek CD-ROM	www.cdrom.com	1.0

Source: PC Meter.

Table 2-17

Top 5 Web Technology/Hardware Shopping Sites Based on Reach, December 1996

Rank	Site	URL	Reach
1	Surplus Direct	www.surplusdirect.com	1.5
2	Gateway 2000	www.gw2k.com	1.5
3	NetBuyer	www.netbuyer.com	1.1
4	Onsale	www.onsale.com	1.1
5	CompUSA	www.compusa.com	0.8

Note that Dell's site (www.dell.com), through which many harware sales are made, is classified by PC Meter in the Marketing/Corporate category. Its reach in December 1996 was 0.9. Source: PC Meter.

Table 2-18

Top 5 Web Non-Technology Shopping Sites Based on Reach, December 1996

Rank	Site	URL	Reach
1	Columbia House Records	www.columbiahouse.com	2.9
2	Amazon Books	www.amazon.com	2.5
3	iMall	www.imall.com	1.6
4	iQVC Shop	www.qvc.com	1.3
5	Catalog Link	www.cataloglink.com	1.0

Source: PC Meter.

Table 2-19

Top 5 Directory Sites Based on Reach, December 1996

Rank	Site(s)	URL(s)	Reach
1	Four11 Network	www.four11.com, www.lookup.com, www.wp.com	9.8
2	Switchboard	www.switchboard.com	7.5
3	WhoWhere?	www.whowhere.com	3.4
4	BigBook	www.bigbook.com	1.9
5	BigYellow	www.bigyellow.com	1.4

Source: PC Meter.

Table 2-20

Top 5 Travel/Tourism Sites Based on Reach, December 1996

Rank	Site	URL	Reach
1	Travelocity	www.travelocity.com	1.5
2	American Airlines	www.americanair.com	0.9
3	Internet Travel Network	www.itn.com	0.9
4	State of California	www.ca.gov	0.8
5	State of Texas	www.state.tx.us	0.7

Source: PC Meter.

Table 2-21

Top 5 General Interest Sites Based on Reach, December 1996

Rank	Site	URL	Reach
1	Pathfinder	www.pathfinder.com	6.8
2	USA Today Online	www.usatoday.com	3.7
3	MSNBC	www.msnbc.com	3.5
4	TV Guide	www.iguide.com	2.0
5	The Nando Times	www.nando.net	2.0

Source: PC Meter.

Table 2-22

Top 5 Technology News Sites Based on Reach, December 1996

Rank	Site(s)	URL(s)	Reach
1	CNET	(1)	11.8
2	ZDNet	(2)	11.0
3	PC World	www.pcworld.com	2.0
4	Hot Wired	www.hotwired.com	1.6
5	NetGuide	www.netguide.com	1.6

(1) CNET sample includes www.cnet.com, www.gamecenter.com, www.search.com, www.shareware.com, www.download.com, www.news.com, www.activex.com, and www.mediadome.com.
(2) Ziff-Davis sample includes www.anchordesk.com, www.cdrom.com, www.cieurope.com, www.cobb.com, www.compint.com, www.complife.com, www.computerlife.com, www.cshopper.com, www.downloadnow.com, www.egm2.com, www.egmmag.com, egr www.cdrom.com, www.familypc.com, www.gamespot.com, www.hotfiles.com, www.interactive-week.com, www.macuser.com, www.macweek.com, www.netbuyer.com, www.nuke.com, www.pccomp.com, www.pccomputing.com, www.pcmag.com, www.pcmagazine.com, www.pcmagcd.com, www.pcweek.com, www.pview.com, www.techlocator.com, www.thesite.com, www.topfive.com, www.transfusion.com, www.underground-online.com, www.videogamespot.com, www.wsources.com, www.yahoocomputing.com, www.yil.com, www.zd.com, www.zdbop.com, www.zdil.com, www.zdimag.com, www.zdlabs.com, www.zdnet.com, www.zdtv.com, www.zdu.com, www.ziff-davis.com, www.ziff.com.

Source: PC Meter.

Table 2-23

Top 5 Business News Sites Based on Reach, December 1996

Rank	Site	URL	Reach
1	CNN	www.cnn.com	3.6
2	NewsPage	www.newspage.com	1.8
3	New York Times	www.nytimes.com	1.6
4	CNNfn	www.cnnfn.com	1.3
5	Washington Post	www.washingtonpost.com	1.3

Source: PC Meter.

Table 2-24

Top 2 Weather Sites Based on Reach, December 1996

Rank	Site	URL	Reach
1	The Weather Channel	www.weather.com	4.9
2	IntelliCast*	www.intellicast.com	3.4

* part of the MSNBC site.

Source: PC Meter.

Table 2-25

Top 5 Entertainment/Kids Sites Based on Reach, December 1996

Rank	Site	URL	Reach
1	Disney	www.disney.com	4.8
2	Warner Brothers Online	www.warnerbros.com*	4.0
3	United Media	www.unitedmedia.com	2.2
4	Internet Movie Database	www.imdb.com	1.8
5	Discovery Channel Online	www.discovery.com	1.6

* Warner Brothers Online sites frequently change as new sites are rolled out and taken down in conjunction with the promotion of movies, TV shows, etc.

Source: PC Meter

Table 2-26

Top 5 Sports Sites Based on Reach, December 1996

Rank	Site	URL	Reach
1	ESPNet SportsZone	www.sportzone.com	3.9
2	SportLine USA	www.sportsline.com	2.9
3	NFL	www.nfl.com	2.7
4	NBA	www.nba.com	1.2
5	NASCAR	www.nascar.com	0.9

Source: PC Meter

Table 2-27

Top 5 Games Sites Based on Reach, December 1996

Rank	Site	URL	Reach
1	Happy Puppy (Attitude Network)	www.happypuppy.com	2.2
2	CNET's Gamecenter	www.gamecenter.com	1.9
3	GameSpot	www.gamespot.com	1.5
4	Riddler	www.riddler.com	1.1
5	Sega	www.sega.com	1.0

Source: PC Meter

And Then There's Barter

Since most Web sites are unprofitable and advertising revenue is still small, these companies often form relationships, advertising on one another's sites and gaining "ad revenue" (as well as expense). This practice is known as barter. There is a great deal of ad bartering that takes place between Web companies, and it is no coincidence that there is noticeable overlap between top ad advertisers and publishers. Netscape, which "charged" the major search engines (Yahoo!, Infoseek, Lycos, Magellan, and Excite) $5 million to be placed on Netscape's Net Search page, in reality received $2 million apiece from each company but received $3 million in advertising placement from each site. It is important to be aware of how ad revenue statistics are compiled, as each study and each site may report differently in this respect.

Barter is not a new phenomenon, of course, and is relatively common in other media. Figure 2-7 demonstrates the steady increase in barter revenue in the TV industry.

A Summary of How the Ad-Math is Done on the Web

The importance of measuring page views accurately becomes very clear in the context of the advertising business model. Advertisers pay an agreed-upon multiple of the number of "guaranteed" impressions delivered. This limits the site's responsibility for ad delivery, and the ad revenue generated is simply the product of the traffic (and subsequent pages downloaded) times the multiple, which is generally priced in terms of the cost per thousand impressions (CPM). Internet CPMs range as high as Riddler's $250 and NewsPage's $200 CPM down to average CPMs at sites

like Discovery Channel Online ($50) to lower CPMs at sites like the search engines, where CPMs can range from $12 to $20 (Table 2-28). Generally, CPMs seem to average on the order of $30, resulting in a per unit cost of $0.03 per impression delivered.

The wide price spread suggests that the Web functions both as a mass medium and a direct-marketing vehicle, and that context, audience, technology, and results all play a part in determining what price an advertiser will pay.

If past is prologue, as the medium evolves (as in the cable analogy), we believe a few well-branded sites in a very broad range of categories (such as news, entertainment, and sports) will come to dominate, and these sites will be able to charge a premium for ad space. Note, however, that there are some fundamental differences between Internet publishing/programming and cable programming, and the Internet's lack of barriers to entry may prevent, to some degree, the same narrowing we saw in cable (cable stations with little viewership are entirely too expensive to support, but Web sites are not). There is, therefore, an almost unlimited amount of content (and therefore inventory) available for advertiser purchase on the Internet, in contrast with the limited amount of inventory available in radio and on TV. This Internet inventory glut may therefore heat up the competition for ad dollars (which, as it increases, lowers ad rates). The ability of premium sites to command pricing should play a key role in setting the acceptable boundaries for CPM, and ultimately, revenue.

Figure 2-7

10-Year Evolution of TV Barter Revenue ($MM)

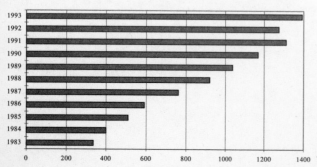

Source: TV Dimensions '96.

Table 2-28

Selected CPMs from Various Media

Web/Online Site	CPM	Web/Online Site	CPM
Riddler	$250	ESPNET SportsZone	$35
Individual Inc.'s NewsPage	$200	DOWNLOAD.COM	$30
HotWired	$150	Netscape	$30
NEWS.COM	$100	SEARCH.COM	$30
CNET.COM	$75	SHAREWARE.COM	$30
GAMECENTER.COM	$75	Yahoo!	$23
America Online	$38	PointCast Network (PCN)	$3
General Web/Online	*CPM*	*General Web/Online*	*CPM*
Targeted content sites	$45-260	Other search engines	$12-18
High traffic sites	$35-65		
Traditional Medium	*CPM*	*Traditional Medium*	*CPM*
Magazines -- niche	$70 - 150	Television	$13
Magazines -- general	$25 - 50	Radio	$5

Source: Morgan Stanley Technology Research.

There is an inventory paradox on the Web. While there is tons of available inventory on the Web in aggregate, the highest traffic sites have a limited amount of high traffic inventory. This paradox can govern revenue growth for the Web in aggregate by keeping CPMs low and govern revenue growth for the highest traffic sites by keeping CPMs high, but for limited space.

And Now a Look at Some of the Hot Areas by Channel/Category . . .

In thinking about who the future "contenders" to dominate each channel may be (according to our cable analogy; see Chapter 3), we thought the best place to start would be to look at some of today's top sites.

A Web Ad Revenue Cut . . .

We take a pass at the current annualized revenue run-rates of the top site in several major categories (ranked by Jupiter Communications' 3Q96 revenue estimate) in Figure 2-8. The revenue run-rate is derived by annualizing Jupiter Communications' 3Q96 revenue estimate for each site. There are several leading sites in each category of content on the Web. In sports, there's ESPNet SportsZone, in technology news, CNET, and in financial news, the Wall Street Journal Interactive. For search engines, Yahoo! currently leads on a revenue and page view per day basis, though Excite's late November announcement that it would become the exclusive search engine for AOL (and its 3Q acquisition of Magellan) has altered the competitive landscape in this category to some degree.

Figure 2-8
1996 Web Advertising Revenue for Today's Top Publishers by Channel/Category (by Estimated 3Q96 Revenue)

Channel/Category	No. 1 Web Site	Annualized Revenue Run-Rate (1), ($ Millions)
Browser	Netscape	$33
Search Engine*	Yahoo!	$22
General News	USA Today	$14
Technology News	CNET	$12
Sports	ESPNet SportsZone	$7
General Interest	Pathfinder	$6
Financial News	Wall Street Journal Interactive	$6
Special Interest	Playboy	$2

Source: Jupiter Communications.
(1) based on annualized 3Q96 Internet advertising revenue estimate from Jupiter Communications for each site.
* On November 25, 1996, Excite became AOL's exclusive Internet search service and acquired WebCrawler, significantly altering the competitive landscape in this channel.

An America Online Traffic Cut

America Online has over 8 million subscribers, putting it in the position of delivering more effective "page views" than any other site by a long shot. Though each screen that AOL users see is not the technical equivalent of a Web page, for advertisers it is virtually the same vehicle and delivers an ad impression in an equivalent fashion. We therefore think it useful to extrapolate AOL subscriber usage and take a pass at the number of pages AOL can deliver for advertisers.

Figure 2-9 shows the estimated number of pages AOL delivered per day in November across its highest-traffic channels. These estimates are based on America Online research, which found that, on average, users view each page for 30 seconds. Page view estimates are then extrapolated from the amount of use for each channel. Some channels, based on the nature of the content, have longer or shorter average viewing times per page and are adjusted accordingly. Figure 2-10 shows similar estimates of amount of use across broad categories (chat, e-mail, Internet, etc.), though this does not apply as directly to activities such as e-mail.

These data suggest to us that America Online drives more traffic than most comparable Web sites in each content channel.

Figure 2-9

November 1996 Estimated U.S. Daily Page Views Delivered by America Online for Selected Content Channels (1)

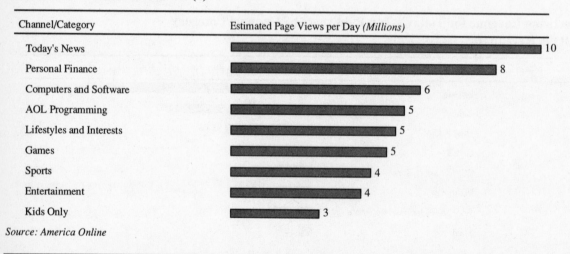

Channel/Category	Estimated Page Views per Day *(Millions)*
Today's News	10
Personal Finance	8
Computers and Software	6
AOL Programming	5
Lifestyles and Interests	5
Games	5
Sports	4
Entertainment	4
Kids Only	3

Source: America Online

Figure 2-10

November 1996 Estimated Daily Page Views Delivered by America Online by Broad Category (1)

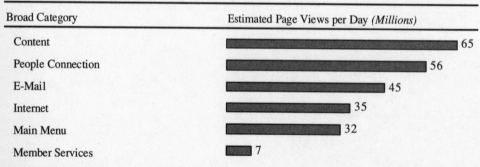

Broad Category	Estimated Page Views per Day *(Millions)*
Content	65
People Connection	56
E-Mail	45
Internet	35
Main Menu	32
Member Services	7

Source: America Online

(1) America Online estimates that, on average, users view each page for 30 seconds. Page view estimates are then extrapolated from hours of use for each channel. Some channels, based on the nature of the content, have longer or shorter average viewing times per page and are adjusted accordingly.

Chapter 3: Where Are Advertising Dollars Spent in Traditional Media? What's the Value of an Eyeball or an Ear?

Summary

◆ **Media usage is staggeringly high, and advertising support of media has been, and should continue to be, the major component of media company revenue streams**.

◆ In 1995, the average American watched TV for 1,575 hours, read newspapers for 165 hours, and used consumer online and Internet services for 7 hours (average use for an America Online user is 100 hours per year and rising — this is active use, as opposed to the passive use of other media). And the number of Internet users (estimated at 7% of the U.S. population and 0.4% of the worldwide population) is still quite small compared with the audiences for mass media.

◆ **Domestic annual measured media advertising spending (including television, radio, daily newspapers, and magazines) was $100 billion in 1995** (broadcast television accounted for 32% of the total; cable television, 5%; daily newspapers, 37%; magazines, 15%; and radio, 11%).

◆ **Broadcast television and broadcast radio are 100% funded by advertising,** while 80% of newspaper revenue, 50% of cable network revenue, and 63% of magazine industry revenue are derived from advertising.

◆ **To date, advertising revenue in the Internet space has been small (but growing rapidly), and, according to Jupiter/AdSpend's 3Q results, the annual revenue run-rate for Web advertising revenue is $264 million.** Jupiter/AdSpend also notes that 1996 Internet-based advertising should be nearly $311 million, up from $55 million in 1995. Our bet is that, in time, successful Internet sites will support significant advertising revenue, and that the interactive nature of the Web could assist the rollout of transaction-based revenue and point-of-purchase sales for Web sites.

◆ **Traditional media buying has been based on CPMs (cost-per-thousand impressions).** So far, this model has been the standard advertising rate card pricing tool for Web sites. **While CPMs on the Web vary widely, on average they have been at higher levels than they are in most other media** due to: 1) the lack of accurate measurement of a potentially desirable Web audience; 2) the focused nature of Web advertisers (for now, mostly Internet, technology, and telecommunications companies); 3) the small supply of highly trafficked Web sites; and, to some degree, 4) the experimental nature (and relatively small size) of Internet ad budgets to date, which may be less price-sensitive at this stage. It is possible that direct-marketing nature of the Web could continue to put upward pressure on CPMs for the hottest Web sites.

One of the biggest problems that hot Web sites deal with is the creation of high-quality inventory — while millions of Internet users may come to the "front door" (a great place for ads and high CPMs), once users go through the door, they have sometimes thousands of different potential routes — subsequently, user traffic levels spread and diminish quickly, thus limiting high-traffic inventory on even the highest traffic sites.

◆ **Growth in Internet advertising may affect advertising growth in other media.**

Figure 3-1

Number of Years for New Media To Reach 50 Million U.S. Homes

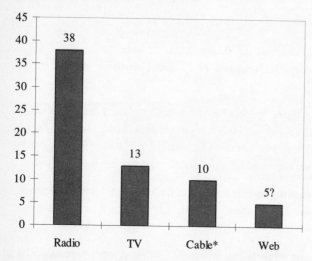

*Source: McCann-Erickson, Paul Kagan Associates, and Morgan Stanley Technology Research. * We use the launch of HBO in 1976 as our estimate for the beginning of cable as an entertainment/advertising medium.*

Media usage has reached a staggering level. As depicted in Table 3-1, the average American watched TV for an estimated 1,575 hours in 1995, read newspapers for 165 hours, and used consumer online and Internet services for seven hours.

It took decades for each new medium to develop, although each developed faster than its predecessor (Figure 3-1), and these early stage cowboy days of the Internet look and feel

like the early days for other media. In our opinion, there is loads of upside for Internet usage.

Call us early adopters, but the team that put this report together already averages at least 400 hours per person per year in this emerging new medium, and we are not alone. The average America Online user (and there are more than 8 million of them) uses AOL for 100 hours (and rising) per year.

Traditional Advertising Market Is Huge

The traditional advertising market is huge (and growing). In the U.S., measured media ad spending (including television, radio, daily newspapers, and magazines) totaled $100 billion in 1995 (Table 3-2). Of this, broadcast TV advertising spending was nearly $32 billion; cable TV spending was $5 billion; newspaper spending was $38 billion; radio was $11 billion; and magazines were $15 billion.

According to Veronis, Suhler & Associates and Paul Kagan Associates, total U.S. advertising and promotional spending, through measured media (broadcast and cable TV, radio, daily newspapers, and magazines), non-measured media (direct mail, yellow pages, outdoor, weekly newspapers, sports or event sponsorships, and so forth), and promotions (consumer promotions such as point-of-purchase, coupons, and premiums, and trade promotions such as meetings, conventions, trade shows, and incentives), totaled more than $293 billion in 1995 (Table 3-3).

Table 3-1

U.S. — Hours Devoted Per Person Per Year to Use of Various Media, 1990-2000E

Year	Broadcast TV	Cable TV	Total TV	Radio	Recorded Music	Daily News-papers	Consumer Books	Consumer Magazines	Home Video	Movies in Theaters	Home Video Games	Consumer On-Line/ Internet Services	Education Software	Total
1990	1,120	350	**1,470**	1,135	235	175	95	90	42	12	12	1	<1	3,267
1991	1,065	430	**1,495**	1,115	219	169	98	88	43	11	18	1	<1	3,257
1992	1,073	437	**1,510**	1,150	233	172	100	85	46	11	19	2	1	3,329
1993	1,082	453	**1,535**	1,082	248	170	99	85	49	12	19	2	1	3,302
1994	1,091	469	**1,560**	1,102	294	169	102	84	52	12	22	3	2	3,402
1995	1,019	556	**1,575**	1,091	289	165	99	84	53	12	24	7	2	3,401
1996E	1,028	567	**1,595**	1,082	290	163	102	83	54	12	27	11	2	3,421
1997E	1,023	587	**1,610**	1,067	296	161	104	82	55	12	31	16	3	3,437
1998E	1,024	601	**1,625**	1,057	315	160	105	81	56	12	34	21	3	3,469
1999E	1,006	634	**1,640**	1,047	331	159	106	81	56	12	37	25	3	3,497
2000E	999	651	**1,650**	1,047	357	158	107	81	57	12	39	28	4	3,540

Source: Veronis, Suhler & Associates, Wilkofsky Gruen Associates.
E = Estimate.

Table 3-2

U.S. — Measured Media Advertising Spending

($ Millions)

Year	Broadcast Television	Cable Television	Radio	Daily Newspaper	Magazines	Total
1987	$22,941	$1,192	$7,206	$29,412	$9,687	$70,438
1988	24,490	1,561	7,798	31,197	10,692	$75,738
1989	25,364	2,031	8,323	32,368	11,446	$79,532
1990	26,616	2,539	8,726	32,280	11,653	$81,814
1991	25,461	2,874	8,476	30,350	11,274	$78,435
1992	27,249	3,297	8,654	30,639	11,960	$81,799
1993	28,020	3,868	9,457	31,869	12,427	$85,641
1994	31,133	4,594	10,529	34,109	13,441	$93,806
1995	32,220	5,342	11,320	36,045	14,627	$99,554
1996E	34,860	6,180	11,990	37,650	15,700	$106,380
1997E	35,645	7,060	12,850	39,320	16,640	$111,515
1998E	37,985	7,960	13,825	41,400	17,790	$118,960
1999E	39,480	8,900	14,815	43,800	18,920	$125,915
2000E	42,945	9,850	15,880	47,350	20,750	$136,775

Sources: Veronis, Suhler & Associates, Wilkofsky Gruen Associates Data–Paul Kagan Associates. Not adjusted for inflation. E = Estimate.

Table 3-3

U.S. Advertising and Promotional Spending

($ Millions)

Year	Measured Media Advertising	Non-Measured Media Advertising	Promotion	Total
1987	$70,438	$41,063	$86,769	$198,270
1988	75,738	44,687	92,562	212,987
1989	79,532	46,869	102,160	228,561
1990	81,814	49,550	108,300	239,664
1991	78,435	50,707	112,200	241,342
1992	81,799	52,400	114,555	248,754
1993	85,641	55,397	114,150	255,188
1994	93,806	59,704	120,350	273,860
1995	99,554	65,040	128,420	293,014
1996E	106,380	70,230	135,300	311,910
1997E	111,515	74,925	142,820	329,260
1998E	118,960	81,130	150,920	351,010
1999E	125,915	87,445	159,400	372,760
2000E	136,775	95,630	169,900	402,305

Source: Veronis, Suhler & Associates, Wilkofsky Gruen Associates. Cable Data–Paul Kagan Associates. Not adjusted for inflation. E = Estimate.

Media Company Revenue Largely Generated by Ads

Major mass media are largely or entirely advertising supported (Table 3-4). Television and radio receive 100% of revenue from advertising — and the majority of newspaper and magazine revenue is also ad-based. Internet advertising is a new phenomenon; subsequently, there is very little advertising revenue in the interactive media space. Current trends, however, imply that advertising will become an increasingly important part of interactive revenue generation.

What's the Value of an Eyeball and an Ear Or an Advertising Impression?

One of the critical issues in advertising is determining how much advertisers should pay to capture eyeballs or ears (a.k.a., *impressions*). The commonly used metric is CPM (or cost-per-thousand impressions delivered — the industry defines an impression as simply one "media exposure" to an ad). Table 3-5 (courtesy of I/PRO Research) shows average CPM, while Table 3-6 indicates some other sample media buys across various media.

CPMs Vary Widely Across Media — A quick analysis of the data indicates that the more targeted a medium, the more advertisers are willing to pay to obtain user views or impressions. CPMs typically range from $5 and higher for network television and $20-plus for general interest magazines and newspapers (the dotted line for magazines is for

the more highly targeted trade publications, like *PC Week*, which charges more than $100 per thousand readers).

Also, we note that, on average, direct mail carries a relatively high CPM (of $27-plus) because it is a very targeted medium, as marketers can target specific demographic and social groups (for example, by zip code), along with many other techniques. More "shotgun-type" media, like bill-

Figure 3-2

U.S. Measured Media Advertising Spending Market Share 1995

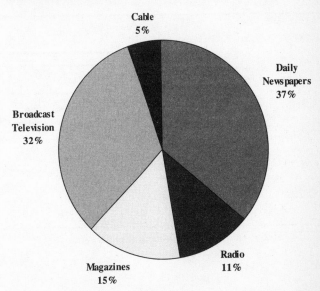

Sources: Veronis, Suhler & Associates, Wilkofsky Gruen Associates, Cable Data–Paul Kagan Associates.

Table 3-4

Shares, by Industry Segment, of 1995 Communications Industry Spending

Industry Segment	Advertising Spending	End-User Spending
Television Broadcasting	100%	0%
Radio Broadcasting	100	0
Newspaper Publishing	80	20
Magazine Publishing	63	37
Interactive Services*	1	99

Source: Veronis, Suhler & Associates, Wilkofsky Gruen Associates.
* Subscription spending by households only.

boards and national radio broadcasts, receive lower CPMs, as advertisers value each impression less.

CPMs on the Web vary widely, ranging from $1 to $200. Why? Well, because, for one, it is very early in the game, and advertisers, agencies, and Web publishers have not yet really proven the inherent value of a Web "eyeball" to advertisers. In addition, confusion reigns because the Web behaves as both a broadcast or mass medium and a direct-marketing vehicle.

CPMs are Seasonal — The seasonality of advertising buying patterns can play a significant role in determining the performance of advertising-related companies. Traditional

advertising media have shown strong advertising spending in 2Q and 4Q, with weaker revenue in 1Q and 3Q. Table 3-7 demonstrates this seasonality, in this case for the major TV networks. The first quarter generally is weaker as, after the traditional Christmas spending blitz, consumers tend to purchase less and companies focus more on direct marketing and promotional campaigns than on advertising. The third quarter suffers from the downturn in spending that characterizes the summer months.

Of course, on TV, summer programming generally comprises reruns, and advertisers usually pay more for the fresh product in late 3Q and 4Q. The second quarter may be characterized more for not having the weaknesses of 1Q and 3Q, and, as one would expect, 4Q is an important selling season for many companies, causing a distinct increase in ad spending. In addition, media buyers tend to buy during the "sweeps" ratings measurements, which occur during the two stronger quarters — programming is better (and newer), branding is thus improved, as are the number of impressions delivered and the overall reach. It should be noted that the size of the audience does not seem to matter, as the two weakest quarters record both the lowest and highest viewership.

Table 3–5
Average CPM Across Media

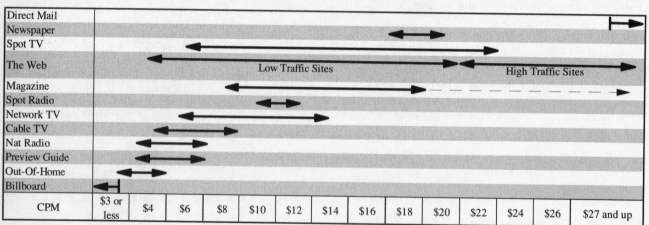

Source: I/PRO Research, Morgan Stanley Technology Research.

Table 3–6
Ad Rate Comparison Across Major Media

Medium	Vehicle	Cost	Reach	CPM
TV	30-second spot on a prime-time program	$120,000	10 million households	$12 per thousand households
Consumer Magazine	Full-page, Four-color ad in *Cosmopolitan*	$86,155	2.5 million paid readers (independently measured and guaranteed)	$35 per thousand paid readers
Online Service	Banner on one of CompuServe's major topic menu pages for one month	$10,000 per month	750,000 to 2 million visits	$13 per thousand visits (at 750,000 visits)
Web Site	Banner on Infoseek (at 500,000 page views) for one month	$10,000 per month	500,000 page views (guaranteed)	$20 per thousand page views

Source: Jupiter Communications.

Table 3–7
Average Prime-Time Network CPMs by Quarter, 1995 (ABC, CBS, NBC, and Fox)

	Prime Time Revenue ($000)	PT Spots	Average Rev./ Spot ($000)	Average PT Rating	Estimated TVHHs (MM)	Average HH Audience (MM)	Average CPM ($)
Quarter 1	$420,689	4,325	$96	11	95	10	$10
Quarter 2	507,261	4,560	109	9	95	8	13
Quarter 3	364,642	4,470	81	8	96	8	11
Quarter 4	541,243	4,410	122	9	96	9	14
Yearly Total/Average	**$7,336,349**	**70,802**	**$104**	**9**	**96**	**9**	**$12**

Source: Paul Kagan Associates, Inc. analysis of published MediaWatch and Nielsen Media Research data.   PT = Prime Time.   HH = Households.

CPMs Have Risen Over Time — Table 3-8 shows the steady rise in CPMs over time for both major network and spot television. CPM trends over time are affected by several macroeconomic factors, such as competitive environment, consumer demand, market stability for each medium, and regulatory changes. As media mature, CPMs tend to rise for the best (most scarce) properties. Note, for example, that while MTV's household coverage has remained steady at 62–63% since 1992, its advertising revenue rose 78% from 1992–95 and its advertising revenue per subscriber rose from $2.40 to $4.03.

Since World War II, there have been four major identifiable periods in measured media advertising.

1) The *postwar era* saw massive growth in advertising revenue after the constraint on such spending during the Great Depression and the war gave way to an explosion in consumer demand. With more consumer spending and the rapid growth of television as a new mass medium, real advertising revenue grew at a 6.0% compound annual growth rate between 1946 and 1960, almost double the 3.2% rate of real economic growth.

2) From *1960 through 1975*, as the postwar boom lost steam, large conglomerates were the dominant forces in the economy, domestic competition declined, there was little in the way of foreign competition, and a relative stability in media. This, in turn, slowed the growth of real advertising spending to a lethargic 1.7% CAGR, half the pace of GDP at 3.3%.

3) The *oil embargo in the early and mid 1970s* caused a large rise in energy costs in the U.S. This decreased the competitive advantage that lower fuel costs afforded domestic companies, and the flow of foreign goods began to increase. The result was heightened competition, which was only augmented by the deregulation of the early 1980s. Accompanying these economic trends were the emergence of two new major media, cable and syndicated programming, and a fourfold increase in the number of independent TV stations. Real advertising spending went on another sharp rise, and from 1975 through 1986, showed a CAGR of 5.3%, versus 2.9% of real GDP growth.

4) As the competitive landscape became more treacherous, companies began looking to consolidate as profit margins declined. The *late 1980s* saw a boom in mergers and

acquisitions, driven further by continued government deregulation in many industries. The high debt loads such consolidation brought began to put additional downward pressure on margins, a trend many corporations attempted to stay through cost-cutting and downsizing. The resulting unemployment meant less consumer spending, and the combination of lackluster sales and cost reduction imperatives forced corporations to spend less on advertising. In addition, advertisers began to put more emphasis on promotional spending (such as mail inserts and sponsored events/atheletes), which decreased to some extent the total budget for measured media advertising.

Real advertising flattened and began to nudge downward in 1986, and by 1988 had begun a severe decline that only began to reverse in 1992, finally surpassing GDP growth again in 1993. In aggregate, real advertising fell at a 0.4% CAGR during the period from 1986–93, with real GDP growing sluggishly at 2.2%.

Since the slowdown of the early 1990s, some of these negative trends seem to be reversing. For the past couple of years, competition has increased, profit margins have been rising, and much of the aforementioned restructuring has been completed. Advertising spending has also been on the rise in the past two years, and Veronis, Suhler and Associates predict that it will grow at a pace of over 6% until the turn of the century.

A Look at Magazine CPMs — In our opinion, a useful way to think about advertising spending statistics is to look at the newspaper and magazine industries. As noted in Table 3-9, we simply take the advertising revenue generated by the 30 most popular magazines in the U.S. in 1995 and divide it by the paid circulation on a magazine-by-magazine basis. *PC Magazine* generated $331 million in revenue in 1995 and its paid circulation was approximately 1 million — over the course of a year, advertisers paid Ziff-Davis Publishing $264 per subscriber per year to print advertisements in *PC Magazine*.

Conversely, the least favorable magazines (which also carry less targeted or demographically desirable audiences) in the top 30 were *National Geographic* (at $7 per sub) and *Star Magazine* (at $8 per subscriber per year). *National Geographic* makes 78% of its revenue from subscribers, and *Star* makes most of its revenue from the newsstand (82%).

A Look at Newspaper CPMs — Newspaper CPMs vary widely, not only because of the usual factors such as market size and demographics but also because the size and creative of ads can be so varied. As a benchmark, a black-and-white ad taking up one-third of a page in a daily newspaper in one of the top 50 markets has a CPM of $17.75. However, newspapers probably have the greatest variety in ad type of all the major media, from the full-pagers on movie opening weekends to one-liners in the help wanted section. In addition, 35–40% of the revenues of the average major market newspaper can come from classifieds. Thus, unlike most other traditional media buys, a large percentage of revenue is not priced in the same CPM-driven fashion (rather, they are fixed-fee per word, per space, and so forth) — to give some perspective on cost, an average help wanted ad in a major market newspaper runs about $1,200. Certainly, the pricing for such advertising is related to the number of "impressions" the paper normally delivers, but the revenue incurred is not.

Newspapers do deliver a valuable audience with great reach — on average, 64% of the adult population reads newspapers daily and nearly three-fourths (73%) read a Sunday paper. And, according to industry studies, as many as 57% of weekday readers read every page. While newspapers are not as effective as other media in building brand through images, readers of newspaper ads tend to be much more interested in buying products (47% of single-copy Sunday readers list advertising as the No. 1 reason for buying the paper).

A Look at Outdoor Advertising CPMs — This type of advertising includes several different media forms used to target consumers while they are in the marketplace or outside the home. It includes billboards, transit advertisements (bus, taxi, and subway advertising), posters in bus, train, or subway stations, neon signs like those in Las Vegas or Times Square, and even skywriting. These ads require short, simple, and easy-to-understand creative, as most users may only be exposed to them for a very short time. The positives of outdoor ads are their broad reach and high frequency levels (good for brand building) at relatively low cost.

However, advertisers have little control over the audience delivered beyond geographical area or setting. The medium seems most effective when supporting and enhancing messages in other media, such as brand name, and is still considered a reinforcing medium by media buyers. Outdoor advertising revenue rose 8% in 1995 to $1.3 billion. CPMs are extremely low, due to the lack of audience targeting and low time of exposure, and generally fall in the $0.50–2.00 range.

A Look at Cable CPMs — It's also interesting to look at similar data for the cable industry. Advertisers are not willing to pay nearly as much to access a customer, and this demonstrates the higher value attributed to active media (a magazine subscriber is much more likely to have a specific demographic or interest profile, and is also more likely to see a particular advertisement than a subscriber to passive media like television). It's important to note, as indicated in Tables 3-10 through 3-12 that advertising revenue per cable subscriber has trended up nicely over the years. (Here we are analyzing cable network revenues, which do not include the local/regional revenues accounted for in our total cable industry revenue estimates, found in Table 3-2.)

As cable TV consolidated and advertisers were better able to define who the audiences for their messages were, gross advertising revenue increased at a rate of 19%, from 1988 to 1995 (Table 3-10), and the revenue that cable networks generated per subscriber rose 11% per year (Table 3-11); at the same time, the number of cable households increased 3% per year (Table 3-12) and the average amount of time Americans spent watching basic and premium cable rose — from 305 hours per year in 1989 to 482 hours per year in 1995 — for a compounded annual growth rate of 8%. And as the major content providers in each genre (ESPN, MTV, and CNN) came into their own, the targeted audience they delivered allowed them, in particular, to generate more revenue per subscriber. We maintain that, for the Internet, similar trends are developing at a rate even faster than they did for the cable networks.

As the popularity of cable has grown, the amount that advertisers have paid for on-air time per household has risen (Figures 1-11 through 1-13; Tables 3-10 through 3-12).

Table 3–8
Advertising Cost to Reach 1,000 Homes (CPMs) for Network and Spot TV 30-Second Units by Day Part, 1955–96

	1955	1960	1965	1970	1975	1980	1985	1990	1995	1996E
Major Network TV										
Daytime	$0.55	$0.65	$0.75	$0.85	$1.00	$2.00	$3.10	$2.35	$3.00	$3.60
Early News	NA	NA	1.40	1.55	1.65	3.20	5.45	6.25	6.35	6.60
Prime Evening	1.50	1.70	1.95	2.20	2.55	4.80	8.25	8.76	9.50	11.00
Late Evening	NA	NA	2.05	1.95	2.00	3.40	5.60	6.35	7.25	8.25
Sports	NA	NA	3.00	2.95	2.60	4.50	7.30	8.75	9.85	10.50
Spot TV										
Daytime	NA	NA	2.00	2.40	2.65	2.75	3.30	4.25	4.35	4.60
Early Evening	NA	NA	1.25	1.65	1.75	2.80	4.05	4.85	5.45	6.25
Prime	NA	NA	2.30	2.60	3.65	6.75	10.00	12.00	12.75	14.10
Late News	NA	NA	1.60	1.85	2.50	4.75	7.25	8.50	10.25	11.40
Late Evening	NA	NA	1.50	1.80	2.35	3.85	5.35	6.50	6.75	7.75

Source: Paul Kagan Associates, Inc. analysis of published MediaWatch and Nielsen Media Research data.

Table 3–9

Top 30 U.S. Magazines by Total 1995 Revenue

1995 Rank By Revenue	Magazine	Parent Company	1995 Revenue ($ mil)	1995 Revenue ($ mil) Advertising	Subscriber	Newsstand	1995 Paid Circulation (subs-mil)	1995 Total Rev/Paid Circulation	1995 Ad Rev/Paid Circulation
1	TV Guide	News Corp.	$1,068	$407	$429	$233	13	$81	$31
2	People	Time	801	438	171	193	3	241	132
3	Sports Illustrated	Time	697	436	246	16	3	221	138
4	Time	Time	672	404	242	26	4	165	99
5	Reader's Digest	Reader's Digest Association	529	187	320	23	15	35	12
6	Parade	Advance Publications	515	516	0	0	37	14	14
7	Newsweek	Washington Post Co.	481	332	123	26	3	152	105
8	Better Homes & Gardens	Meredith	407	274	122	10	8	54	36
9	PC Magazine	Ziff-Davis Publishing	391	331	47	13	1	353	299
10	Good Housekeeping	Hearst Corp.	339	239	67	33	5	63	44
11	U.S. News & World Report	Mortimer Zuckerman	316	222	86	8	2	142	100
12	Business Week	McGraw-Hill	313	268	39	6	1	355	304
13	Woman's Day	Hachette Filipacchi	288	198	34	56	5	61	42
14	Ladies' Home Journal	Meredith	262	158	88	16	5	52	31
15	Family Circle	Bertelsmann (Gruhner & Jahr)	255	164	42	50	5	51	33
16	Forbes	Forbes Inc.	252	206	42	5	1	323	264
17	Cosmopolitan	Hearst Corp.	242	160	21	62	3	94	62
18	USA Weekend	Gannett	230	230	0	0	19	12	12
19	Fortune	Time	226	180	40	6	1	298	237
20	National Geographic	National Geographic Society	202	52	149	0	8	26	7
21	PC Week	Ziff-Davis Publishing	198	196	1	0	–	–	–
22	National Enquirer	American Media	196	29	18	149	3	75	11
23	Money	Time	177	105	60	12	2	92	55
24	Computer Shopper	Ziff-Davis Publishing Co.	174	146	7	21	1	322	270
25	Star Magazine	American Media	174	20	15	139	2	72	8
26	Southern Living	Time	173	100	59	13	2	70	40
27	McCall's	Bertelsmann (Gruner & Jahr)	171	104	57	11	5	38	23
28	Redbook	Hearst Corp.	171	113	37	22	3	54	36
29	Playboy	Playboy Enterprises	165	47	79	39	3	50	14
30	Entertainment Weekly	Time Warner	158	89	57	12	1	132	74
Total/Average			**$10,243**	**$6,351**	**$2,698**	**$1,200**	**164**	**$62**	**$39**
Percentage Contribution			**100%**	**62%**	**26%**	**12%**	**--**	**--**	**--**

Source: Advertising Age, *Morgan Stanley Research (Doug Arthur, Publishing Analyst).*

Similarities Between Cable TV and the Internet

We believe there will prove to be several key similarities between the evolution of cable content providers and Internet content providers, such as: 1) rapid, steady growth in advertising and usage from a low base; 2) rising revenue per subscriber (CPM) trends for the best brands; and 3) emergence of winning/best brands in specific categories, like ESPN in sports, CNN in news/networks, and MTV in music.

Here, we will focus on that last point, winning/best brands in specific categories:

America Online has created 19 channels (in addition to Find, Internet Connection, and People Connection) as a part of its interface/network programming and has organized these channels according to user interest. These channels (in order of usage/interest) are Personal Finance, Games, Today's News, Computers and Software, Lifestyles and Interests, Sports, Entertainment, Marketplace, Kids Only, Travel, Reference, MusicSpace, Learning and Culture, Digital City, Health, Newsstand, International, The HUB, and Style.

Notably, Microsoft is focusing its MSN Web programming efforts on six channels: 1) news, weather, sports; 2) show business, games, drama; 3) arts, nature, history; 4) personal — self, health, wealth; 5) media, zines, attitude; and 6) fun, teens, and comics.

Microsoft-developed media properties are a combination of partnerships, acquisitions, new efforts, and an extension of CD-ROM efforts: news/commentary — the MSNBC and *Slate* partnerships; interactive entertainment — Music Central and Cinemania CD-ROMs, the Internet Gaming Zone (acquired), and MSN (its online effort); services/shopping — The Plaza (the eShop acquisition); and local information and services — Cityscape.

Table 3–10

Basic Cable Networks — Gross Advertising Revenue*

		1985	1986	1987	1988	1989	1990	1991	1992	1993	1994	1995	1996E
ESPN	ESPN	$79	$96	$125	$147	$176	$260	$282	$303	$336	$407	$444	$479
USA	USA Network	58	71	80	114	160	197	228	260	260	295	330	390
CNN + HN	Cable News Network	70	91	111	143	190	221	248	278	269	289	318	343
TBS	TBS	186	204	222	262	266	276	287	302	340	356	283	403
MTV	Music Television	88	82	78	92	108	125	134	158	188	242	282	310
TNN	The Nashville Network	32	23	34	44	51	55	65	75	105	122	248	265
TNT	Turner Network Television	-	-	-	4	40	111	138	173	210	234	248	265
NICK+ NAN	Nickelodeon	10	16	27	32	52	69	93	126	182	234	227	313
LIFE	Lifetime Television	25	35	44	68	87	107	129	149	158	198	225	259
DSC	The Discovery Channel	1	4	6	17	28	46	63	89	120	144	174	211
A&E	Arts & Entertainment Network	6	8	14	23	36	49	71	85	112	138	165	179
FAM	The Family Channel	36	38	46	54	68	82	83	92	108	113	124	136
CNBC	Cable News Business Channel	-	-	-	-	15	23	37	46	58	70	97	110
VH-1	Video Hits One	2	4	8	12	22	28	29	39	52	61	71	82
BET	Black Entertainment Television	5	7	11	13	19	27	35	38	45	54	61	67
COM	Comedy Central	-	-	-	-	-	-	10	18	27	38	49	61
E!	E! Entertainment Television	-	-	1	2	6	10	11	14	17	29	48	54
TWC	The Weather Channel	8	9	11	14	17	20	22	25	34	41	48	55
TLC	The Learning Channel	-	4	4	6	7	9	11	13	18	26	43	61
SCI-FI	Sci-Fi Network	-	-	-	-	-	-	-	3	12	25	35	52
TOON	The Cartoon Network	-	-	-	-	-	-	-	2	6	14	21	30
PREVUE	The Prevue Channel	-	-	-	-	-	-	-	-	5	12	19	27
Court TV	Courtroom Television Network	-	-	-	-	-	-	2	6	7	10	15	21
CMT	Country Music Television	1	2	2	2	3	4	4	7	8	12	15	19
TRAV	The Travel Channel	-	-	2	8	4	2	3	5	6	9	13	16
PSCN	Prime Sports Channel Networks	-	-	-	-	3	4	4	5	8	9	11	13
NOST	Nostalgia Television	-	-	-	0	0	3	5	7	7	9	9	10

	1980	1981	1982	1983	1984									
Industry Total	$50	$105	$195	$331	$487	$634	$748	$891	$1,135	$1,461	$1,802	$2,046	$2,339	$2,725	$3,221	$3,685	$4,127

*Source: Paul Kagan Associates. *Network-specific data not available until 1985. E = Estimate.*

A channel programming strategy (similar to AOL's) worked well in cable and may prove to be the appropriate "channel proxy" for the Web. In order to appreciate what areas are hot and drive traffic, we list, with descriptions, the top 27 cable channels, ordered by 1995 gross advertising revenue — thus implying that where consumer interest levels are highest are where new brands may have the most upside business opportunity.

As we look at the Internet, we believe that old/new media leaders will emerge to dominate these channel categories. For example, ESPN SportsZone and SportsLine USA have presences on the Web that are analogous to ESPN's presence in cable. Clearly, though, ESPN's Web site benefits from the cross-promotion capability provided by its cable programming. On another front, CNET is a leader in information/news about the Internet, computers, and software and, somewhat like ESPN, benefits from its affiliated cable programming through cross-promotion.

Being No. 1 Matters . . .

One thing is clear across all media: Being the No. 1 brand in a market segment is much more lucrative than being No. 2, and after that, life can be very tough. Those companies with a cross-media jump start in a category, like ESPN in sports, should have a huge advantage on the Web.

A Look at Direct Marketing CPMs — Gauging direct marketing as a form of advertising is challenging because it is incorporated, in different degrees, in all media categories and comes in many different forms. For our purposes, we define direct marketing from a broad media perspective, as any direct communication to a consumer or business recipient that is designed to generate a response in the form of an order *(direct order)*, a request for further information *(lead generation)*, or a visit to a store or other place of business (like a Web site) for purchase of specific products or services *(traffic generation)*. Direct-response advertising thus is intended to achieve at least one of these three objectives.

Table 3–11

Basic Cable Networks — Advertising Revenue per Subscriber

		1985	1986	1987	1988	1989	1990	1991	1992	1993	1994	1995	1996E
ESPN	ESPN	$1.87	$2.12	$2.49	$2.62	$2.85	$3.94	$4.12	$4.27	$5.59	$5.46	$5.86	$6.17
USA	USA Network	1.67	1.83	1.79	2.23	2.81	3.20	3.47	3.75	3.56	4.01	4.41	5.08
CNN + HN	Cable News Network	1.24	1.40	1.44	1.57	1.80	1.91	2.02	3.93	3.69	3.89	4.19	4.42
TBS	TBS	4.58	4.61	4.62	4.93	4.53	4.37	4.32	4.36	4.73	4.84	5.09	5.24
MTV	Music Television	2.86	2.32	1.90	1.90	1.95	2.07	2.12	2.40	2.75	3.50	4.03	4.31
TNN	The Nashville Network	1.23	0.73	0.87	0.94	0.94	0.94	1.00	1.12	1.52	1.74	1.94	2.10
TNT	Turner Network Television	-	-	-	-	1.18	2.12	2.19	2.57	2.99	3.24	3.37	3.51
NICK+ NAN	Nickelodeon	0.30	0.49	0.69	0.67	0.94	1.14	1.45	1.87	2.59	3.27	3.80	4.15
LIFE	Lifetime Television	0.91	1.13	1.17	1.50	1.68	1.86	2.09	2.31	2.32	2.85	3.18	3.55
DSC	The Discovery Channel	-	0.34	0.24	0.43	0.56	0.78	0.97	1.31	1.68	1.96	2.34	2.75
A&E	Arts & Entertainment Network	0.32	0.30	0.43	0.57	0.77	0.90	1.90	1.33	1.66	1.99	2.35	2.45
FAM	The Family Channel	1.07	1.01	1.09	1.13	1.26	1.40	1.34	1.40	1.57	1.61	1.78	1.93
CNBC	Cable News Business Channel	-	-	-	-	-	1.26	1.02	0.85	1.00	1.16	1.56	1.70
VH-1	Video Hits One	-	0.21	0.32	0.39	0.58	0.64	0.60	0.72	0.92	1.04	1.20	1.33
BET	Black Entertainment Television	0.46	0.48	0.54	0.58	0.70	0.84	0.97	0.97	1.04	1.15	1.26	1.32
COM	Comedy Central	-	-	-	-	-	-	-	0.62	0.79	1.04	1.28	1.43
E!	E! Entertainment Television	-	-	-	0.22	0.40	0.53	0.53	0.60	0.61	0.89	1.39	1.43
TWC	The Weather Channel	0.39	0.36	0.32	0.34	0.36	0.38	0.38	0.42	0.53	0.63	0.72	0.80
TLC	The Learning Channel	-	0.48	0.46	0.58	0.60	0.60	0.63	0.63	0.64	0.73	1.03	1.26
SCI-FI	Sci-Fi Network	-	-	-	-	-	-	-	0.47	0.77	1.29	1.49	1.81
TOON	The Cartoon Network	-	-	-	-	-	-	-	0.33	1.21	1.11	1.21	1.36
PREVUE	The Prevue Channel	-	-	-	-	-	-	-	-	0.13	0.26	0.42	0.57
Court TV	Courtroom Television Network	-	-	-	-	-	-	-	0.74	0.53	0.56	0.64	0.70
CMT	Country Music Television	0.24	0.21	0.22	0.18	0.28	0.27	0.25	0.37	0.32	0.39	0.47	0.52
TRAV	The Travel Channel	-	-	-	0.81	0.20	0.13	0.12	0.25	0.27	0.39	0.57	0.78
NOST	Nostalgia Television	-	-	-	0.06	0.03	0.29	0.34	0.40	0.49	0.70	0.81	0.82
PSCN	Prime Sports Channel Networks	-	-	-	-	-	-	-	0.16	0.19	0.19	0.22	0.25
Industry Average		$1.32	$1.13	$1.16	$1.14	$1.22	$1.41	$1.48	$1.81	$1.93	$2.16	$2.37	$2.52

Source: Paul Kagan Associates.   E = Estimate.

Direct marketing is widely integrated throughout all advertising media, and includes direct mail, telephone marketing, television, radio, newspaper, magazines, and, of course, the Internet. We believe the form of direct marketing most comparable to the Internet is direct mail. According to the Direct Marketing Association, 1995 U.S. direct-mail expenditures totaled $31 billion (TV, radio, newspapers, and magazines direct-marketing expenditures are the amount of total ad revenue spent to achieve one of the three major direct marketing objectives, as discussed above). While generally recognized as the most "traditional" of direct-marketing media, direct mail is actually the second largest in terms of expenditures (in Table 3-13, telephone marketing is the largest, estimated at $54 billion in 1995, or 40% of all direct marketing spending; however, telemarketing is not considered an advertising "medium" per se and is more aligned with promotional spending).

Direct mail gained initial success in the 19th Century, when consumption patterns in small-town America were significantly changed by the advent of mail-order catalogs from Sears Roebuck and Montgomery Ward. Today, direct-mail advertising still consists mostly of mail-order catalogs, with some local co-op advertising as well. The Direct Marketing Association reports that in 1994, 53% of the U.S. adult population ordered merchandise or services by phone or mail. Of those who did, more than 24% spent $200 or more on such purchases, the most popular of which was clothing. Some of our favorite "direct mail" company Web sites include www.llbean.com, www.dell.com, and www.netmarket.com.

Direct mail is the third-largest "medium" in terms of advertising spending, and follows newspapers and TV. McCann-Erickson states that in 1995, U.S. direct-mail advertising expenditures totalled $33 billion, over 20% of the $161 billion in total U.S. advertising expenditures across both measured media (TV, radio, daily newspapers, magazines) and non-measured media (including direct mail, yellow pages, weekly newspapers, outdoor ads). Chapter 12 features tables of ad spending across these media over time.

Table 3–12

Basic Cable Networks — U.S. TV Household Coverage

		1985	1986	1987	1988	1989	1990	1991	1992	1993	1994	1995	1996E
ESPN	ESPN	43%	46%	51%	55%	60%	63%	64%	66%	67%	67%	68%	69%
USA	USA Network	36	40	46	51	55	59	62	65	66	66	67	68
CNN + HN	Cable News Network	39	43	48	54	59	62	64	66	67	67	68	68
TBS	TBS	42	45	48	53	57	61	62	65	66	66	67	68
MTV	Music Television	32	37	42	49	54	58	59	62	63	62	63	64
TNN	The Nashville Network	29	33	42	47	53	57	58	61	64	63	65	66
TNT	Turner Network Television	0	0	0	22	41	57	60	63	65	65	66	67
NICK+ NAN	Nickelodeon	30	35	40	49	54	59	61	63	65	64	66	67
LIFE	Lifetime Television	28	33	40	46	51	56	58	61	63	62	64	65
DSC	The Discovery Channel	5	16	31	42	51	59	61	63	66	66	67	68
A&E	Arts & Entertainment Network	20	25	36	41	47	54	57	60	62	62	64	65
FAM	The Family Channel	35	39	42	48	52	57	59	62	63	63	64	65
CNBC	Cable News Business Channel	0	0	0	0	14	19	49	51	54	55	56	58
VH-1	Video Hits One	13	20	26	34	38	43	47	51	53	53	54	55
BET	Black Entertainment Television	13	14	20	24	28	33	35	37	42	42	44	46
COM	Comedy Central	0	0	0	0	0	0	24	29	32	33	36	39
E!	E! Entertainment Television	0	0	5	13	15	19	21	23	28	30	32	35
TWC	The Weather Channel	-	-	-	-	-	-	-	-	-	-	-	-
TLC	The Learning Channel	7	8	9	11	13	15	17	20	30	34	40	45
SCI-FI	Sci-Fi Network	0	0	0	0	0	0	0	12	17	18	23	27
TOON	The Cartoon Network	-	-	-	-	-	-	-	-	-	-	-	-
PREVUE	The Prevue Channel	0	0	0	0	0	0	0	8	22	28	29	30
Court TV	Courtroom Television Network	0	0	0	0	0	0	6	9	15	17	25	28
CMT	Country Music Television	7	7	8	9	11	13	16	19	26	27	30	33
TRAV	The Travel Channel	0	0	8	11	15	18	19	19	21	21	21	21
NOST	Nostalgia Television	-	-	-	-	9	14	14	16	12	10	10	11
	Average HH/Network (MM)	25	27	29	32	36	38	39	39	39	37	39	41
	Basic subscribers (MM)	42	45	48	50	54	57	58	59	61	62	63	63
	Cable TV Households*	47	50	52	56	60	64	65	67	68	69	70	70
	TV Household Penetration	75%	79%	82%	85%	90%	94%	96%	96%	97%	97%	96%	96%

Includes basic cable subscribers, illegal subscribers, SMATV, wireless cable, backyard dish, DBS and telco homes.
Source: Paul Kagan Associates.   E = Estimate.

Direct mail grew 11% from 1994 to 1995, as the growth in the economy promoted greater direct-mail advertising to capitalize on a healthy consumer market. Other methods of direct-response selling, like telemarketing, have also experienced strong growth in recent years. This type of advertising can be very effective, as corporations use extensive databases of customer information to target the most attractive segments of the population for their particular product or service.

While costs for direct marketing campaigns can vary widely, CPMs can range up to $1,000 or more, depending on the cost of production, printing, postage, and so on. Using a reasonably wide range for total CPM for the medium ($200–1,000), we derive Table 3-14, which shows the cost per response for direct mail. The Direct Marketing Association reports that the average response rate for direct mail is 17%.

Is the Internet Just Direct-Mail/Response Advertising?

On a grand scale, there are two main purposes for an advertisement: building brand or direct marketing. Brand advertising associates positive qualities or emotions with a company's product or service, while direct marketing attempts to stimulate a direct sale. All advertising falls somewhere on the spectrum between these two points. And in thinking about the Internet as an advertising medium, it is important to clarify how it fits in, what type of advertising works well, and what the specific strengths and weaknesses of the medium are in achieving each of these two goals.

Table 3-13

U.S. Direct Marketing Advertising Expenditure and Sales Growth

	U.S. Direct Marketing Advertising Expenditures ($ MM)			U.S. Direct Marketing-Driven Sales ($ MM)			DM Advertising Expenditures as a Percentage of DM Sales	
	1990	1995	1990-95 CAGR	1990	1995	1990-95 CAGR	1990	1995
Direct Mail	$23,400	$31,200	6%	$250,000	$356,100	7%	9%	9%
Direct Order	9,600	12,500	5	95,900	131,200	7	10	10
Lead Generation	10,400	14,200	6	115,900	173,200	8	9	8
Traffic Generation	3,400	4,500	6	38,200	51,700	6	9	9
Telephone Marketing	40,500	54,100	6	272,800	385,600	7	15	14
Direct Order	13,600	17,500	5	83,800	114,300	6	16	15
Lead Generation	21,700	21,300	6	164,300	239,500	8	14	14
Traffic Generation	3,200	4,400	7	24,700	31,800	5	13	14
Newspaper	11,100	13,600	4	105,600	137,000	5	11	10
Direct Order	3,200	3,900	4	27,500	35,700	5	12	11
Lead Generation	5,400	6,600	4	53,600	70,500	6	10	9
Traffic Generation	2,400	3,000	5	24,600	30,800	5	10	10
Magazine	5,200	6,800	6	43,700	60,700	7	12	11
Direct Order	1,400	1,800	5	12,400	17,000	7	11	10
Lead Generation	3,300	4,300	5	26,000	36,700	7	13	12
Traffic Generation	600	700	3	5,300	7,100	6	11	10
Television	10,100	14,100	7	49,600	72,700	8	20	19
Direct Order	1,900	2,700	7	10,600	15,400	8	18	18
Lead Generation	7,100	9,800	7	29,500	44,200	8	24	22
Traffic Generation	1,100	1,500	6	9,500	13,100	7	12	12
Radio	3,100	4,100	6	18,000	25,500	7	17	16
Direct Order	600	800	6	3,900	5,500	7	16	15
Lead Generation	2,100	2,800	6	10,100	14,600	8	21	19
Traffic Generation	400	500	5	4,000	5,300	6	9	9
Other	7,900	10,200	5	40,400	55,000	6	20	19
Direct Order	2,800	3,600	5	14,400	19,300	6	20	19
Lead Generation	3,800	4,900	5	16,800	23,800	7	23	21
Traffic Generation	1,300	1,700	6	9,300	11,900	5	14	14
Total	**$101,300**	**$134,000**	**6%**	**$780,100**	**$1,092,600**	**7%**	**13%**	**12%**
Direct Order	33,100	42,800	5	248,400	338,400	6	13	13
Lead Generation	55,800	74,600	6	416,100	602,500	8	13	12
Traffic Generation	12,400	16,200	6	115,600	151,700	6	11	11

Source: The WEFA Group, Direct Marketing Association.

We submit that, although brand-building through advertising is possible on the Internet, it is not as effective as other media (especially TV) in achieving this objective (at least in its current state). The lack of bandwidth (and the resulting lack of great sound and animation) makes it less powerful than the life-like images and sounds that TV and radio provide. In other words, youthful, suntanned frolickers who "Tap the Rockies" in a Coors Light TV commercial (or even those early Infiniti ads, with no product in them whatsoever) build brand — the Internet cannot currently deliver such effective branding.

However, for direct marketing, the Internet offers the ability to target and deliver messages to an audience with specific demographics and interests, and allows the user to interact instantly with that message. In essence, direct response advertisers sell goods and services to customers individually, and no other medium affords users such immediate access at the point of sale.

The advent of electronic commerce over online services and the Internet, as well as the growth of televised shopping channels, might be seen as a threat to direct mail. On the contrary, we think these new advertising methods have not had a material impact and may in some circumstances complement or increase the amount of direct-mail advertising spending. Direct-mail advertising provides a method for sellers to enter the home without having to wait for the initiative of the buyer, and that can be extremely effective. This intrusiveness is, in fact, direct marketing's appeal, and once a consumer makes an online or televised home shopping purchase, that customer is then sent catalogs in the future.

In comparing the relative effectiveness of media buys, some similarities can be drawn between a successful response in direct mail and delivering a user directly to an advertiser's Web site when he or she clicks on an advertisement (we will refer to these as "transfers").

Table 3-15 uses what we believe is a reasonable range of CPMs for the Web ($10–90) and calculates the cost per transfer based on the rate at which users click on the ad (the "click rate"). The most recent average click-through rate released by I/PRO (a Web measurement company) and DoubleClick (a Web rep firm) was 2.1%, though, as we discuss in Chapter 6, this rate can vary widely.

For direct mail, at a 17% response rate (the industry average) and a $600 CPM (the midpoint of our range), the cost per response is $3.53. If we take the average online ad click-through rate of 2.1%, and solve for the same cost per response, we arrive at a reasonable CPM of $74. Thus, we can see that online advertising can certainly compare favorably with direct mail on a cost-per-lead basis, especially if the click rate can be nudged higher. If the direct-mail market is indeed that large, there is thus a sizeable opportunity through the use of similar techniques on the Internet.

And There are Always the Home Shopping Channels

Another example of the size and power of direct marketing is the success of the home shopping channels, which marked the advent of a whole new type of promotional advertising and purchasing in the TV world. Below, we provide brief descriptions of the two major ones that benefitted, yes, from a new medium:

The **Home Shopping Network (HSN)** sells a variety of consumer goods and services by means of live, customer-interactive electronic retail sales programs, which are transmitted 24 hours a day, seven days per week, via satellite to cable television systems, affiliated broadcast television stations, and satellite dish receivers. HSN reaches over 69 million television households, and the company estimates that there are 5 million "member" HSN households (HSN defines "members" as simply households which have made more than one purchase). In 1995, HSN generated $1.0 billion in revenue, down 10% from 1994. In terms of reach, cable accounted for 45 million, broadcast accounted for 20 million and satellite accounted for 4 million households. HSN's product offerings include: jewelry; hard goods, which include consumer electronics, collectibles, housewares, and consumables; soft goods, which consist primarily of clothing and fashion accessories; and cosmetics. In 1995, jewelry accounted for 39% of net sales, hard goods 37%, soft goods 14%, and cosmetics 10%.

Quality Value Control (QVC) was founded in June 1986 by Franklin Mint's founder, Joseph Segel. In the U.S., QVC operates two cable shopping services — the original QVC plus 2Q, which are broadcast from West Chester, Pa. Although QVC has a diverse programming mix (it distributes over 5 million monthly program guides), 35% of programming is derived directly from jewelry lines, making QVC one of the world's largest sellers of 14-karat gold jewelry. In 1995, the company fielded over 70 million phone calls and shipped over 46 million packages, for total sales that topped $1.4 billion, up 14% from 1994.

Table 3-14
Cost per Response for a Direct-Mail Advertiser

		$200	$400	$600	$800	$1,000
	30%	$0.67	$1.33	$2.00	$2.67	$3.33
Response	25%	0.80	1.60	2.40	3.20	4.00
Rate	20%	1.00	2.00	3.00	4.00	5.00
	15%	1.33	2.67	4.00	5.33	6.67
	10%	2.00	4.00	6.00	8.00	10.00

Source: Computer Advertisers' Media Advisor, Morgan Stanley Technology Research.

Table 3-15
Cost per Transfer for a Web Advertiser

		$20	$40	$60	$80	$100
	5%	$0.40	$0.80	$1.20	$1.60	$2.00
Click	4%	0.50	1.00	1.50	2.00	2.50
Rate	3%	0.67	1.33	2.00	2.67	3.33
	2%	1.00	2.00	3.00	4.00	5.00
	1%	2.00	4.00	6.00	8.00	10.00

Source: Computer Advertisers' Media Advisor, Morgan Stanley Technology Research.

QVC signs an impressive 150,000 new members each month. On average the company fields 113,000 orders a day — 35,000 through automated voice response units. At full capacity, there are more than 5,300 phone lines, and QVC's customer representatives can handle close to 50,000 purchases an hour. QVC operates four distribution centers that cover more than 1.2 million square feet, the size of 27 football fields. At full capacity, QVC can pack over 400,000 packages daily and ship 80% of the packages within 24 hours of taking the order.

Here, TV home shopping offers another example of the opportunity that the Internet offers marketers. There are prohibitive production costs for TV, limited channel capacity, and the information offered for each product is almost entirely programmer-driven. With the Internet, users can seek out the products and services they want (and not have to wait for the TV to deliver it to them) and obtain deeper information when desired. In addition, Internet sites are much cheaper to run than TV channels (and each company can have its own site, tailored to its particular message). TV also requires that you go "out of band" and use a different medium to order the product, whereas the Internet can facilitate online transactions.

Will Internet Advertising Growth Affect Other Media?

As technology and society changes, so does the mix of advertising spending across various media. Figure 3-3 and Table 3-16 display the change in this mix between 1975 and 1995. While radio and magazine revenues maintained a consistent percentage of total advertising revenue, newspapers declined by 10%, with broadcast TV (with an increase of 3%) and the introduction of cable TV revenue (which grew to 5% of the total) taking up most of the slack. The increase in broadcast TV can be attributed to the growth in the number of TV households (from 72 million in 1975 to 95 million in 1995) and the continued increase in the reach, branding, and buying efficiency that TV has been able to deliver. We mark the beginning of cable TV as an entertainment/advertising medium with the launch of HBO in 1976, and cable, too, has grown in its ability to deliver better efficiency. The marked decline in newspaper advertising has been attributed to many factors, including a slower rate of audience growth and societal changes like the reduction in leisure time and the shifting of demographic focus to younger audiences (who read newspapers less frequently than older demographic groups).

Figure 3-3
Change in Advertising Revenue Mix From 1975 to 1995

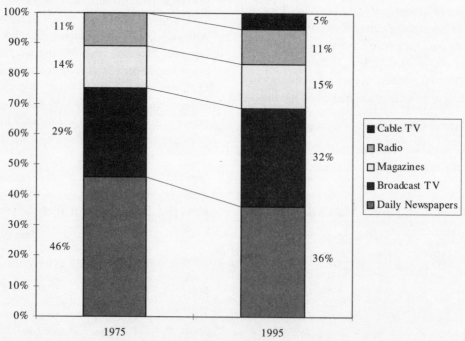

Sources: McCann-Erickson, Veronis, Suhler & Associates, Wilkofsky Gruen Associates, Cable Data–Paul Kagan Associates.

In time, growth in Internet advertising will likely nab spending from other media. Forrester Research (Figure 3-4 and Table 3-17) believes that newspapers (especially classified ads) will be affected the most, followed by yellow pages, then radio, and finally, TV.

Forrester notes that classified advertising carries the greatest risk because the distribution/access for classified ads benefits most from the strength of online features: search function; rapid change/updating; and availability of local/personal information. We note that 35–40% of newspaper advertising revenue is derived from classified advertising.

Morgan Stanley's cable analyst, Rich Bilotti, believes that even though cable television advertising has grown rapidly over the past several years, peak performance has occurred when the overall television advertising market was growing at its most rapid pace. The reason for this phenomenon is that most media buyers at the top 20 advertisers are reluctant to reduce their purchases of conventional broadcast television, and generally increase those purchases by some level in all but the worst years. Therefore, availability of funds to spend on new activities tends to increase most sharply in years when overall advertising budgets are ballooning.

In general, total advertising has been increasing on the order of $5 billion per year, and in most cases, about $3 bil-

Table 3-16
Change in Advertising Revenue Mix From 1975 to 1995

($ Millions)	1975	1995
Daily Newspapers	$8,234	$36,045
Broadcast TV	5,263	32,220
Magazines	2,458	14,627
Radio	1,980	11,320
Cable TV	0	5,342
Total	**$17,935**	**$99,554**

Sources: McCann-Erickson, Veronis, Suhler & Associates, Wilkofsky Gruen Associates, Cable Data–Paul Kagan Associates.

lion, or 60%, is a "locked-in" amount that each medium gets across the board. The $2 billion remaining is, in effect, a "jump ball." In a very strong year, the incremental increase generally appears in the latter category.

For the Internet, significant drivers of growth should be both the amount of "jump ball" revenue up for grabs and the rate at which the medium can win it away from the typical winners of such secondary spending, such as cable, syndicated programming, and radio.

For now, Internet spending as a percentage of total advertising spending is too small to significantly affect most budgets for other media — but this will likely change in time.

Figure 3-4

Forrester's View of Percentage of the Traditional Advertising Revenue to be Lost to Internet Advertising

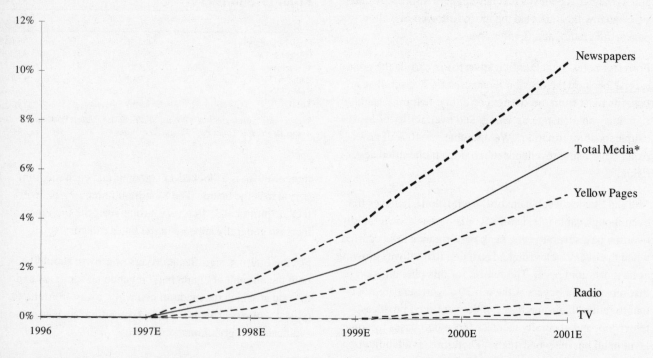

*Source: Forrester Research.   * Includes other media not explicitly listed. E = Estimate.*

Table 3-17

Forrester's View of Percentage of the Traditional Advertising Revenue to be Lost to Internet Advertising

	1996	1997E	1998E	1999E	2000E	2001E
Newspapers	--	--	1.5%	3.7%	7.0%	10.5%
TV	--	--	--	--	0.1	0.3
Radio	--	--	--	--	0.4	0.8
Yellow Pages	--	--	0.4	1.3	3.4	5.1
Total Media*	--	--	0.9	2.2	4.5	6.8

*Source: Forrester Research.   * Includes other media not explicitly listed. E = Estimate.*

Chapter 4: An Update on Internet Usage Trends/Forecasts

Summary

◆ **The Internet is growing at an unprecedented pace**, and, for now, most market data are suspect. There are numbers that seem solid, like the 8 million-plus America Online users (largely consumers) and the 50 million users of Netscape Navigator (although Netscape believes that 80% of those users are Intranet users, and frequency of usage "beyond the firewall" is tough to predict).

◆ We believe there **are currently 20–35 million Internet users (our point estimate for the end of 1996 is 28 million)**. That's a huge range, but big at both ends, nonetheless, and it's especially compelling since we believe there were only about 9 million users one year before. These users are a mix of both business people and consumers.

◆ We project **compounded annual growth in Internet users for the next four years of 54%,** and we believe that **more than 150 million people will use the Internet by the year 2000** — in fact, this assumption may be conservative, since there are already 150–200 million PC users worldwide.

◆ **Web demographics are compelling for marketers**.

A Perspective on the Evolution of the Internet

Everyone's heard the hype surrounding the Internet and the Web, yet we think there is ample cause for it — we continue to believe that the Web may be the single most important development in technology since the debut of the PC, and that, in time, it should have a pervasive effect on our daily lives.

In general, we still believe that development of the Internet industry will follow a pattern similar to that of the personal computer, which emerged in the early 1980s and has seen three distinct phases (Figure 4-1). In the early years of the Internet, we believe, hardware/**infrastructure** will dominate, but over time, value will shift first to enabling technology (like an operating system and the necessary **software** and **services** to manage an interactive environment) and ultimately to programming, **content,** and **aggregation**.

Although we think advertising revenue can assist growth for certain Internet-related companies, advertising-supported media companies typically trade at lower multiples than subscription-based media companies (e.g., professional publishing and information services), even on a growth-adjusted basis, due to the cyclicality of ad spending. Investors prefer recurring, stable revenue streams to big

advertising dollars. Thus, many traditional media companies have been strategically focused on reducing advertising revenues as a percentage of total revenue (in favor of subscriptions, transactions, and the like).

Internet Market Size — Big and Bigger

The Internet is growing at an unprecedented pace (Figure 4-2), creating enormous opportunities for investment and wealth creation (as well as massive capital losses). At the same time, because of this rapid growth, it can be difficult to gather accurate market data and make informed business decisions. As we discussed in *The Internet Report*, back in

Figure 4-1

**Timing and Development
Of the Three Internet Market Segments**

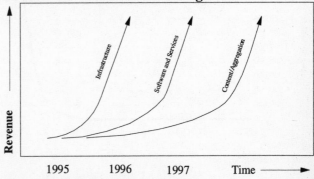

Source: *Morgan Stanley Technology Research.*

4-2

Figure 4-2

Internet Domain Name Registrations, 1985–1996

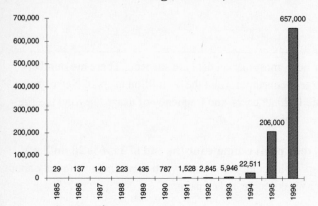

Source: InterNIC, Internet.org.

December 1995, such fast growth should inevitably lead to breakage and dislocations in the Internet market.

Currently, Internet measurement seems somewhat analogous to Heisenberg's uncertainty principle — in that it's nearly impossible to determine exactly where the Internet is and where it is going at the same time. Current estimates place the number of Internet users at 20–35 million (if we include Intranet usage, the number would be much higher), with projections of the number of users by the year 2000 ranging from 120 million to 200 million.

According to a first-half 1996 analysis of Web usage by I/PRO, of 1.5 billion visits to 75 ad-supported sites, site-traffic jumped 67% between January and May — clearly, these data have directional significance. This growth

should only accelerate as mass-marketed Internet access products, from such companies such as AOL, AT&T, Sprint, MCI, Microsoft, and many others, make getting online easier.

In addition, corporate America has been moving online. IDC has estimated that the number of Fortune 500 companies with a Web presence increased in 1996 from 175 to nearly 400 (an increase from 35% to 80% penetration) — an important barometer for how quickly the Web is becoming a mainstream channel for major corporations' marketing, communications, and business transactions.

InterNIC reports that, through December 1996, there were 897,662 registered Internet domains (these are the unique names, such as microsoft.com, that identify an Internet site), of which 73% were created in 1996 alone. Of the total sample, 796,039 (or 89%) were commercial (".com") domains (Table 4-1). The number of Internet hosts (a host is any computer whose services are available to other computers on the Internet), tracked by Network Wizards,

Table 4-1

Internet Domain Share through December 1996

Domain Type	Number	Share
.com	796,039	89%
.org	53,141	6%
.net	44,431	5%
.edu	3,309	<1%
.gov	548	<1%
Other	194	<1%
Total	**897,662**	**100%**

.com = commercial; .org = organization; .net = network; .edu = education; .gov = government. Source: InterNIC.

Figure 4-3

Internet Host Growth (Normal Scale), 1969–1996

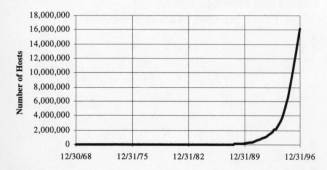

Source: Network Wizards.

Figure 4-4

Internet Host Growth (Semi-Log Scale), 1969–1996

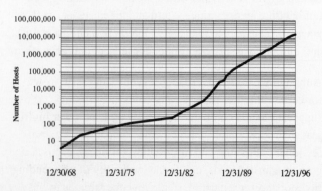

Source: Network Wizards.

Figure 4-5
Daily Hits Against Netscape's Web Site, 1/96 Through 11/96

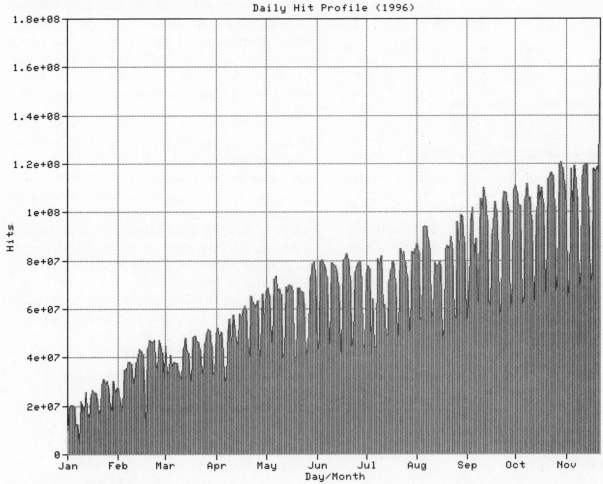

Source: Netscape Communications.

has shown similarly explosive growth (Figures 4-3 and 4-4). *At its ever-increasing pace, the Web is adding roughly 2,500 new domains daily, or about 75,000 per month. That's real growth!*

As a specific example of the tremendous growth in site traffic, Figure 4-5 graphs the daily hits that Netscape's Web site has received in the year to date — average traffic has risen from fewer than 20 million hits per day at the beginning of 1996 to 120 million in late November (for 500% growth). Note: the dips are due to weekend decreases in site traffic.

We estimate 167 million PC users worldwide by the end of 1996 (Table 4-3), and we expect about 84 million PCs to

ship in 1997. PC shipments are expected to pass TV shipments in the next year or two. Moreover, record-high sales of modems and networking equipment imply that PC connectivity is on the rise. All of this lends credibility to the idea that the Internet as a medium for delivering information and entertainment content may become a significant alternative to TV. Coopers & Lybrand recently reported that 58% of Internet users indicated that their online time comes at the expense of watching television. We estimate that, at the end of 1996, 28 million PC users, or 14%, had Web access (Table 4-2). By the year 2000, we could see as many as 157 million PC users with Web access.

Table 4-2

Worldwide Connectivity Market 1996–2000E

(Millions)

	1996	1997E	1998E	1999E	2000E
Users of:					
PCs	167	191	219	246	269
E-Mail	60	80	130	180	200
Internet/Web	28	46	82	134	157
Online/Hybrid	13	18	23	27	30

Source: Morgan Stanley Technology Research.
E = Morgan Stanley Research Estimate.

Web Usage — Noontime, During the Week

Although the amount of Web traffic is rapidly increasing, Web usage patterns remain fairly stable. In a recent study, I/PRO found that daily traffic, which has a heavy business-user bias, is highest on weekdays (Figure 4-6), and that about 60% of all traffic occurs during the nine-hour workday (9 a.m. to 6 p.m.), as recorded by each server in its time zone; the highest traffic level is around noon (Figure 4-7). America Online, unlike the Web, experiences a traffic surge during the prime-time evening hours.

Web Demographics Are Compelling

In considering how much the Internet audience is worth to advertisers, it is useful to highlight the makeup of the market into which they are selling. Information about the demographics and purchasing patterns of Internet users is emerging, and current data offer what we think is compelling evidence for advertisers to consider the Internet as a viable option for branding, promoting, and selling products and services.

Contrary to some popular perceptions, Internet users are not young, poverty-stricken nerds — in fact, the median Internet age has been placed by various studies at between 30 and 34. A.C. Nielsen conducted a study that found only about one in ten Internet users is under the age of 18. The study also showed that 64% of users are college-educated, that the median income is about $60,000, with 25% above $80,000, and that 50% hold professional or managerial jobs. Further, at least 60% of these users are online more than two hours a week and about 50% have Internet access at work. For many advertisers, these are strong demographics, which we believe will mean an increased willingness among advertisers to spend, or spend more, for Internet exposure.

Figure 4-6

Percentage of Web Traffic by Day of Week

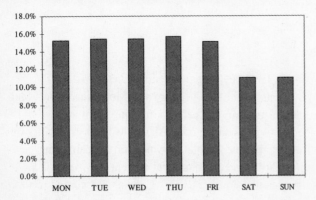

Source: I/PRO Research.

Figure 4-7

Percentage of Web Traffic by Time of Day

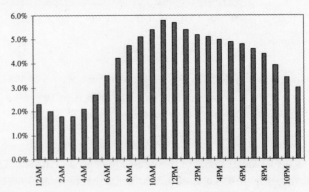

Source: I/PRO Research.

Table 4-3
Base Case Estimates for PC, E-Mail, and Internet Users, 1984–2000E

	1984	1985	1986	1987	1988	1989	1990	1991	1992	1993	1994	1995	1996	1997E	1998E	1999E	2000E
Worldwide																	
PC Unit Shipments (MM)	9	9	10	12	14	16	19	24	31	41	50	60	71	84	98	114	130
Y/Y Growth	--	2%	12%	17%	17%	14%	19%	26%	29%	32%	22%	20%	19%	18%	17%	16%	15%
PC Lifetime Shipments (MM)	23	32	42	54	68	84	103	127	158	199	249	309	380	464	563	677	807
PCs in Use (MM) (a)	23	28	35	40	45	52	61	73	90	115	146	182	222	265	313	367	426
Pct. with Two PCs (b)	2%	2%	3%	5%	6%	7%	8%	10%	15%	20%	22%	23%	25%	28%	30%	33%	37%
Actual # of PC Users (MM)	23	27	34	38	43	49	56	66	77	92	114	140	167	191	219	246	269
Y/Y Growth	--	22%	24%	13%	11%	14%	16%	17%	16%	20%	24%	23%	19%	15%	15%	12%	9%
U.S.																	
PC Unit Shipments (MM)	6	6	6	7	7	7	8	9	12	16	19	23	26	30	35	40	46
Y/Y Growth	--	-6%	3%	8%	6%	0%	12%	18%	31%	31%	23%	17%	15%	16%	16%	14%	15%
U.S. Pct. of PC Unit Shipments	70%	65%	60%	55%	50%	44%	41%	38%	39%	38%	39%	38%	37%	36%	36%	35%	35%
PC Lifetime Shipments (MM)	16	21	25	30	34	37	42	49	61	77	97	117	140	169	201	240	286
PCs in Use (MM) (a)	16	18	21	22	23	23	25	28	35	44	57	69	82	96	112	130	151
Pct. with Two PCs (b)	5%	6%	7%	8%	10%	15%	20%	22%	23%	25%	28%	30%	33%	37%	42%	48%	50%
Actual # of PC Users (MM)	15	17	20	20	20	19	20	22	27	33	41	48	55	61	65	68	76
Y/Y Growth	--	12%	14%	5%	0%	-5%	3%	9%	23%	24%	23%	18%	14%	11%	7%	4%	12%
Worldwide Connectivity Estimates																	
# of PC Users (MM)	23	27	34	38	43	49	56	66	77	92	114	140	167	191	219	246	269
# E-Mail Users (MM) (c)	1	1	2	3	4	5	6	8	12	18	25	35	60	80	130	180	200
Pct. PCs with E-Mail Access	4%	4%	6%	8%	9%	10%	11%	12%	16%	20%	22%	25%	36%	42%	59%	73%	74%
# Internet/Web Users (MM)	<1	<1	<1	<1	<1	<1	<1	<1	1	1	3	9	28	46	82	134	157
Pct. PCs with Internet Access	1%	1%	1%	1%	1%	1%	1%	1%	1%	1%	3%	7%	17%	24%	38%	55%	58%
# Online/Hybrid Users (MM)	<1	<1	<1	<1	<1	<1	<1	1	2	3	5	8	13	18	23	27	30
Pct. PCs with Online/Hybrid Access	1%	1%	1%	1%	1%	1%	1%	2%	3%	3%	4%	6%	8%	9%	10%	11%	11%
Windows Installed Base (MM) (d)	<1	<1	<1	<1	<1	<1	3	8	23	44	77	115	--	--	--	--	--

(a) Assumes that PCs have an average useful life of four years. (b) Estimated number of PC users that use second PCs: home, office, and portables.
(c) Estimates of all e-mail accounts. We estimate that 50% of 1995 e-mail users could be connected to the Internet. (d) Estimated legal (non-pirated/copied)
shipments of Microsoft Windows. Arrows added to compare Windows ramp with Internet ramp.
Source: Morgan Stanley Technology Research.
E = Morgan Stanley Technology Research Estimate.

Chapter 5: The Latest and Greatest From Some of the Hottest Web Sites

Summary

◆ In this section, we show **examples of how various content providers are approaching their online content offerings, in the hopes of gaining traffic/users, luring advertisers, and generating revenue in other ways.**

Clearly, if Web site traffic grows and advertising benefits can be garnered, advertisers will only crank up the volume of advertising dollars spent on the Web. In this chapter, we take a quick look at what some of the best and brightest companies are doing to boost traffic on their sites (or their service, in AOL's case) and to encourage advertisers to ante up by offering them eyeballs and good demographics and data. We look at information aggregators (Yahoo! and AOL); a content provider (CNET); a hybrid site (Intuit's QFN); and a commerce site (Amazon.com).

Each of these companies takes a different approach to attracting users and advertisers. Yahoo!s business model relies exclusively on advertising revenue (and, in search of merchandising and transaction revenue, the company just launched a shopping site). CNET relies largely on advertising but is ramping up several sites that should generate transaction revenue. AOL relies largely on subscription revenue but is ramping up merchandising, advertising, and transaction revenue. QFN relies largely on revenue generated from placement and aggregation of ads from financial institutions and lead-fees generated from providing customers to financial institutions. And Amazon.com relies on the margins from sales of books on its site.

Aggregators

Yahoo!s Web site offers one of the leading search engines based on traffic — it is, in effect, an online *TV Guide* for the Internet. Yahoo!s marketing goal is to create the leading branded search engine, and thereby become every Web user's "front door" to the Internet. When a Web user becomes perplexed because the Web has countless channels (and everything's on), Yahoo! would like that user to go directly to www.yahoo.com to find what he or she wants. And if Yahoo! can continue to be a Web front-door-of-choice, and if Web traffic continues to grow, then space near that front door should have a rising value for advertisers.

Yahoo! is broadening its offerings of media properties and Internet programming within www.yahoo.com — the company is creating various destinations/channels to provide compelling target-market opportunities for advertisers and to expand its inventory of available advertising vehicles. For example, Yahoo! is expanding its destinations by: geography (e.g., Yahoo! New York and Yahoo! France); subject (Business/Economy and Entertainment); demographic (Yahooligans! for Kids); and personalization (My Yahoo!, a self-customizable home page for users). In addition, Yahoo! is getting into television co-branding and cross-promotion to boost its brand name and drive traffic to its site by providing technology information for TV newscasts.

Yahoo.com Home Page

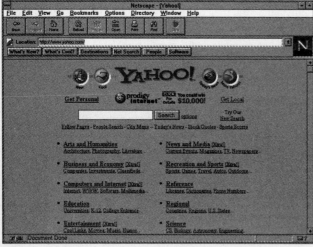

Yahoo! Entertainment Page

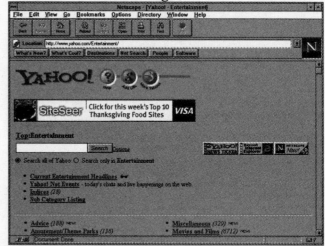

Yahoo! New York

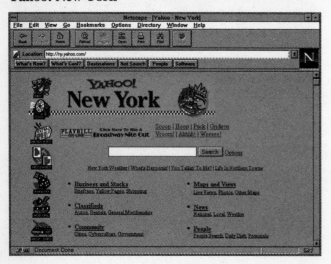

My Yahoo!

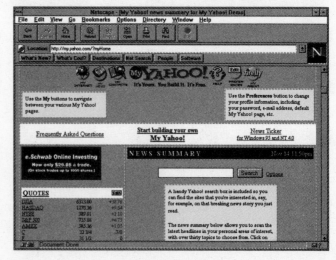

America Online (AOL), the world's leading Internet online service, also provides an online *TV Guide*-like product for its own offerings and the Internet. AOL's offerings, in comparison to Yahoo!, are in our view easier to use and more mainstream. AOL has a broad variety of media properties that are segmented by channel, including Personal Finance, Games, Today's News, Computers and Software, Lifestyles and Interests, Sports, Entertainment, Marketplace, Kids Only, Travel, Reference, MusicSpace, Learning and Culture, Digital City, Health, Newsstand, International, The HUB, and Style (see AOL's Channels screen, displayed below). In addition, AOL's Welcome screen, the first thing an AOL user sees after logging on, alerts users to the five or so events that it deems to be most important or interesting at the time. Like Yahoo!, AOL is keenly interested in providing advertisers with segmented demographics based on its channel approach. And the company is aggressively ramping up its efforts to increase revenue from merchandising and transactions.

AOL's approach to the Internet is driven by its success in the online market over the last decade. AOL offers a full-service, easy-to-use product to consumers. The idea is that AOL makes the following things easy: installation of software; obtaining access on a nationwide basis; billing (with reasonable pricing); and customer support. In addition, AOL's approach to online programming is *USA Today*-like, in that its channel programming (and programming within channels) is well done and mainstream.

Over the years, AOL has worked to develop a sense of community with its customers through services such as chat and e-mail. In time, we believe that AOL will work to develop even stronger relationships with its customers by more effectively targeting items of interest, based on user profiles. AOL has, in our view, an impressive database of user demographics and online usage patterns that has been developed over many years. As long as AOL can curb its subscriber churn, we believe the company's base of 8-million-plus active users should provide advertisers with an attractive marketing opportunity and provide AOL with the opportunity to boost revenue streams that are incremental to subscriber fees.

America Online Channels Screen

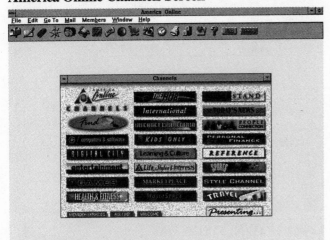

America Online Sports Channel

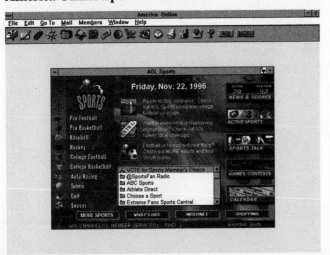

America Online Travel Channel

America Online Marketplace Channel

5-4

Content Provider

CNET is a leading Web/TV-based provider of news and information about technology. The CNET team believed early on that one of the most compelling early market opportunities on the Web would be related to the advertising and marketing of technology products (after all, by default, everyone who visits CNET's sites is a Web-enabled PC user). Taking a cue from the computer-oriented magazine success stories of the last decade (such as Ziff-Davis, IDG, and CMP), CNET has launched a family of technology-news-oriented Web sites that it cross-promotes through its TV programming efforts.

The company's key sites are CNET.COM (for broad-based technology information), NEWS.COM (24-hour coverage of technology news), GAMECENTER.COM (information for computer gamers),

SHAREWARE.COM (an online warehouse for downloading free software), DOWNLOAD.COM (a warehouse for purchasing software), SEARCH.COM (an aggregation of different Internet search engines), BUYDIRECT.COM (a site for purchasing software directly from developers), MEDIADOME.COM (a site created in a joint venture with Intel which showcases cutting edge multimedia content), and ACTIVEX.COM (for the ActiveX development community).

In addition to offering technology advertisers compelling demographics and high traffic, CNET has also been aggressive about creating tools to provide advertisers with key data and facts about usage. CNET has been aggressive about launching sites that we believe should generate transaction revenue for the company.

CNET.COM

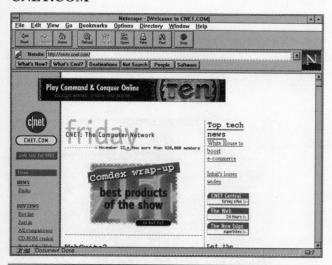

CNET GAMECENTER.COM

CNET NEWS.COM

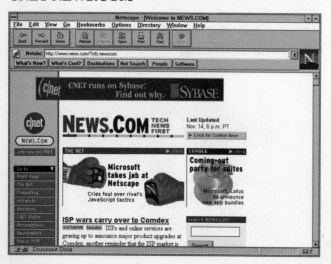

CNET DOWNLOAD.COM

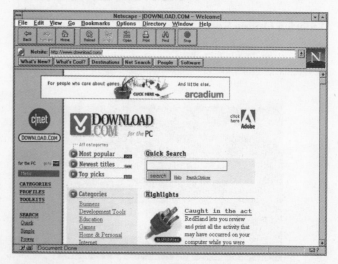

Hybrid Site

Intuit's **Quicken Financial Network (QFN)** has two objectives: 1) provide a customer service and support area for the 10-million-plus users of its personal finance software (Quicken and TurboTax), and 2) create a leading financial-services aggregation site (or hub) on the Web. Quicken is one of the most successful software products ever, in our view — over the years, Intuit has built a strong brand name and developed expertise in creating easy-to-use software for a variety of financial needs. With its Web efforts, Intuit hopes to: 1) sell more software by expanding the need for its product offerings; 2) encourage more users to use PC-based online banking; and 3) generate revenue from its financial-services aggregation efforts. To the last point, because of the Web's interactive nature and volume of information, it has the potential to significantly change the way financial services business is conducted. We believe that, over time, there will be major business opportunities for several financial services superstores operated by intermediaries on the Web.

Intuit's Web sites already contain: 1) data on about 60 mutual fund families, plus Morningstar data; 2) the ability to obtain real-time insurance quotes and purchase policies from six of the top 20 insurance companies; and 3) information about online banking and bill payment with financial institutions. Intuit generates revenue from its Web efforts through: 1) selling placement/advertising space on its sites to various financial institutions — it has 100 advertisers on its site, the largest being American Express, Charles Schwab, Merrill Lynch, and Lotus; 2) generating leads or sales commissions for, or from, financial institutions; 3) generating royalties related to online banking efforts; and 4) making software sales. Intuit hopes to reduce its relative operating expenses by providing online product support.

QFN Home Page

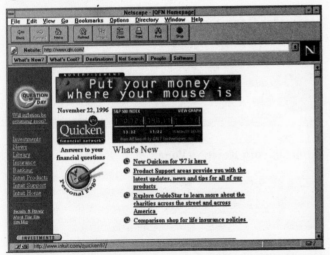

QFN Investment Page

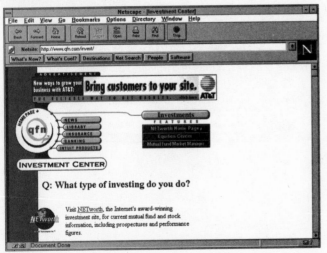

QFN Insurance Page

QFN BankNow Page on AOL

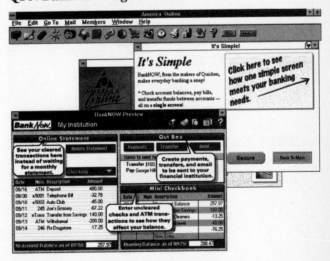

Commerce Site

Amazon.com has one goal — to sell books — and to date, the company has not aggressively pursued advertisers for its site. Amazon.com is the leading bookstore on the Web, providing users with the ability to easily search through its database of over 1 million books. And it's very easy, with a credit card, to purchase books from the company's Web site (at competitive prices) for delivery by mail.

The company has expanded its offerings to include book-club-like services and book reviews. It highlights hot books, compiles a best-seller list (which, yes, included *The Internet Report* for a while), groups books by interest area, offers interviews with authors, and provides customer book reviews.

Amazon.com Home Page

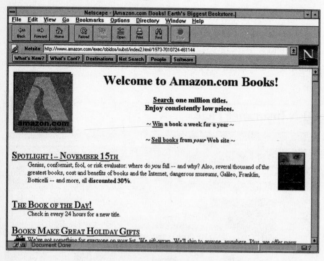

Amazon.com Spotlight Page

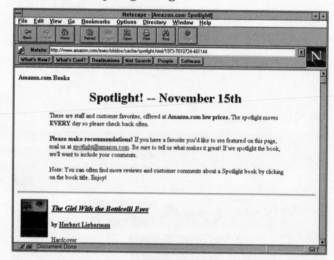

Amazon.com Subject/Title/Author Page

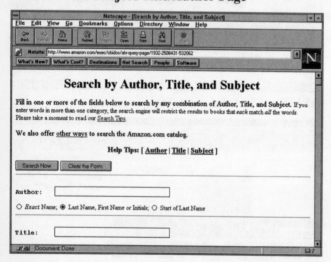

Amazon.com Reviews Page

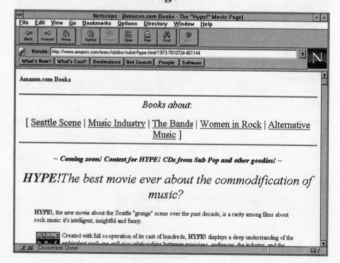

Chapter 6: Buzzword Mania —
The Nuts and Bolts of Internet Advertising

Summary

◆ In this section we describe **the current offerings of the ever-changing array of Internet advertising products/methods**, including banner ads (the "billboards of the information superhighway"), buttons, key words, portals, hot corners, "offline" ads, sponsored content, targeted direct mail, and pay-per lead.

◆ We also discuss **the current state of, and potential for, other revenue models for the Web related to transactions and subscriptions**.

◆ In a new medium, there is a natural tendency initially to adopt the business models of those media that have preceded it (i.e., the traditional CPM model). **No doubt, Internet advertising dynamics/methods will change — Netizens are already calling for the "death of the banner" ad. The bottom line is that we think advertisers will shift spending to where they can find the best advertising/marketing value and get the most bang for the buck; agencies will strive to change or improve their offerings to make advertisers happy; and Web content providers will scramble to provide relevant demographics to advertisers. As technologies improve, the very nature of Internet advertising should change, too.** We believe that America Online, thanks to the current features of its service (plus upcoming rollouts for members like streaming media, new offline technology, and AOL Phone), will be a hotbed for innovation in online advertising.

Just What You've Been Waiting For —
A Tutorial on Web Advertising Methods

In his book *Confessions of an Advertising Man*, advertising maven David Ogilvy wrote that "the market you are advertising to is not just a crowd, but a passing parade." While these words aptly summarize the nature of all media, they seem especially appropriate for the Internet.

On the Internet, efforts to capture the attention of this parade center on several different products (or ad-related methods) that are currently being sold to advertisers. At its core, Internet advertising is similar to many other forms of advertising — it's all about reaching potential customers and making an impression. And as in any business, advertisers on the Internet want to maximize profit by selling as much product as possible — and in any way possible. Web publishers are responsible for attracting traffic (eyeballs) for advertisers, while advertisers are responsible for developing great creative to capitalize on the traffic.

Of course, we shouldn't miss the forest for the trees. Quality advertising on the Web should, along with building an advertiser's brand, lead to increased traffic at the advertiser's Web site, which, in turn, should lead to additional purchases of the advertiser's goods or services.

Even so, an advertiser can find a shorter path to Internet users by creating its own site with content that's compelling enough to bring the user there without advertisements. A quality Web site can be an advertisement in itself. For example, Absolut Vodka (www.absolutvodka.com) and Clinique (www.clinique.com) have attempted to create compelling content and interesting and informative resources for users about their products, industry, or even content (through games, and so forth). Check out Absolut Kelly, which is Kevin Kelly's quote generator, which can be found at www2.absolutvodka.com/cgi-bin/fortune.

Well-designed advertising creative, delivered in the right environment with complementary content, is a key driver of advertising success. It is important that ads not be too intrusive, and we believe the more an advertisement seems like a value-added service to the user and less like an invasion of privacy, the more successful that ad will be in driving traffic or business to wherever it is connected. (At the opposite extreme is "spam," which refers to the practice by some advertisers or promoters of sending unsolicited, mass-mailed e-mail advertisements. Although some Internet users don't seem to mind receiving this type of ad, a large number of users have been vocal in their complaints. This kind of junk mail and invasion of privacy most likely will be ongoing issues on the Web.)

This brings us to the concept of links, which basically are anything on a Web page that drives traffic to another site. Links can be buttons, "hypertext," advertising banners, or some other form, but they all provide pathways from one Web site to another, and are major drivers of site traffic (perhaps the most critical).

To get a sense of how important well-placed links are (and how valuable), look no further than the major search engines — Yahoo!, Excite, Infoseek, Lycos, and Magellan. Each company anted up $5 million (a rather large chunk of their current annualized revenue) for the right to be placed on Netscape's Internet search page. This positioning, however, helps them drive part of the enormous amount of traffic that comes through Netscape's pages (Netscape is the most visited site on the Web) toward their own Web sites.

Another important strategy for driving traffic (and thereby for revenue) is to cross-promote a site through different media. CNET, for example, produces cable and network television programming through which it not only expands brand awareness but also drives traffic onto its Internet sites. This strategy has been employed somewhat successfully by other sites with a cross-media presence, most notably ESPNET SportsZone (with parent company ESPN's TV programming), MSNBC (the cable channel was launched in concert with the Web site and NBC's major network programming), ZD Net (on both its print pages and its TV programming on MSNBC's cable channel), and HotWired (with its well-known parent magazine, *Wired*). PC Meter, an independent consumer measurement company, reported very well-defined spikes for site traffic at MSNBC immediately after each time the site was mentioned during NBC's Olympic coverage. Point is, it works.

In a new medium, there is a natural tendency to initially adopt the business models of those media that have preceded it. To date, the most prevalent business model for pricing ad products (the majority of which are banners, discussed below) is the CPM (cost-per-thousand impres-sions, or ad views, delivered) model employed in traditional media.

A discussion of the various Web-advertising products and methods follows.

Banners

Figure 6-1 shows Netscape's SuiteSpot banner ad on CNET's NEWS.COM home page. Banner ads revisit the traditional cost-per-impression advertising model, employed in print and broadcast media. Banners are by far the most common advertising product sold on the Web, and most companies have adopted this product for the majority of the advertising they sell. Banner ads can be thought of as mini-billboards for advertisers on the information superhighway.

Typically, a banner ad is a horizontal, rectangular graphic image appearing at the top of a Web page, and often using GIF, Java, or Shockwave animations. The banner usually includes some text (such as a phrase or slogan and the advertiser's name and Internet address). If the user finds the ad intriguing enough, he or she will then click on the ad, which activates an embedded link, to visit the advertiser's Web site.

In banner advertising, each page of Web content delivered to a user contains an area displaying the advertising creative, in this case a banner, which is counted as a single impression. The banner product generally appears much like a print ad on a magazine or newspaper page.

Each time the page is downloaded by a user, a designated space on the page (in the example in Figure 6-1, a rectangle across the top) is automatically filled with a banner. The method by which a site determines which ad to put into which download may depend on agreements or contracts with advertisers, the capability of the technology involved, the demographics of the user, and other factors.

To put it simply, one could think of the Web page being downloaded as a post card and the banner ad as a stamp. As the page is delivered, it is just like slapping the stamp on the post card as it goes out to the post office (the Internet) to be delivered to the addressee (the user). The method of selecting the ad (stamp) to be added to each page is handled by ad management software (see our discussion of inventory allocation below). Thus, if the same page of content is downloaded a second time, the same content would appear, but the advertisement inserted would be a function of these allocation rules (downloading a page again should not be confused with viewing "cached" pages, which a user sees after pressing the Back button on a browser — in that case, the page will contain the same ad because the page file comes from the browser's storage on the user's own computer hard drive, and not from the Web site's server).

Each time a download occurs, it is called a *page view*. When a page view contains an ad, it can also be called an ad view, or, more commonly, an impression (akin to the term used in traditional media). However, the number of page views does not necessarily map to the number of ad views, as some pages may contain more than one ad and some pages may not contain any ads at all.

This brings us to the concepts of inventory management and allocation, and ad tracking and rotation. The most important goal of advertising is to deliver to each person the message most appropriate to their tastes, buying habits, and so forth, and with the most effective frequency — in other words, to execute a campaign tailored to each individual. To this end, many Web sites use software packages to impose ad delivery schema over on-the-fly allocation of advertising inventory. By schema, we mean sets of rules governing which ads get delivered when. This software can be either off-the-shelf (from companies like Net Gravity, Bellcore, and Accipiter) or developed in-house (as HotWired and CNET, for instance, have done). The importance of the quality, flexibility, and reliability of ad management software is simple: more targeted, reliable, and verifiable advertising delivery translates directly into the ability to charge more per impression.

CNET has gone to great lengths to provide advertisers with good data, and the company has developed its own proprietary dynamic-delivery system (including DREAM — delivery of real-time enhanced advertising messages — an advanced technology for enhancing ad targeting) to seamlessly integrate advertising throughout its sites. The system performs three major custom delivery functions: 1) it guarantees that the impressions purchased are actually delivered (if the entire graphic does not appear on the page, CNET does not count it as an impression); 2) it delivers all advertising banners to the top of the page, and loads them first,

to guarantee to advertisers that their messages are seen; and 3) it rotates advertising banners throughout CNET's several sites according to dynamics defined by the publisher and advertisers.

Targeting gives advertisers the opportunity to filter messages to selected audiences based on certain criteria. This may be the most powerful aspect of the Internet as an advertising medium — the ability to dictate the exact composition of an advertisement's audience. Though there are opportunities to target audiences in traditional media (such as radio stations selling for cell-phone companies during drive time, or ESPN selling for auto parts companies during NASCAR races), in our view there is nothing akin to the targeting that the Internet affords.

This targeting ability has two pieces: 1) the process for ad delivery and measurement is precise and directed (e.g., each ad is individually delivered in response to a user-generated request — there is no TV- or radio-like "shotgun" delivery — followed by statistical sampling and averaging to determine the actual composition of the receiving audience); and 2) each individual delivery can be tailored, based on user information. The power of the second aspect is increased substantially with more detailed user data, potentially collected through registration or in the course of using the site. Thus, with the right user information, one could know that every advertisement delivered is received by teenage women using a Macintosh, or by college-educated middle-age men in specific (perhaps high-

Figure 6-1
Sample Banner Ad

income) zip codes, and so on. Essentially, it's a marketer's dream.

Currently, CNET's systems can determine a user's platform (Macintosh, PC, UNIX), browser type (Netscape, Internet Explorer, or others), affiliation (such as AOL, Prodigy, CompuServe, Netcom) and domain (.edu, .gov, .com, etc.). As the technology continues to improve, further filtering by age, gender, zip code, CD-ROM-drive ownership, and connection speed may become possible.

For more information on banners, check out these Web sites:
www.linkexchange.com/compare.html
www.wmo.com/Articles/Banners/Build.html
www.sharat.co.il/teneta/banners/known.html
doubleclick.net/advertising/testit!.htm
www.photolabels.com/betterbanners.shtml

Factors That Skew Page Views

Reliability is important to advertisers. In television, for example, reliability of ad delivery is lessened because viewers can channel surf all through commercials, and impressions that an advertiser might pay to be "delivered" never really get there. There is no guarantee that each page of a newspaper magazine is opened and viewed by each reader.

The Internet, on the other hand, offers some important improvements on the reliability of ad delivery. This can be a double-edged sword, though, as user control of the ad delivery environment (as well as middlemen like America Online, ISPs, etc.) could potentially have real impact — imagine if viewers could fast forward or remove all the ads on their TVs? Since ad delivery measurement and tracking are done on the server side, one must take into account that the actual number of pages viewed by users may differ from the number of pages downloaded by the server, for several reasons.

1) *Caching* — The phenomenon of caching occurs when OSPs (online service providers, like America Online or CompuServe), ISPs (Internet service providers, like PSINet or UUNet), or even browsers store or buffer Web page data in a temporary location on their networks or in their disk space. They do so to speed up subscriber access to commonly accessed Web content, and caching pages reduces the time it would take to get pages off the original site server and reduces traffic on the networks. A certain page may then be downloaded once, cached, and then viewed many, many times by users. This, of course, translates into a higher actual number of page views than the original site's server is able to record.

Another form of caching occurs with products like Freeloader, which uses a robot or other "agent"-type software to seek out the content at specified sites and download to a local cache for a user's viewing convenience. However, the user may or may not actually look at the content, though the site has recorded each page downloaded as an ad delivery.

2) *Text-only browsing* — It is possible to turn off the loading of images in some browsers and only load text when pages are viewed. For users with low connection speeds, where pictures slow the viewing process significantly, these ads can be a hindrance. Although studies indicate that users are, in general, rapidly upgrading their equipment to overcome such problems, they do still exist. Estimates vary widely about the extent to which this occurs, but the overall effect is that of lowering the real number of pages actually viewed by users.

In addition, software products have been developed that can strip out ads from Web pages. For example, PrivNet, Inc. has developed a product called Internet Fast Forward that uses database technology and artificial intelligence to remove ads from pages as they are downloaded. Though not a significant threat as of yet, it is unclear how pervasive such products might become.

3) *Ad Position* — If the page is longer than the browser viewing space, and the ad comes at the bottom of the page, then the user may move to a new page before having scrolled to the bottom of the page and seen the ad. This also lowers real user page views.

4) *Errors* — At times, when a page is loaded, not all the images load correctly, and various parts of the page may not be displayed properly. The frequency with which this happens may well be a function of the user's computer memory profile and configuration, the network the computer is on, or other technical factors. The net result is that the site server records a page as viewed, but the ad is not actually delivered to the user.

5) *Interruption* — Users can select their browsers' Stop, Back, or other commands, or click on hyperlinks and leave a page before an ad downloads. Many ad management/tracking systems are unable to prevent this and are unable to detect when it happens. This is becoming more prevalent with larger banners and pictures that take longer to load.

6) *Lack of Attention* — According to a 500-person study by I/PRO, 42% of users never look at ad banners. We know our eyes have developed a keen ability to ignore the ads, though this may become less of an issue as more eye-catching techniques/technologies are developed.

All of these factors influencing true page-view/impression statistics need to be weighed by advertisers when they make decisions about purchasing and attempt to quantify what they are really getting for their dollars.

Click-Throughs

A notable existing model used for some banner ads charges for the number of "click-throughs" delivered (the number of times users click on the ad, taking them to the advertiser's Web site, or any other advertiser-specified location), and can be categorized more as cost-per-response. In this model a site's revenue is a function not only of delivery but also of the subsequent action taken by users when the ad is displayed. This can be affected by several external factors, most notably the advertising creative, the ad frequency (the number of times each user sees the same ad), and the content within the page. The latest data from I/PRO and DoubleClick found that the average ad-click rate is 2.1%, though this can vary widely based on the factors mentioned.

Companies generally charge between $0.31 and $1.36 per click-through for their Web sites, with general-interest sites seeing click-through rates of between 0.36% and 2.8% and highly targeted sites generating rates upwards of 20%. Using the 2% click-through rate as a benchmark, this puts the CPM range between $12 and $52, but the decision to purchase advertising in this form is clearly a context-driven issue for advertisers, as the site, the advertiser's products, and the creative all come to bear on the return the advertiser will receive from such an investment. In May 1996, Procter & Gamble signed a well-publicized deal of this type with Yahoo!, but the click-through model has not caught on to the same degree as the banner/impression model to date.

An alternative on the click-through model can be seen on the Riddler site (www.riddler.com). Users win prizes through accruing "caps," which may be won each time a user is successful at playing a round of one of the site's several games (the prizes aren't bad — Riddler has given away several cars). The only thing required of users is that, each time one round of any game is played, they view a page containing only an advertisement. This way, the click-through rate for each ad is technically 100% (though the clicks do not take users to the advertiser's Web site).

CyberGold is a company that pushes the click-through concept even further. The company's business model is simple: since the attention of a specific audience has a value for advertisers, pay people for their attention and charge advertisers for delivery of the audience, profiting from the difference. To participate, users are required to give CyberGold demographic data, and are then offered the opportunity to view personalized menus of ads. They are then paid at least 50 cents for each ad that they click all the way through. When their credit amount reached $20, the company pays out. The value of having the user data is threefold — it allows an advertiser to select the specific demographic groups to which its advertisements will be shown, it aids in delivering the most relevant ads to each user to make his or her experience more engaging, and the synergy created by these two points allows CyberGold to sell a much more valuable product (because, as we have said time and again, it's all about creating a value proposition for advertisers).

Figure 6-2
Sample Button Ad

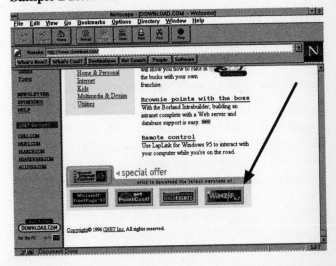

Buttons

Another Web advertising product offered by Web publishers is the selling of "buttons" on their pages. On CNET, for example, these buttons are advertisements for such software products as Netscape Navigator and Microsoft's Internet Explorer (browser clients), Macromedia's Shockwave software, and PointCast's client software. Each of these companies pays CNET a royalty for placing its button on a page that, if the user clicks on it, will take the user to the company's download site — direct marketing at its finest. Figure 6-2 shows a button advertising Microsoft's Internet Explorer in the left-hand column of the page. Clicking on that button takes the user to a "Featured Product" page, where he or she can read a description of the product and access links to download the software directly.

Key Words

Search engines, by definition, use text input by users to conduct searches of relevant content on the Web. Since advertisements are displayed along with the search results, these companies allow advertisers to buy "key words," which display the advertiser's banner when a user searches for the word purchased. It follows that the word or words purchased are generally related in some way to the advertiser's products or services. Infoseek and Yahoo! charge $1,000 per month per keyword, and based on a target of 20,000 impressions, this would yield a CPM of $50.

For example, Figure 6-3 shows how the results of a search for the word "router" yielded a typical list of sites but also netted an advertisement for Cabletron Systems (a maker of switches, considered an alternative to routers). In fact, any time this word was searched for, the same ad came up. A search for "hub" consistently resulted in a different ad for the same company. (Yes, we searched for "beer," and each time we got a Miller Genuine Draft ad).

Portals, Hot Corners, and Other Ad Products. . .

In addition to banners, buttons, and keywords, there are a variety of products that publishers can sell to advertisers — they are limited only by what the market will bear and what technology will allow. For example, we cite two more product offerings from CNET, which the company calls portals and hot corners, the rotating banner structure used by the Happy Puppy site (www.happypuppy.com), and "interstitials," a more intrusive, TV-like form of advertisement.

A portal is a linkable graphic that resides within the tool bar of CNET's NEWS.COM site pages (the tool bar is the distinctive vertical yellow stripe on the left-hand side of all CNET's pages). The portal can be static or animated, and it links to a URL (which is a Web address/location, like www.news.com) specified by the advertiser. Even this product is segmented into three types: principal, section, and radio, with principal portals located on NEWS.COM's "front door," section portals located on the front door of each news department (The Net, Computing, Intranets, Business, and so on), and radio portals are located on CNET's Radio page and include one 15-second "commercial spot" within each CNET Radio Webcast.

Hot corners are linkable graphics that reside in the upper-right corner of DOWNLOAD.COM site's pages. The ad is linked to a hot-corner advertisement area, where the company can display corporate and product information (the area consists of four interlinked and external-linked pages supplied by the advertiser to CNET). Hot corners are also segmented into principal and section types.

Happy Puppy (happypuppy.com), an online gaming and entertainment software site, uses rectangular banner ads on the left hand column of the screen (similar to CNET's portals), but the ads rotate every 30 seconds (the length of a TV ad). This is analogous to the ads one sees along the sidelines of basketball courts, or behind home plate in a baseball stadium, which rotate during the course of the game, creating additional inventory. Thus, in the course of reading one page of content, the user is exposed to several different ads. The impact of each ad may even be augmented by the rotation, as users' eyes are drawn to the movement while they read the page's content (in addition, when users try to go back to previous pages, using the browser's Back button, the page first rotates through each ad already displayed with each click of the mouse before moving to the previously viewed page).

Figure 6-3

Sample Keyword-Generated Ad

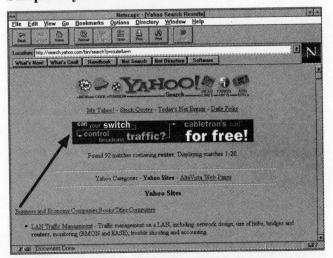

Figure 6-4

Sample 'Portal' Ad

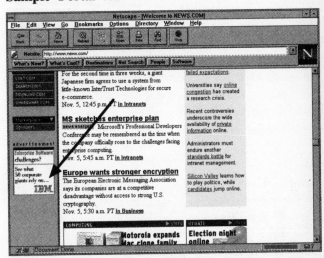

Another step beyond normal banners is the use of "interstitials," which pop up to snare the user's attention in a more active, TV-like manner. This type of ad can come in various forms, including a "cover page" of ads that a user must click through to get to the home page of the Women's Wire site (www.womenswire.com); the quick "billboards" flashed between a site's pages (check this out at "Word," www.word.com), or a full-color, full-sound, animated spot like the one Berkeley Systems uses to begin the online version of its "You Don't Know Jack" game show (for which a user must download a separate application). The idea is to use more animation, color, sound, and complexity to attract users' attention more effectively than passive banner ads. These techniques help to deliver some of the advantages TV and radio advertising have over more print-like banners (the better branding and intrusive message delivery that sound, color, and animation provide).

Animation can be powerful. A recent study by I/PRO and Double-Click found that adding animation to a simple image boosts response rates as much as 25%. Other techniques the study found effective included using cryptic messages (like "Click Here") unaccompanied by any other text, which increased response rates 18%; questions such as "Look down. Need shoes?" (a 16% boost); and calls to action ("See us now"), which yielded a 15% increase in response.

The point is that sites will continue to invent different value-added products and services for advertisers, depend-

ing on content, format, site design, technology, business model, and so on, and we are likely to see the number of alternatives to, and variations on, banners continue to grow.

'Offline' Ads

Another variation on the banner ad model is the selling of "offline" ads. Currently, there are many companies looking to tap in to the demand for "pushed" content, where the user requests the type of news and information he or she would like delivered to the desktop at specified intervals (instead of having to go out and search for it). Many of these companies offer client software (that can be easily and freely downloaded and installed on a PC), which they use to deliver this tailored content through what amounts to a customized broadcast network. Several notable companies (such as PointCast, FreeLoader, and Juno) generate revenue by including advertisements with their content or service. This is attractive to advertisers, as it allows them to customize ad delivery to users with specific demographic or psychographic profiles.

Sponsored Content

Taking a page from the 1950s TV soap opera playbook, when HotWired ran the first Web ad two years ago it offered a 12-week sponsorship for a flat rate of $30,000 to AT&T and ran an ad for "The Virtual Museum," along with ads from Sprint, MCI, Volvo, and others. Many sites still sell flate-rate sponsorships, but typically they guarantee a minimum number of impressions, essentially functioning as a variation on the CPM theme.

However, there are signs that companies are taking sponsorship a step further. HotWired has rolled out a new advertising strategy to create "micro-sites" sponsored by HotWired advertisers. Sponsored sites are less intrusive than banners, and the hope is that users will more closely associate the content with the advertiser. As an example, HotWired has a site called Dream Jobs (sponsored by

Dockers) that is designed to promote the idea that, in your dream job, you can wear Dockers at work.

In our opinion, the best example of a mutually useful online service using Web technology is Physicians' Online (www.po.com). The company generates 80% of its revenue from sponsorships/advertisements from pharmaceutical and

Figure 6-5
Sample 'Hot Corner' Ad

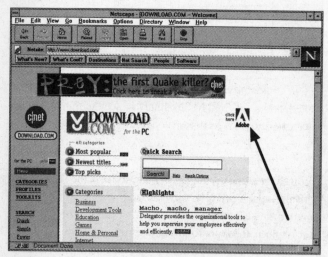

Figure 6-6
'Offline' Ad Delivery

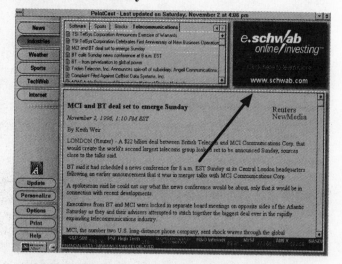

Figure 6-7
AOL's Brokerage Center with Sponsorship Ads

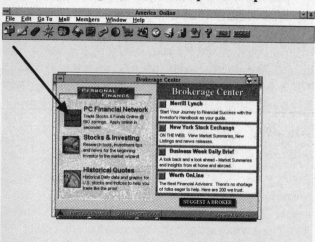

Figure 6-8
AOL's Mutual Fund Center with Sponsorship Ads

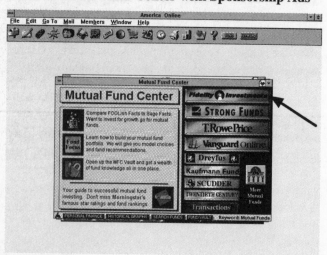

healthcare organizations, such as Abbott Laboratories, Astra Merck, Pfizer, Bayer, Eli Lilly, Glaxo Wellcome, Hoechst Marion Roussel, Teva Marion, Aetna Health Plans, Cigna HealthCare, Oxford Health Plans, Humana, and Harvard Pilgrim Health Care.

Physicians' Online is the world's leading medical information and communication network. It connects its growing base of physician members with the largest online community of their peers while offering the most up-to-date medical resources, Worldwide Web access, and direct links to associations, health plans, pharmaceutical sponsors, and healthcare organizations.

The service can be accessed only by registered physicians (it has in excess of 130,000 members, or almost 25% of practicing physicians in North America). This targeted demographic creates an especially compelling market for advertisers in the medical field.

Another example of sponsorship is in the Brokerage Center of AOL's Personal Finance Channel, where PC Financial Network has purchased the sole spot on the page — one click allows a user to launch into online trading via PC Financial Network (Figure 6-7). In addition, AOL sells sponsorship advertorials in its Mutual Fund Center area (note the efforts of Fidelity, Strong, Vanguard, T. Rowe Price, and others in Figure 6-8) and in its Celebrity Circle area (sponsored by Oldsmobile, shown in Figure 6-9).

Direct E-Mail and 'Push' Services

Direct e-mail is a technique used by a variety of Web sites to keep their products fresh in users' minds. This is an opportunity for companies to reverse the normal "pull" methodology of Internet surfing (where the users have to go out and find the content) to more of a "push" paradigm.

Many sites use interesting ploys to get hold of a user's e-mail address, and then leverage this knowledge by sending e-mails that detail updates to the site, promotions, newsletters, and so on. Additionally, sites can sell their user information (along with any other demographic details) to marketing firms, which use them for other direct marketing campaigns. Whereas, at one time, netiquette (that's Internet speak for online etiquette) would have considered such use of e-mail an abomination, user sentiment seems to be increasingly accepting of the idea. It's hard enough for people to stay abreast of what's happening at their favorite

sites — if it's actively delivered to them, ready for consumption, then it saves them time and effort. Of course, many sites ask users first if they'd like to receive e-mail updates, as unsolicited e-mail (or "spam") has been strongly opposed by many users.

This desire for tailored information delivery has spawned several software and service companies that are beginning to implement this "push" framework by delivering user-configured content to subscribers. PointCast is a notable example, as is IFusion Com. Netscape's Inbox Direct for Navigator 3.0 is an innovative new content delivery service, which bundles content supplied by more than 40 content providers, such as *The New York Times,* CMP Media, Gartner Group, HotWired, Times-Mirror Magazines, *U.S. News and World Report,* and Ziff-Davis's ZD Net AnchorDesk). Inbox Direct is proving extremely popular, receiving over 500,000 subscriptions in its first two weeks alone. Other notable examples of the "push" framework include My Yahoo! and Individual's NewsPage Direct.

In another variation on the e-mail/push theme, Juno Online Services (www.juno.com) offers free Internet e-mail service to its subscribers, with the aim of exploiting the resulting "digital shelf space" to generate revenues through selling the space to advertisers, for direct product sales, or for the provision of optional billable services. In exchange for this free service, the only requirement of users is that they fill out a registration form which allows Juno to target very specific and well-defined demographic groups. With a sizable user base, this can make for an extremely powerful

Figure 6-9

AOL's Celebrity Circle with Sponsorship Ads

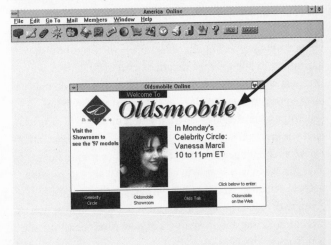

direct-marketing tool. Thus, an advertiser can choose to only have ads displayed to males, 25–40, with household income above $30,000 — a proposition for which they would likely be willing to pay a premium. The service, however, is limited in functionality to just e-mail, and we believe the test of this model will be whether Juno or any other similar service can attract a large enough subscriber base to make the business work. To date, Juno reports it has 1.5 million users of its product.

Intelligent Agents

We reiterate our belief that the ability to marry content to creative will be a key driver of pricing. Essentially, this requires that the advertising be targeted at the audience for the particular site's type of content. The next logical step in this process would then be to tailor not just to the audience, but also to each individual user according to his or her buying and browsing habits. Several makers of personalization software, most notably Firefly Network (formerly Agents, Inc.), provide products that personalize ad delivery based on a user's past behavior or profile. If a user has come to an advertiser's site three times, looked at the same item each time, but has yet to purchase it, delivering an ad for that product as the user again enters the site would certainly be more valuable to an advertiser than the delivery of that ad indiscriminately. Once again, the more targeted the audience delivered, the higher the price advertisers will pay.

Pay-Per Lead

Some companies in the industry have begun to propose an advertising model based not on impressions or click-throughs but on activity at client's Web sites. Though sites are compared primarily on impressions delivered and on visits, future models might use such measurements as total viewed minutes per month (the number of monthly visits multiplied by the average length of visit). Of course, advertisers would love a proposition where they would only have to pay for results. It is one step further down the spectrum toward a pay-per-transaction model, where revenue is a function of business generated. For example, after Amazon.com experienced initial success at selling books over the Web, it was able to convince host sites to provide links to Amazon.com's home page in exchange for a percentage of sales resulting from the link. (See our section on direct marketing for an analysis of how direct-mail pricing compares with click-throughs.)

Advertising Networks are Emerging for the Web

There are thousands of disparate sites on the Web, each of which has a potential audience (however small) to deliver to advertisers. Networks aggregate these sites, creating a huge total inventory of pages from many different types of publishers. For media buyers, it's more efficient to buy as many "eyeballs" from as few players as possible, and networks allow advertisers to simply make one purchase, specify basic criteria for where they want creative delivered (for instance, all entertainment sites), and the networks act as the distributor.

This saves publishers time and money related to direct sales, cushions them somewhat from price fluctuations, and relieves them from continuous update and investment in ad server and measurement technologies. In turn, networks can offer advertisers a much larger audience than any one site with a much greater reach. For example, a company in this space, DoubleClick, attracted 10 million unique visitors to its network in six months.

We especially like the business models of companies like the LinkExchange, which uses a barter business model — the company displays one banner ad for a given member site elsewhere in its network (helping the site drive traffic) in exchange for two ads displayed on the member site's own pages. As the size of the member base grows, the size of available inventory for reselling to paying advertisers dovetails with the size and reach of the audience. In addition, this eliminates the hassle of transactions between member sites and the network (no billing, collection, etc.). If a large enough inventory and membership can be accumulated, the challenge becomes selling the excess inventory (and withstanding the competitive pressures of the market once such a model becomes successful).

Running an ad campaign through a network can also reduce frequency (the number of times each user sees an ad, on average). For example, Figure 6-10 shows data collected by DoubleClick which suggest that after two impressions, the value of delivering additional ads declines. There is some debate over exactly how much (if at all) frequency affects click-rate. Since users often return to the same sites, advertising on one site means that users see the same ads repeatedly, so there may be some merit to the idea. Networks are able to spread impressions out over many sites, potentially providing a more effective delivery.

We concur with Forrester Research, which has forecast the emergence of five distinct types of ad networks (Table 6-1): 1) *Ad-reach networks* will aggregate sites numbering to the thousands from a wide range of categories (such as news, entertainment, sports, health, and financial); 2) *Local networks* are geography-based and function as the Web equivalent of local TV or radio programming, selling classifieds and store listings; 3) *Personal broadcast* networks offer advertisers access to the desktop, as companies like PointCast and IFUSION deliver personalized news and information to users, with advertiser creative attached; 4) *Content networks* are aggregates of thematically related site properties, like AOL's Greenhouse or CNET's several sites, oriented toward marrying the content to the advertising delivered; and 5) *Navigation hubs,* like the search engines, provide high-traffic volumes.

**Other Revenue Models for the Web That Use
An Advertising Front to Generate Transactions
(Internet Interactivity Should Be a Very Good Thing)**

In addition to the creation of a whole new mass medium for advertising-based businesses, we also believe the Internet represents the potential **creation of the greatest, most efficient distribution vehicle in the history of the planet**. In time, we expect an e-mail address to be as common as phone numbers are today.

Figure 6-10
Response Rate vs. Frequency

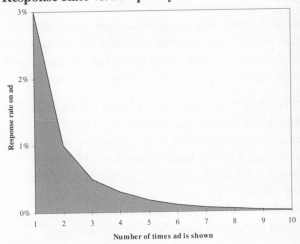

Source: DoubleClick.

History has taught us that **changes in the distribution of goods and services create substantial business opportunities for deft companies**. Note the following cause-and-effect successes: Postal mail order — Sears; telephone mail order — Lands' End and Dell; automobile/door-to-door-based marketing — Avon; overnight package delivery — Federal Express; television mail order — QVC; direct-mail membership marketing — CUC; superstores — Wal-Mart;

Table 6-1
Five Network Types Will Emerge

	Number/type of sites	Value proposition	Pricing models	Contender
Ad-reach Networks	10s to 10,000s of highly varied content sites	Mass reach plus individual targeting	CPM plus response rates	DoubleClick, BURST!, Commonwealth, Internet Link Exchange
Local Networks	50 to 200 cities	Promotions tied to local retail classifieds	Response rates and percentage of sales	Digital Cities, Hometown Network, CityScape
Personal Broadcast Networks	15 to 20 channels	Intrusion on the desktop	Mostly CPM-based	PointCast, IFUSIONcom, Marimba
Content Networks	10 to 15 sites per network	Ads relate to content	Higher CPM based on context	CNET, ZD Net, Starwave, iVillage, America Online's Greenhouse, Pathfinder, CMP TechWeb, Attitude Network
	2 to 3 networks per major content provider	Support relationships between advertisers and consumers	Response rates and percentage of sales for related direct marketing	
Navigation Hubs	2 to 3 hubs	Mass traffic, short visits, key words	CPM only: Response-based ads compromise their positions as independent guides	Yahoo!, Excite, Netscape, AltaVista, Magellan WebCrawler, Infoseek, Lycos

Source: Forrester Research, Morgan Stanley Technology Research.

PC OEMs for software — Microsoft; and Internet for software — Netscape.

With the Internet, which offers ubiquitous points-of-sale processing, advertising should eventually become, in effect, a precursor to executing transactions, thus making the total business opportunity created by the Web quite substantial.

In time, the **Internet will likely drive lots of commerce to maximum efficiency,** and purchases will be made at wholesale (plus shipping) plus n% (where n% represents advertising). Efficiency in all areas should be key, and time will tell if vendors become aggregated or disaggregated. We argue for aggregated — the bigger, the better, the cheaper, the better, the critical mass, the economics 101, and perhaps the Wal-Marting of all businesses.

The beauty of retailing on the Internet for businesses is that customer service and support costs can be reduced dramatically; companies with scale, critical mass, and/or unique value-added services offered through their Web site(s) have opportunities for market share gains and the ability to acquire new customers on a global basis; and first mover advantage, building a Web brand name, and a loyal customer base may create new business opportunities for fast-moving companies.

For customers, the beauty of retailing on the Internet is that it offers: maximum choice, 24 hours a day, 7 days a week; low cost (by eliminating the middleman); nearly instant feedback and tailoring; and close to immediate (overnight in many instances) delivery of goods to the consumer's front door — **yep, when customers order something quickly and easily at a low price, we think there's a good chance that they also want it *delivered* quickly and easily. Hello, air-express companies.** Early stage due-diligence calls to leading Web-based retailers, for the most part, support the thesis that air express companies should benefit from the growth in this new form of retailing.

In addition, over the last three years, mail-order companies have significantly ramped up their offerings of overnight shipping to consumers at reduced rates (sometimes absorbing the cost of shipping internally!), in order to compete more effectively at peak seasonal selling times with traditional retailers and to extend the life of their own Christmas season.

We are clearly in the cowboy stage of retailing on the Internet and, in aggregate, the dollar volume of Web-based transactions is tiny (like really tiny), but it's growing very fast, just like the Web. We don't want to put the cart before the horse — Internet retailing should take a long time to evolve (product sectors with early stage transaction appeal include software, PC equipment, audio CDs, and books) — but the infrastructure *is* being built, and over the next one to four years, we think they will come.

To give a sense of trend and scale, we profile some of the early stage consumer and business-to-business Internet-based brands with commerce/retail success stories. Traditional retailers that have launched transaction-based Web sites include Wal-Mart (www.wal-mart.com), LL Bean (www.llbean.com), Lands' End (www.landsend.com), J Crew (www.jcrew.com), Eddie Bauer (www.ebauer.com) and Spiegel (www.spiegel.com). We have collected data for various periods — week, month, quarter, and year — and in the following table have annualized the data to determine (admittedly, shoot-from-the-hip) revenue run rates.

Company Profiles: Early Stage Internet-Based Brands

CUC <www.cuc.com> — With more than 63 million members worldwide, CUC is the leading provider of membership-based consumer services (primarily serviced through telephone efforts). The company reported brisk online and Web-related sales (more than 75% were online-based) in November and generated $90 million in gross sales of various products, and it indicated sales could reach in excess of $400 million for 1996. November traffic was busy, with over 60,000 transactions, representing a sales gain of over 100% in each category. This implies a hefty average purchase price of $1,500, thanks in large part to sales of cars through AutoVantage.

The top-selling categories, by total dollar amount, were cars, travel, phones, VCRs, TVs, stereos, exercise equipment, consumer software and video games, books, and cameras. On a per member basis, the average dollar amount spent (excluding cars) increased 61% year-over-year. On an annualized basis, **CUC is ramping to well over $1 billion in gross sales,** seasonally adjusted. In June/July, CUC plans to launch an online "mega-mall" for membership-based Web shopping that will include many of its traditional services. CUC notes that to date, its interactive-shopping members spend approximately twice as much money as phone-based members.

Table 6-2

Transaction-Based Web Sites' Annualized Online Revenues

Company	Business Line(s)	Stated Online Revenue/Period	On...
CUC	Various consumer products	$90MM — 11/96	$1,080MM
America Online	Various consumer products	$89MM — C4Q96	$356MM
Amazon.com	Books	NA	NA
1-800-FLOWERS	Flowers, gifts	$4MM — 12/96	$48MM
E*TRADE	Securities trading	$25MM — C4Q96	$100MM
ONSALE	Auctions	$9MM — C3Q96	$36MM
Cisco	Internetworking products	$75MM — (6/96-12/96)	$1,000MM run-rate by 7/97E
Dell Computer	Personal computers	$6MM — per week (2/97)	$312MM

* To calculate annualized online revenue (or value of goods/services sold through the site), we have simply annualized stated online revenue — we have not factored in seasonality or growth. These respective businesses are growing rapidly, so actual annual revenues will likely be higher than our annualized estimates. For Cisco, we have not annualized stated online business line revenue, but have used Cisco's own projection for mid-C1997 revenue run rate for its online business. E = Morgan Stanley Technology Research Estimate. NA = Not available.

America Online — AOL is the world's leading online service, with more than 8 million members. AOL estimates that C4Q96 gross product sales through its service were nearly $89 million, up 57% quarter-to-quarter and up from $31 million a year earlier. AOL gets a cut of each of these transactions. The best-selling products are CD-ROMs, books, PC hardware (such as modems and Zip drives), AOL merchandise (such as AOL Tourbooks), flowers, audio CDs, and chocolates.

At the end of C4Q, AOL had 58 online stores on its Marketplace channel, up from 43 in C3Q and 16 a year ago. Key stores (anchor tenants) included CUC, 1-800-FLOWERS, @Once (for downloading computer software), Tower Records, Sharper Image, JCPenney, and Omaha Steaks. Barnes & Noble launched on AOL in February.

In addition to increasing the number of traditional retailers on its Marketplace channel, AOL has added lots of merchants to other channels, most notably the Personal Finance channels' Banking Center, Mutual Fund Center, and Brokerage Center. AOL gets revenue from these sites through up-front payment for screen positioning, cuts of transactions, advertising, and referral fees from brokers — thanks to an SEC ruling on January 16, 1997, stating that online services can take referral fees from brokers without coming under the SEC's jurisdiction.

Participating financial institutions include Bank of America, Wells Fargo, Citibank, Chase Manhattan Bank, First Union, E*Trade, PC Financial Network, Merrill Lynch, Charles Schwab, Fidelity Investments, Vanguard, T. Rowe Price, The Kaufmann Funds, and Dreyfus.

Amazon.com <www.amazon.com> — Amazon.com is the leading bookstore on the Web, providing users with the ability to easily (and quickly) search through its database of over 1 million books. It's simple, with a credit card, to purchase books from the company's Web site (at competitive prices) for delivery by postal mail. The company has expanded its offerings to include book-club-like services and book reviews. It highlights hot books, compiles a best-seller list, groups books by interest area, offers interviews with authors, and provides customer book reviews. Going forward, we think it will be important for the company to foster a sense of community among its users.

Amazon.com is one of the highest profile Web commerce success stories, and the company has been especially guarded about disclosing revenue data. We won't wing it here, but suffice it to say that the run-rate is impressive: Revenue in C4Q96 was up 20-fold versus C4Q95; it appears that January revenue will exceed seasonally strong December revenue (we believe that revenue has risen sequentially every month since the site's inception in July 1995); and the company has indicated that an impressive 40% or more of its customers are repeat buyers.

1-800-Flowers <www.1800flowers.com> — During December 1996, 1-800-Flowers placed about 80,000 flower and gift orders via the three leading online services (AOL, Compuserve, and the Microsoft Network) and generated more than $4 million in sales (up 150% year-over-year). In addition, the company's rate of sales growth is even higher on its Web site, though the base is much lower. 1-800-Flowers expects to report about $30 million in online sales for fiscal 1997 (June), which would represent about 10% of the company's total revenue.

E*Trade <www.etrade.com> — E*Trade is an electronic financial services company that, through its subsidiary E*Trade Securities, is a leading provider of online investing services. E*Trade offers independent investors the convenience and control of online access to securities markets and access to value-added information, such as new charts and fundamental data, along with attractive commission rates on trades. The company provides access to brokerage services through the Internet, online services (such as AOL and Compuserve), touch-tone telephone, and direct modem connection. The company also offers automated order placement, portfolio tracking, market information and news, and other information services 24 hours a day, seven days a week.

Revenues for C4Q96 were $25 million, up 189% year-over-year and 46% quarter-to-quarter. New account growth, up 24% sequentially and 187% year-over-year in C4Q96, has for the past year grown consistently between 8% and 10% per month, with more than 112,800 active accounts at the end of December 1996, versus 39,000 the previous year.

E*Trade has also reported an impressive 96% annualized customer retention rate — the company says that 0.3% of active accounts are closed or moved elsewhere each month. EGRP indicated that it is processing about 10,750 transactions per day (averaging 12,200 a day in December alone), up 131% year-over-year — more than 50% of these trades are being made via the Internet service, which began in February (other transactions are made via touch-tone phone or by calling the customer service reps). Given current trading volumes, E*Trade believes it handles a whopping 0.7% of all trading on the NYSE and NASDAQ.

Onsale, Inc. <www.onsale.com> — Onsale is the leading retail auction service on the Web. The company specializes in selling refurbished and close-out computers, peripherals, and consumer electronics. In the first 19 months of operations, as of late December, the company had sold over $35 million in merchandise to more than 50,000 customers. Gross merchandise sales (the total amount paid for goods and services sold through or by Onsale) were $9.2 million in 3Q96, up 75% quarter-to-quarter from $5.3 million. Total gross merchandise sales from July 1994 through 3Q96 were $17.6 million.

To date, the company has auctioned over 200,000 items, with over 65,000 in C3Q96. More than 1 million unique users have visited the company's auctions, with over 100,000 having registered as bidders (over 30,000 in C2Q96). The company currently auctions over 1,500 items a week, usually ranging in value from $50 to $1,500 and sold in quantities of one to several hundred per auction.

Cisco Systems <www.cisco.com> — Cisco, the internetworking company, established a business-to-business commerce area (Cisco Connection Online) on its Web site in June 1996. Recently, the company indicated it had generated $75 million in product sales through mid-December. Note that the company's products sell at prices ranging from hundreds of dollars to hundreds of thousands. Cisco believes its Web-related sales could reach a $1 billion run-rate by July 1997 (upwards of 30% of its total sales). The efficiencies and gross margins that Cisco can achieve through selling on the Web look pretty sweet — and, yes, the company is keeping customers happy and providing fast response time and around-the-clock service and support.

Dell Computer <www.dell.com> — Dell has indicated that it is generating Web-based sales of about $6 million per week — up from zero a year ago. Dell believes that a number of customers use the service to price product and then end up securing actual product over the phone. So actual Web-based sales may be low relative to actual use of the Web site.

Dell plans to offer two Web-based sales plans over time: one for consumers and one for businesses. The consumer version will essentially be the evolution of the company's current Web site, while the business offering will consist of customized Web pages for specific accounts — for example, Dell will build and customize versions of its current Web site with customers' preset configuration, standards, and approval priorities. For Dell, this corporate offering is important for two reasons: It builds another tie to customers, and it should eventually save substantial sales costs by replacing sales people with online access.

Dell believes that having a strong online presence will be incremental to revenue, but it also believes adamantly that it will be an important tool to drive down selling costs while delivering a comparable level of service to customers.

Currently, technology products seem to be very popular, of course, as the nature of the medium makes its users more likely to use services that provide software, hardware, peripherals, games, and so on. CNET, for example, has recognized the opportunity in software distribution and is moving aggressively in the direction of enabling transactions at its DOWNLOAD.COM site and with its recently launched BUYDIRECT.COM site. The company is attempting to capture market share and leverage its increasing brand in what is likely to be the most fundamental change to the way software is distributed and sold that the industry has ever seen.

And while we don't completely cover online shopping opportunities in this report, we believe that Forrester Research's estimates have directional significance. Forrester believes that online shopping revenue will ramp from $518 million in 1996 to $6.6 billion in 2000 (Figure 6-11 and Table 6-2), with computer products and travel services generating the highest revenue levels.

The Web Provides One-to-One Marketing Capabilities

As discussed in our section on direct-response advertising, direct marketing is an essential piece of the Internet advertising puzzle. The Internet provides the ultimate in one-to-one tailored marketing — the ability to interact with users at the point of ad/site/content viewing may well prove to be the most important facet of this medium. We think the distinction between the advertising on TV, radio, and in print and the actual purchase of items that results from this type of promotion will become blurred on the Internet, as advertising seamlessly becomes integrated with the purchasing process. This entails services in the form of transaction processing and online help directly to the user through the Web. Additionally, until high-speed networks

Table 6-2
Forrester's View:
Total Online Shopping Revenues

($ Millions)	1996E	1997E	1998E	1999E	2000E
Computer Products	$140	$323	$701	$1,228	$2,105
Travel	126	276	572	961	1,579
Entertainment	85	194	420	733	1,250
Apparel	46	89	163	234	322
Gifts and Flowers	45	103	222	386	658
Food and Drink	39	78	149	227	336
Other	37	75	144	221	329
Total	**$518**	**$1,138**	**$2,371**	**$3,990**	**$6,579**

Source: Forrester Research.   E = Forrester Research Estimate.

Figure 6-11
Forrester's View:
Total Online Shopping Revenues
($ Millions)

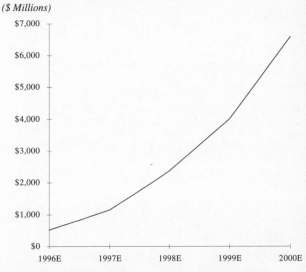

Source: Forrester Research.   E = Forrester Research Estimate.

deliver video to the desktop, cyber-marketing will remain largely a direct-response medium, rather than a brand-building one (that's what TV does so well).

The real "sweet spot" for Internet ad revenue may not be from selling ad space on a cost-per-thousand basis, comparable to print and broadcast media, but instead may reside in getting advertisers to understand and act on the possibilities this technology affords them — to reach out and touch each potential customer in a unique, timely way. Indeed, advertising pricing models may well evolve more along the cost-per-response lines of direct marketing than on CPMs. In other words, we'll start thinking about ad pricing more in terms of $2 per click or lead generated than $20 per thousand impressions.

Web-Based Subscriptions Models, Except for AOL's, So Far Aren't Sticking

In the Web content business, so far, if users pay, they rarely stay. Magazines and book publishing yield examples of successful print businesses based partially, or even completely, on revenue from user subscription fees. A number of companies (e.g., *The Wall Street Journal, Penthouse,* and the *San Jose Mercury News),* usually owned by a print or other media content provider, have attempted to convert this print-based model to the online world by charging sub-

Figure 6-12

Jupiter's View of Advertising Vs. Subscription Online Revenues

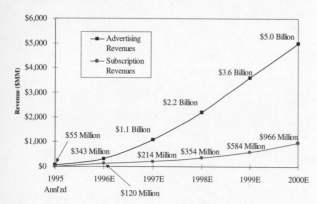

Source: Jupiter Communications. E = Jupiter Communications Research Estimate.

scriptions for content. It has been fairly unsuccessful in most cases, for several reasons. First, given the incredible amount of free content on the Web, there is little incentive for people to pay for information they can simply get for free, which at best puts severe price pressure on subscriptions.

The absence of users who would be willing to pay, combined with this price pressure, makes the critical mass of users required to generate enough revenue to cover costs very difficult to acquire. Even a publication with the incredible branding of *The Wall Street Journal* is having a tough time making this model stick. If one of the biggest brands in media, with no comparable competition, with content that is almost a daily necessity for a large number of people, and which charges only a small premium for its

product, cannot make it work so far, then it makes the outlook for other subscription-based Web efforts pretty bleak. The *Wall Street Journal* has indicated that, within three weeks, from a base of 600,000 registrants for its free Web version, it had only signed up 30,000 subscribers to its interactive version; those who signed up paid $49 for an annual subscription fee, or $29 if they were already print subscribers.

Several companies use hybrid models, allowing some of their content to be viewed for free (with ads), and making certain premium portions available only to users who subscribe. ESPNET SportsZone, SportsLine USA, and Pathfinder, to name a few, have seen some success to date. That success seems to be connected, however, to the amount of content available for free. The more valuable and compelling the "free" area is, the better, in general, these experiments seem to go. If the free area generates more usage, the benefit is twofold: Even if the subscription penetration rates stay the same, the net result is more subscribers and increased revenue, plus the benefit of increased ad revenue (more eyeballs equals more page views).

While a complete analysis of the future of subscription-based businesses is outside the scope of this report, we do believe that Jupiter's estimates (Figure 6-12) are directionally correct. Jupiter forecasts that the revenues incurred from online subscriptions will grow from $120 million in 1996 to $966 million in 2000 — these estimates suggest that there will be a market for such products, but it is unlikely that subscription-based revenue will be on the same scale as advertising revenue in the future.

Chapter 7: The Whys and Hows of Advertising Measurement

Summary

◆ **The principal element that drives advertising in all media is ratings.** And each medium uses a different unit to judge viewership.

◆ **Advertisers will not be totally comfortable advertising on the Web until confidence builds that Web advertising measurement is accurate and auditable by a reliable third party in a "Nielsen-like" way.** This relates to accurate information and tracking of site traffic and activity, advertisement delivery accuracy, and user response. Scores of new companies are emerging to create solutions for these problems — but one difficulty is that, for now, the addressable market is quite small.

◆ **The power of ratings was evident in the recent skirmish between TV broadcasters and Nielsen Media Research. Nielsen claims that TV lost viewers this fall, especially those in the 18-to-34-year-old demographic, to, yes, other pursuits, like online services and the Web.** The TV networks claim that the Nielsen ratings, which they have relied on for years to gauge viewership and revenue, are now unreliable and suspect — NBC and Fox are considering lawsuits against Nielsen, and the six commercial-broadcast networks could end up owing advertisers something like $100 million for lost airtime. Meanwhile, the FCC has launched an investigation of the issue. We don't have all the facts here, but we do know that America Online alone has seven million-plus subscribers (93% of whom are in the U.S., or 3% of U.S. households), who pay AOL an average of $17 or more per month and, on average, use the service for eight hours per month. So, our instincts tell us that Nielsen is on to something. Coopers & Lybrand recently reported that 58% of Internet users indicate that their online time comes at the expense of watching television.

Traditional Advertising Measurement — Ratings Rule!

The principal element that drives advertising in all media is *ratings*. Each medium, be it print, TV, radio, or the Internet, may use a different unit to judge viewership, but the concept remains the same: broadcasters (in the most general sense possible) sell time or space that is used for the dissemination of advertising messages. Ratings are a measure of the number of people exposed to that message. For traditional media (TV, radio, and print), ratings are defined as the percentage of a given population group consuming a medium at a particular moment. One rating point equals 1% of the population in question (e.g., U.S. households). Ratings in this sense are generally used for broadcast media, but the concept is relevant for any medium.

Ratings are not equivalent to *advertising message delivery* (i.e., commercial exposure), though they are probably the strongest indicator and driver of this metric. Ratings simply point to the percentage of a group that has the opportunity to be exposed to the advertising. This *"commercial rating"* can be influenced by many factors, such as the

number of people paying attention, the relative position of the commercial within a pod of different commercials (first, middle, last), the number of different commercials, the length of the commercial, its creative content, and the rele-

Table 7-1

Measurement/Audit Providers for Various Media

Medium	Who Performs Measurement?	Who Performs Audit?
TV	Nielsen	EMRC (Electronic Media Research Council)
Radio	Arbitron	EMRC (Electronic Media Research Council)
Magazines	MRI, Simmons	ABC (Audit Bureau of Circulation), BPA International
Internet	I/PRO*, NetCount**, Intersé, Accrue, Accipiter	I/PRO*, Audit Bureau of Verification Services (subsidiary of ABC), BPA International

Source: Morgan Stanley Technology Research.
* I/PRO is affiliated with Nielsen.
** NetCount is affiliated with Price Waterhouse.

vance of the message to the interests of the given audience. Because many of these factors can be difficult to measure or interpret, ratings are the most fundamental measure in determining how much advertisers are charged to place commercials.

Ratings, however, are also a measure of the total available audience (e.g., people who own TVs). There may only be a certain percentage of the available viewing population that is currently viewing any form of the medium, and the relative popularity of one particular program can be higher than another shown at a different time. In short, a radio program that has half the audience currently listening at 4:30 a.m. has far fewer listeners than a program that has a quarter of the current listening audience at 8:00 p.m. This concept of relative popularity is called *share*. Share is also a major factor in determining ad pricing.

Although the cost of advertising time or space has a high correlation with rating, the relationship between the two is not necessarily linear. Other important influences on price are the size of the rating across specific demographic groups, the program's share of audience, the cost to produce the medium, the cost paid by the supplier to secure the rights to broadcast its content (e.g., the Superbowl), and the "invisible hand" — the greater the demand, the greater the price. The *inherent value of a ratings point* can also be debated in terms of program environment — a ratings point on ESPN's "SportCenter" is inherently more valuable to *Sports Illustrated* than to *Cosmopolitan*.

Turning to non-broadcast media, while "ratings" imply the same concept, slightly different measures (and subsequent terminology) may be used. *Newspapers are measured in terms of penetration* — the circulation divided by the population base. *Magazines are measured in terms of coverage.* Coverage is the percentage of a population group exposed to a medium, generally described within defined demographic or purchasing groups (i.e., the number of readers divided by population base). *Outdoor or "out-of-home" media are also measured in terms of circulation,* which in this context is defined as the number (not percentage) of people who pass by a given poster or billboard.

Gross ratings points (GRPs) are the sum of all ratings delivered by a given list of media vehicles. They are the absolute value of the sum, regardless of duplication of audience. *Impressions* are also the sum of all advertising exposures, but differ from GRPs in that GRPs are expressed as percentages and impressions are expressed in terms of numbers of individuals. *CPM,* then, is defined as the cost associated with the delivery of 1,000 impressions.

Measuring Media, Anyway You Cut it, Is Weird Science

Web content providers argue that in no other medium is the ad publisher responsible for anything more than delivering the advertisement to the audience (measured in various ways like ratings, impressions, reach, and frequency). Certainly, traditional media companies are never directly responsible for what happens after customer exposure. On the Web, though, should it be the content provider's burden to bear the risk of bad advertising creative, poor Web site design, ineffective sales execution once the lead is delivered, oversaturation of exposure, poor public perception of the advertiser or their products, or any of the myriad reasons that businesses can't convert a large audience into sales?

Conversely, advertisers might contend that the current paradigm of ratings, reach, frequency, circulation, penetration, exposure, and so forth are simply a function of the technical limitations of these other media. Traditional media measurement and ratings are an inexact science at best, and the Internet may provide a much better metric of dollars earned from dollars spent. This then begs the question: Won't advertisers just spend their budgets with those publishers that can provide the highest quality service? And if such measurement is feasible, and the competition for ad dollars continues to heat up, won't publishers simply be forced to play the game on the advertisers' terms?

Site Measurement/Tracking — There's Good News and Bad News . . .

The Internet certainly provides more accountability to advertisers than any other medium simply because of the measurability associated with digital computers. Even on the Internet, though, measuring viewer usage is done in an indirect fashion. The promise of Internet advertising is increased feedback to advertisers through the use of greater levels of interactivity, targeting, and precise measurement of user behavior.

In time, the accuracy of this measurability may be both a blessing and a curse — accountability in an industry that has always had soft results/data can be a disturbing thing.

On the Web, research can be done in real-time, and creative can be changed mid-campaign, whereas in print advertising, the concept-to-finish effort takes weeks or months.

Pricing on the Web potentially can be tied more closely to direct results, rather than to the simple per-impression pricing to which the traditional media are limited. In fact, Forrester Research conducted a survey of 52 Web advertisers (Figure 7-1), and found an aggregate of 85% would prefer a pricing other than straight CPM. To provide the information necessary to implement such pricing models, the infrastructure for advertising sales, tracking, and reporting will need to evolve to meet ever-changing advertiser requirements and desires.

The Demand (and Market) for Standards and Audit

As advertising on the Web has exploded in recent months, the need for accurate information and tracking of site traffic and activity, advertisement delivery, and user response has grown increasingly important, for both the publishers of content and the advertisers on their sites. The market has begun to demand standardized methods for analyzing advertising opportunities and quantifying return on advertising investment.

Web Publishers and Advertisers Need Simple Stats . . .

Web publishers need a simple way to understand and communicate the results of ad delivery on their sites. Advertisers and media buyers need reliable, standardized reports in order to plan their buys. In making buying decisions, media buyers look at pre-buy reports, which provide usage data about each potential site (total traffic, average per day, visit length, and so forth). During a campaign, they need to monitor audience response to determine if adjustments need to be made in frequency, creative, and the like. After the campaign is over, these buyers also need post-buy statistics about how many impressions were delivered, the delivery rate, click-through rates, and other related performance information. In addition, when choosing a specific vehicle for their creative, buyers need to have an understanding of the opportunity cost of a given purchase, which requires reports detailing not only specific site traffic and demographic data but also, to provide context, the averages for comparable sites.

Currently, many of the measurement options available to Web sites use unstandardized and undefined methodologies

and tools. Publishers must choose from several different alternatives, including: shareware products (like Getstats and WWWStat); log software bundled with Web servers, from the likes of Netscape and Microsoft; off-the-shelf products (from Intersé and net.Genesis); ad management products (from Net Gravity, Focalink, and Accipiter); and even their own, custom-built solutions (HotWired's Hotstats and CNET).

The need to resolve increasingly complex advertising inventory management issues (keeping ads fresh, updated, changed while complying with scheduled levels of delivery) and simultaneously to improve the level and quality of tracking and measurement provide substantial opportunities for many of these companies. We think it is likely that the industry will standardize on certain tools and products, and that those who make these tools and products will surely see a lot of demand.

. . . And Standardized Metrics . . .

Along with the confusion over products, the definitions for the metrics being reported are also still evolving. Concepts like hits, visits, page views, page requests, visitors, unique visitors, impressions, and click-throughs are not always well defined. Even if they are, exact measurement requires some standardization in order to provide apples-to-apples comparisons across sites (which, as noted earlier, are critical to the media planning/buying process).

One example of potential confusion is the difference between hits and page views. Often, these terms are consid-

Figure 7-1
Results of Pricing Model Survey Of Web Advertisers

(Of 52 advertisers interviewed, percentage preferring each pricing model)

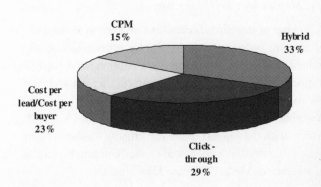

Source: Forrester Research.

ered either equivalent or as having a direct relationship. Neither is true, however, as a hit is simply any request by a browser for data from a Web page or file, and it results in an entry into the log file of the Web server. The number of hits in a particular period is often cited in attempts to compare the popularity or traffic of one site with another.

It's a common mistake to equate hits with page views (or even visits, which are discussed below). A single page view is recorded for each user request of a given page. The same single request, however, is usually recorded as several "hits," as it may take several packets of data to deliver all of the page information. Thus, depending on the browser, the page size, and other factors, the number of hits per page can vary widely (if you've spent time on the Web, you probably have a sense that there is a wide variance in the amount of information any particular page may deliver or display).

An example of a metric that is universally understood in concept but lacks precise definition is that of a visit. Though intuitive in nature, there are technical issues concerning when one visit ends and a new one begins. We define a visit as a sequence of hits made by one user at a site (see our Glossary section). As Internet technology does not maintain a continuous "connection" (like a radio signal) to a site (data are sent in discrete packets), there is no way to know when a user has ended a visit after the initial packets requested are sent. Thus, if such a user makes no request for data from the site during a predetermined period of time (and a discretionary one — there's the rub), the user's next hit would constitute a new visit. This length of time is known as the "time-out" period. Depending on how the publisher, or an auditor, chooses to define this time-out period, the number of visits recorded can vary significantly.

. . . Metrics May Be On the Way . . .

A number of standards bodies have evolved to attempt to bring some order and definition to the Internet advertising industry. Foremost is CASIE (the Coalition for Advertising Supported Information & Entertainment), a joint project of the Association of National Advertisers (A.N.A.) and the American Association of Advertising Agencies (A.A.A.A.), which, with the support of the Advertising Research Foundation, has drafted a document on the "Guiding Principles of Interactive Media Audience Measurement."

The document focuses on supplying guidelines for providing quality audience measurement of interactive media, including the Internet and interactive television. It discusses the importance of, and makes recommendations on, third-party measurement/auditing, full-disclosure methods and data, comparability of vehicles within total medium measurement, non-intrusiveness, and best practices based upon industry consensus. In addition, it offers guidelines for which metrics should be used in advertising sales and delivery, and how they should be defined. CASIE also has issued documents outlining standards and goals for privacy in marketing, as well as definitions of "standard advertising units."

Auditing, Auditing, Auditing . . .

One of the principles emphasized most by CASIE is the need for reliable, independent third-party auditing. Third-party audience estimates are the primary or exclusive audience data that advertisers and their agencies use to determine media buys. Thus, third-party measurement is, as CASIE put it, "the foundation for advertiser confidence in information. It is the measurement practice of all other advertiser supported media." An audit provides assurance that a Web site's activity counts have not been misrepresented (counted incorrectly), manipulated (where counts don't reflect actual activity), or reported in a nonstandard format (which leads to a lack of comparability).

Though we have used the terms "auditing" and "measurement" somewhat interchangeably up to this point, it is important to make a distinction. The best way to differentiate the two is to define the purpose of each. Third-party measurement is the timely reporting of data by an outside source that are used to make informed business decisions. For example, in TV, Nielsen provides third-party measurement like "overnights" and the weekly ratings, as does Arbitron in radio. These numbers are used by media buyers in deciding when and where to place ads. While measurement focuses on accurately tracking the activity at a site, an audit is a review of these measurement numbers performed at a later date, done to ensure the accuracy of the original measurement.

There are Standards in Other Media . . .

In each traditional medium, generally one or two companies end up as the default audit or measurement bodies. As mentioned, Nielsen does ratings measurement for TV and

Arbitron for radio (there is no auditing of measurement data in radio or TV, although EMRC, the Electronic Media Research Council, audits the processes of both companies); in print, ABC (the Audit Bureau of Circulation) and BPA are the major auditors of publication readership and circulation data, but do no real measurement, while MRI and Simmons provide third-party measurement research.

And Standards Appear to be Emerging for the Web. . .

To fill the demand for measurement and audit on the Internet, a handful of companies (most notably I/PRO and Net-Count for third-party measurement and the Audit Bureau of Circulation's subsidiary, the Audit Bureau of Verification Services, BPA International, and I/PRO for third-party audit) are vying to become the Nielsen-equivalent for Internet advertising/usage information. The rapid growth in this area, the potential size of the market, and the fact that only one or two entities tend to dominate measurement in a medium have spurred several traditional measurement companies to get "skin in the game," either through partnership (Nielsen with I/PRO and Price Waterhouse with NetCount) or by forming new areas (ABC and BPA).

I/Pro — I/PRO (Internet Profiles Corporation) has formed a partnership with Nielsen Research, the dominant force in TV ratings, to provide both third-party measurement and auditing. I/PRO's measurement and audit offerings are NetLine, and I/AUDIT, respectively.

• NetLine, a service for internal site measurement, resides on a Web-site owner's server and counts the number of visits, pages served, and most frequently accessed files and directories. The names of visiting organizations can be identified and analyzed based on industry (SIC) codes, organization size, or other criteria. Reports are delivered to users via a Windows application and can be generated by time, date, geographic or organizational data, and site location/access. The NetLine data are collected nightly and transmitted to I/PRO, where it is processed, encoded, indexed, and loaded into I/PRO's database.

• I/AUDIT, I/PRO's auditing service, independently tracks a Web site's daily and weekly visits, average visit length, pages accessed, and most requested files. As with NetLine, I/AUDIT data are collected and transferred to I/PRO's central database, analyzed, and then delivered by postal

mail in the form of printed reports, generally two months after the beginning of an audit period. Visitor reports are broken down by day of week, time of day, industry, region, country, organization, and several other categories. Whereas NetLine measures and reports Web site traffic for internal analysis, I/AUDIT data provide an independently audited report of Web site activity in a standard format.

NetCount — NetCount offers several measurement products, including NetCount Basic, NetCount Plus, and Net-Count AdCount. In June, NetCount announced that Price Waterhouse was licensing its name to NetCount and taking an equity stake in the company (this is the first time that Price Waterhouse has licensed its name to another company's product or service in its 100-year-plus history).

NetCount Basic is an introductory service that provides the bare bones of information for measuring and managing a Web server. It tracks requests by their distinct points of origin (an IP address), graphically compares the types of requests by domain, and reports on Web page delivery and abandonment rates.

NetCount Plus offers the information included in Basic, as well as data about site performance and requests made both to the site and to the users making those requests. It breaks down file types, time spent in those files, and reports on the number and rate of file transfer successes and failures.

NetCount recently introduced AdCount, which provides third-party Web advertising measurement reports on a weekly basis. The reports are designed in a standard format so that advertising performance may be analyzed across sites. AdCount adds a level of tamper-resistance to third-party measurement by requiring that sites install the AdCount software in the background of the publisher's server, where it passively monitors and records advertising usage. Data are securely transferred to NetCount's central data facility and processed hourly.

There are two other players in this space, and they compete strictly as site auditors, offering site audits independent of any other site measurement. These are the Audit Bureau of Verification Services, a subsidiary of the Audit Bureau of Circulation, and BPA. Both have been central to the auditing process in print for many years, and each is attempting to position itself in a similar fashion on the Web.

The Audit Bureau of Verification Services — The ABVS is a subsidiary of the Audit Bureau of Circulation, which has been the central auditing force in the print industry for many years, and ABVS is attempting to position itself in a similar fashion on the Web. Using software developed by WebTrack, ABVS employs a "gatekeeper" approach by sitting on top of a publisher's Web server and monitoring its activity. In this manner, ABVS can monitor and verify site statistics. ABVS is incorporating CASIE's guidelines for third-party site auditing into its technical specifications.

BPA — BPA International is fast becoming a major player in Web auditing and plans to release quarterly audits of Web site and advertising usage. BPA takes a different approach than ABVS, in that it does not place software on servers. Instead, it relies on services like NetCount and I/PRO to provide the third-party measurement, and then it provides a quarterly audit, in compliance with the CASIE guidelines for measurement.

PC Meter — One additional player (in a slightly different, but related, game) that deserves mention is PC Meter, which approaches Web measurement not from the server side but from the client side, by installing its tracking software in 10,000 U.S. households with Windows-based PCs. This is the Nielsen approach to media measurement — select a representative sample of the medium's user population and extrapolate based on its behavior.

This approach has three important advantages over server-side measurement: 1) its estimates are not skewed by the caching of pages on proxy servers, browsers, and so forth; 2) the company is able to capture individual and demographic usage, as opposed to simply unique IP addresses, which is the only differentiation server-based measurement can make (without additional user input); and 3) the ability to track URLs accessed per user. PC Meter uses client software that records a date and time stamp for each unique URL or executable file (.exe) accessed or used, and the sample of households is balanced to reflect U.S. Web-active households.

Unfortunately, the PC Meter methodology does not track individual usage in the Web's *.edu* domain (which represents all colleges, universities, and the like, such as www.harvard.edu) or in the commercial sector in its measurement sample, so its results are skewed toward the consumer base. We believe that a great deal of future Web growth will occur in the corporate sector, and that the presence of educational institutions will also be substantial (a vast majority of college students have paid-for Internet access at their institutions). The PC Meter approach, though it solves some of the thornier measurement issues of server-side measurement, lacks any input from these sectors.

The ability to measure individual use, record the spectrum of URLs that each user accesses, and make comparisons with demographic data affords the ability to more accurately measure metrics like reach and frequency across a broad range of sites. The drawback is a less accurate picture of individual site data, and one restricted to consumers (again, the sample is taken from households only, and misses the entire corporate user base). Therefore, for understanding larger trends and the potential audience by site, or category of site, such data can be valuable. To measure the performance of a specific campaign, though, different types of creative, server-based management, and tracking and measurement tools are required.

. . . And, Now, for the Samples . . .

Figures 7-2 through 7-5 are excerpts from a sample measurement report (NetCount) and a sample audit report (I/PRO). For a given publisher/site, these reports include a description of the site, its content, its audience, and so on. The report details statistics for visits (such as the total, the average per day, and the average visit length) and pages (total delivered, average pages per visit, etc.) for the site, its industry as a whole, and for ad-supported sites in general. In addition to these overall metrics, more detailed results provide insight into day-by-day performance of the site, as well as metrics like click-through rate.

These reports can validate advertising buys and increase advertisers' willingness to spend on Internet campaigns by giving them confidence that they are receiving a real return on their purchases. They also aid in differentiating the value of one potential purchase from another.

Figure 7-2

Excerpt from a Sample NetCount Measurement Report

Ad Impressions and Click-Throughs Report*

Publisher:	Snob Review
Advertisement Name:	"Merlot to go"
Advertisement Site:	http://www.frenchywines.com
AdCount Activation Date:	August 19, 1996
Report Run Date:	09/2/96
Report Period:	8/26/96 - 9/1/96

In this example, Snob Review publishes the advertisement "Merlot to go" for advertiser Frenchy Wines.

	This Week 8/26/96 - 9/1/96	Last Week 8/19/96 - 8/25/96	Percent Change
Graphical Ad Impressions	63038	71517	- 13.5
Cached/Textual Ad Impressions	33791	39514	- 16.9
Total Ad Impressions	96829	111031	- 14.7
Click-Throughs	5253	4228	+ 24.2
Graphical Click-Through Rate	8.3%	5.9%	+ 41.0
Total Click-Through Rate	5.4%	3.8%	+ 42.4

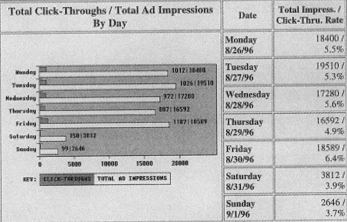

Total Click-Throughs / Total Ad Impressions By Day

Date	Total Impress. / Click-Thru. Rate
Monday 8/26/96	18400 / 5.5%
Tuesday 8/27/96	19510 / 5.3%
Wednesday 8/28/96	17280 / 5.6%
Thursday 8/29/96	16592 / 4.9%
Friday 8/30/96	18589 / 6.4%
Saturday 8/31/96	3812 / 3.9%
Sunday 9/1/96	2646 / 3.7%

Graphical Ad Impression
The delivery of a graphical advertisement to a Browser.

Cached/Textual Ad Impression
The delivery of an advertisement to a Browser that has cached the advertisement, has graphics turned off, or does not support graphics.

Total Ad Impressions**
The total of all Graphical, Cached & Textual Ad Impressions.

Click-Through
A click by a user on an advertisement.

Graphical Click-Through Rate
The percentage of Graphical Ad Impressions that result in Click-Throughs.

Total Click-Through Rate
The percentage of Total Ad Impressions that result in Click-Throughs.

Percentage Change
The percentage of increase or decrease between the current figure and the previously recorded figure.

**If a Web site uses certain methods to dynamically display advertisements, or if a Web site subscribes to a remote Ad management service or an advertising network, the Web server may only record graphical advertisements. In these cases, cached/textual advertisement statistics are not available (N/A).

*This report is not NetCount HeadCount (TM) enhanced.

Copyright © 1996 NetCount, LLC

Source: NetCount.   Reprinted with permission of NetCount.

Figure 7-3

Excerpt from a Sample NetCount Measurement Report

Top Site Pages Report *

NET COUNT, LLC PriceWaterhouse LLP ⊕ Plus			
Prepared for:	Company XYZ		
URL:	http://www.companyxyz.com/		
Run Date:	April 15, 1996		
Report Period:	4/14/96		

Document Title - Document Path	PITs - URL Type	%Failure - % Abandoned	Peak Hour ~(PST)~ Peak Volume in PITs	Avg Time On Page	Hourly Performance in PITs (Previous Day Shadowed)
Welcome to Company XYZ /index.html	3413 HTML	0.2% 0.3%	4pm 203	141 secs	
Trees Around the World /Trees/index.html	1100 HTML	0.7% 24.7%	7pm 95	63 secs	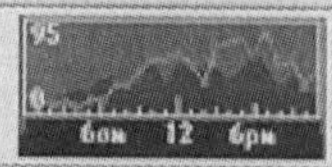
Italy /cgi-bin/card.cgi	638 CGI	0.0% 0.0%	5pm 56	85 secs	
Trees Around the World /Trees/Html/loon.html	503 HTML	0.0% 0.0%	5pm 39	67 secs	
Italy - Pasta /Italy/pasta.html	474 HTML	0.0% 0.0%	7pm 43	75 secs	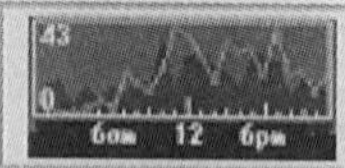
World of Apples /Trees/Html/apple.htm	334 HTML	0.0% 0.0%	7pm 35	52 secs	
Phones /html/Phones/index.html	212 HTML	0.0% 0.0%	7pm 24	60 secs	
Greenface /greenface/wow_01.htm	183 HTML	0.0% 0.0%	11am 19	87 secs	
Wild Roses /Wild/rose10.html	163 HTML	0.0% 0.0%	5pm 19	54 secs	
Media Services /Media/Html/media.html	143 HTML	0.0% 0.0%	5pm 18	52 secs	

PIT-Page Information Transfer
The successful transfer of the text of a web page to a Browser.

*This report is not NetCount HeadCount(TM) enhanced.

Copyright © 1996 NetCount, LLC

Source: NetCount.   Reprinted with permission of NetCount.

Figure 7-4

Excerpt from a Sample I/PRO Audit Report

I/AUDIT

This report is a standard, verifiable means for Web sites to report traffic to advertisers and media buyers/planners in order to facilitate effective placement of advertising.

I/PRO certifies that these results are an independent, accurate, and complete summary of this web site's activity.

Nielsen I/PRO I/AUDIT is based on census analysis of raw log files provided by the site. I/AUDIT is a consistent, conservative report of site activity that is reviewed and verified by I/PRO's Audit Analysts.

SUMMARY OF SITE ACTIVITY

@COMPUTERWORLD Computerworld

505 Sansome Street, 6th Floor • San Francisco, CA 94111 • 415.676.3000 • www.computerworld.com

Site Content
Computerworld features computer and software industry news and targets the IT community.

Computerworld	AUGUST 1996
▶ VISITS Indicates the number of times visitors came to your site	
TOTAL	165,051
AVERAGE PER DAY	5,324
AVERAGE VISIT LENGTH	3:47 minutes
▶ PAGES Indicates the extent of a visitor's interaction with the site	
TOTAL VIEWED	428,124
AVERAGE VIEWED PER VISIT	2.6 pages

AFFIDAVIT

Internet Profiles Corporation

Source: I/PRO.   Reprinted with permission of I/PRO.

Figure 7-5

Excerpt from a Sample I/PRO Audit Report

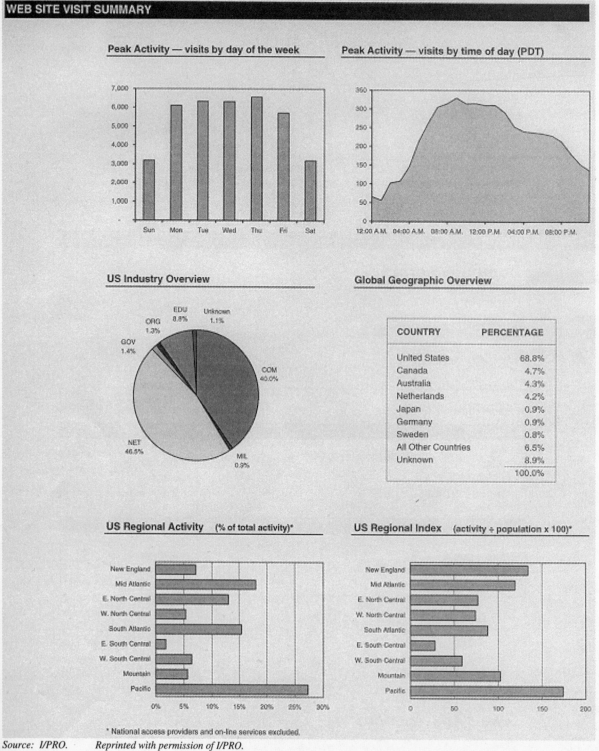

Source: I/PRO. *Reprinted with permission of I/PRO.*

Point-of-Sale Purchasing Could Be Key

As the nascent electronic commerce industry evolves, users increasingly will be able to make purchasing decisions precisely at the point of exposure, an advantage not supplied by any other form of media advertising. Once users have this ability (and moreover, perhaps, feel secure in exercising it), it will likely be a significant boon to those companies with a well-developed Web presence and the transactional capability and infrastructure to execute online purchases. Although average click-through rates seem low (2–3%), these still compare favorably to average response rates for other media, including direct-mail and traditional advertising.

Certain industries are inherently more conducive to this type of purchasing, with perhaps the best example being the software industry itself. Software (especially freeware and shareware) is currently distributed widely across the Internet by companies as a means of inducing subsequent purchases by consumers. This trend may be best evidenced by CNET's own software download site, SHAREWARE.COM, which has proven to be tremendously popular. The future of software sales and distribution undoubtedly will include the Web, and software companies are well on their way to leveraging this new medium in marketing their products. We think CNET understands the potential of this new paradigm of software sales, as it is aggressively working to incorporate the ability to purchase software directly into its sites (through its recently launched DOWNLOAD.COM and its coming transactional back-end, BUYDIRECT.COM).

Cookies: You Can Rely on Them for Weight Gain, And Now, for Web Stats

Another development in this area is the use of cookies, wherein a server-specific file is sent by a Web site server and automatically stored by a browser on a user's hard disk. This cookie file's data can be anything, like a date/time stamp, an IP address, or a unique user ID. Once a cookie is received from a given server, whenever that browser makes a request to that server for an HTML page, it will include the cookie with the request. The browser will only send a cookie to the server site that originally sent it, so it is not possible for one Web site to look at or request cookies from other sites.

Cookies provide a signature, so that Web sites can track an individual's number of visits and the path he or she took through a site. This information can be employed in a number of creative ways, including obtaining behavioral data, crafting marketing messages for a site owner's or advertiser's products, keeping track of purchasing activity at a site (if you visit and read all of my pages on espresso makers, but don't buy one, I can still show you the product each time you return), and overall personalization of the user's experience at the site.

Some potential downsides to the use of this technology is the possibility of tampering by users or third parties. Cookies are located on a user's local hard drive, and if altering the cookie data is beneficial enough to a user, it is likely that many will attempt to do so. In addition, third-party sites might have cause to tamper with the cookie data of competitors (or partners), or invade the privacy of users by reading their stored data for behavioral, purchasing, or other purposes.

Despite these potential security and privacy issues, this tailored marketing approach adds significant value, we believe, that may be enhanced further by demographic information gained through user registration data, which are collected at such sites as CNET, ESPNET SportsZone, *The Wall Street Journal* Interactive, and the online services. In our view, it would make a very compelling value-added proposition if advertisers could be certain of the age, gender, occupation, or purchasing preferences of each person who views an ad.

Chapter 8: How Companies Can Succeed in Internet Advertising

Summary

◆ Given the potential size of the opportunity for advertising on the Web, we think **companies that want to be successful in the Internet ad game need to prove there is a business model that works, determine growth factors, provide good feedback to advertisers, and make the right friends.**

So What's an Advertiser to Do?

Choosing the right place to advertise on the Web is similar to the approach used in traditional advertising. When advertisers make media buying decisions, they use a rate card supplied by each of the potential sites, magazines, and the like. The rate card lists the rate (most likely in CPMs) that the publisher charges for each type of advertising product it offers. A magazine, for example, might have one CPM for an ad on the back cover, one for an ad on the inside cover, one for the middle of the magazine, and so on. Similarly, Web sites might list the CPM for their banners, along with prices for products like buttons or keywords, all tailored to the particular vehicle that site might provide. An advertiser might then make a purchasing decision based on such criteria as the nature of the product or service being advertised, the target audience of the advertiser, the size and nature of the audience the publisher commands, the size of their budget, and many other factors.

We believe there are several criteria that media planners and buyers need to focus on in making purchasing decisions. How much does the space cost? (With banners, this is generally CPM.) What positioning will an advertisement receive? (The top of the page versus the bottom of the page makes a big difference.) To what content is the advertisement, product, or brand being married, and does that make sense? Which audience will see the ad? How much control do planners or buyers have over reach, frequency, change of creative, market testing, and so forth? How reliable is the management, delivery, and auditing of the buy?

For example, CNET has seven active sites — CNET.COM, NEWS.COM, SHAREWARE.COM, SEARCH.COM, GAMECENTER.COM, BUYDIRECT.COM and DOWNLOAD.COM. The value for advertisers to purchase banners on each particular site varies due to factors such as the nature of the content on the site, the profile of users who view the site, the traffic on the site, and the perceived value of advertising in that space. Figure 2-14 shows this to be true, as the CPM for these sites varies widely. For example, NEWS.COM carries the highest CPM, due in part to the very targeted nature of its content and the demographic that the content carries with it. Each site has a different audience, and the ads on each are married to different types of content; thus, the value proposition (and resulting CPM) is different for advertisers on each.

I/PRO Research conducted a study called *The Web In Perspective,* which found a loose but positive relationship between site traffic and ad pricing. This is a very broadband relationship, and there are exceptions to the rule, but it follows that the more engaging, useful, and popular a sight is, the more advertisers want to brand or promote themselves on that site. The study stated that ads on home pages tended to generate a lower click-through rate than ads on specific content pages, suggesting that editorial context is, in fact, a significant driver of traffic. Also, advertisers will pay more for a better audit of their investment, and the more traffic a site has, the more robust and detailed its data collection likely is.

Furthermore, the greater the traffic, the higher the response rate (click-through) — essentially meaning that higher traffic indicates a generally more engaged user. Factors that significantly increase traffic growth, I/PRO found, include cross-media promotions and non-Internet events (e.g., there was a dramatic uptick in traffic at sports information sites during the NCAA college basketball tournament).

The study indicated that increases in site traffic allowed ad-supported sites to attract more advertisers at higher rates, emphasizing how crucial the ability to attract eyeballs will be as competition heats up. Advertisers recognize that higher traffic is a result of a better product, and aligning themselves with a quality site adds to the marginal return on each dollar invested. Even more value can be added to this proposition if the advertisers and site work together to marry advertisement and content in a synergistic fashion, which, if the content is compelling, creates a more natural segue to the purchase of an advertiser's product.

An example of the variance in traffic between sites with different types of content can be found in Figure 8-1. In the I/PRO study, navigational sites (defined as search, directory, and indexing services used to find content located elsewhere) were segmented from content sites (all other sites that provide text, graphics, or sound). The graph shows that while traffic at both sites increased significantly from January, the total traffic for navigational sites is more than four times greater than the traffic at content sites.

The bottom line in making media buys and determining the effectiveness of when, how, where, or with whom an ad is placed is that, although the Internet makes it easier to measure the effects of advertising, it does not make it easier to define what real success is — this is particular to each campaign. Though the purpose of marketing communications is to drive sales and revenues, direct measurement of sales made is not a complete measurement of the effectiveness of any one campaign. Campaigns can affect image, awareness, knowledge, attitude, intention, and consumer

behavior, and effective Web-based marketing can affect all of these.

A Thumbnail Sketch for Web Ad Success

Given the size of the opportunity, we think companies that want to be successful in the Internet ad game need to do a handful of things:

Prove there is a business model that works. As yet, ad-based revenue models are unproven, and it will be important to monitor new developments in revenue generation as the medium evolves. It's important for companies to explore revenue opportunities related to transactions and subscriptions. No doubt, in the early days of the Internet, many content providers that seek to drive revenue from advertising will be disappointed. However, the sites that can provide quantifiable returns on investment to advertisers are in the best position to succeed, in our view.

Determine growth factors. Companies need to determine the factors that drive traffic and learn how to make them work for their business. In these early days, it will be more important to grab market share than to run a profitable business. Again, more eyeballs almost always equal increased revenue in the advertising world.

Provide useful feedback to advertisers. Companies need to explore the relationship between site traffic and ad rates, and to design a sales and marketing strategy around them. A whole cottage industry has sprung up around advertising measurement. Companies like NetGravity make software that runs on servers and collects detailed information about hits, visits, page views, demographic information, and the like, so that companies can give accurate, timely feedback to advertisers on the performance of their purchases.

Make the right friends. The space will inevitably become competitive (if it's not already). Choosing the right ad strategy for ad revenue competition and seeking out the right relationships in the Internet community will likely make or break many companies.

Web Successes to Date

Several companies have made much forward progress in achieving these goals (although we would add that none of these potential "successes" has provided proven methods):

Figure 8-1
Average Weekly Visits
Navigational vs. Content Sites

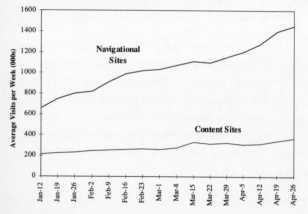

Source: I/PRO Research.

The Business Model — CNET has certainly made significant progress in making an advertising-based business model work — only Netscape and four search engines currently generate more online ad revenue — and the company has done so without the aid of a major corporate parent, such as ZD Net (Ziff-Davis), Pathfinder (Time Warner), and CNN Interactive (Time Warner, after acquisition of Turner). We expect the company to turn profitable in 3Q97.

The Growth Factors — No one has access to more eyeballs and a larger user base than AOL. And as for driving growth from this opportunity, we think AOL's new flat-fee pricing plan will certainly drive huge amounts of new traffic, which equals many more pages served, which equals many more ad dollars. Assuming that the company can withstand this onslaught of new traffic, this should be a very positive step toward advertising revenue success.

The Feedback — This will increase across the board as standards and measurement tools evolve — it is in everyone's best interest to do so, in our view. Advertisers will like it (as it gives them more targeted exposure to a more attractive audience), publishers will like it (higher CPMs/pricing, more revenue), and users will like it, too (advertising more targeted to their needs and tastes, more along the lines of additional services than ads).

Making Friends — Finally, we expect to see a continuing scramble to lock arms with the key players in the Internet space. Yahoo! is a good example, as it has leveraged strong relationships on many fronts, especially technology (DEC's AltaVista search engine) and sales (Softbank Interactive Marketing).

Chapter 9: A Look at the Histories of Traditional Media
Yes, Been There . . . Done That . . .

Summary

◆ In a sentence: Been there, done that. **There have been five major media that have developed in the U.S. since the Pilgrims landed at Plymouth Rock. And while we haven't spent a lot of time trying to figure out if Steve Case was separated at intellectual birth from Ben Franklin or William Paley, we think a few key points (articulated in Chapter 3) can be gleaned from a little journey through time to look at the evolutions of newspapers, magazines, radio, broadcast TV, and cable TV. And, yes, we conclude: Been there, done that.** In this chapter, we devote snippets of air time to five media time capsules.

◆ Our conclusions and analogies? In **Newspapers,** it's easy to say that Will Hearst (of @Home Networks) was "separated at birth" from William Randolph Hearst (of The Hearst Corporation); in **Magazines,** Steve Case (America Online) was separated at birth from Henry Luce (*Time* magazine); in **Broadcast TV,** Marc Andreessen (Netscape) was separated at birth from David Sarnoff (American Marconi/RCA/NBC), while Halsey Minor (CNET) was separated at birth from William Paley (CBS), David and Tom Gardner (The Motley Fool) were separated at birth from Chet Huntley and David Brinkley (NBC's "The Huntley-Brinkley Report"), and Ted Leonsis (AOL) was separated at birth from Brandon Tartikoff (NBC); in **Cable TV,** Steve Case was again separated at birth from a unique combination of John Malone (TCI) and Ted Turner (Turner Broadcasting), and, in the easiest call, Bob Pittman (AOL) was separated at birth from himself, Bob Pittman (MTV). Finally, Bill Gates (Microsoft) may end up being separated at birth from all of the above.

◆ The good news? We don't yet know who was separated at birth from Elsie the Cow, Captain Kangaroo, Mister Magoo, and Doris Day (much to our surprise, Martha Stewart doesn't have a Web site yet). And we can't wait to figure out who was separated at birth from George Burns and Gracie Allen.

When considering the viability of the Internet as an advertising medium, historical parallels may be helpful in predicting future trends. Here, we take qualitative and quantitative trips down U.S. media memory lanes. On the qualitative side, we sourced Shirley Biagi's book *Media/Impact,* (Wadsworth Publishing), extensively; on the quantitative side, we have sourced data provided by McCann-Erickson. In addition, we consulted with Morgan Stanley's U.S. media research team: Doug Arthur (Publishing), Mike Russell (Advertising), Frank Bodenchak (Broadcasting), and Rich Bilotti (Cable and Entertainment/Programming).

Evolution of a Medium: U.S. Newspapers

In the late 1690s, American newspapers began as one-page sheets that consisted primarily of overseas news and ship arrival and departure postings. Yet as dissatisfaction over British rule in colonial America grew, newspapers began taking on an important political role.

By the 1800s, the advent of the telegraph, automated printing presses, and less-expensive paper allowed publishers to lower newspaper prices and boost circulation.

The first newspapers were too expensive for most Americans and were confined to Eastern cities and highly educated urban audiences. But by the late 19th Century the penny paper had arrived, via Benjamin Day's *New York Sun.* His business model was remarkably simple and incredibly successful — sensationalism and gossip at an affordable price — and he sold advertising space in lieu of subscription revenue. In addition, he hired newsboys to sell the paper on street corners. Advertising comprised over one-quarter of printable space.

As Day's model proved feasible, other penny papers were introduced, including Horace Greeley's *New York Tribune* and Henry Raymond's *The New York Times.*

As America expanded to the West, the demand for local and national news increased, and new markets were formed. The most significant advances in the newspaper industry included the launch of the wire services (such as the Associated Press and the United Press), beginning in 1848, which allowed for cooperative news gathering; the development of rural routed delivery systems; the debut of photojournalism in the early 1900s; the growth in tabloid journalism; and industry consolidation.

The three most significant characters in the dynamic growth years of the newspaper industry were Joseph Pulitzer (*St. Louis Post-Dispatch* and *New York World*); E.W. Scripps (*Cleveland Press*), and William Randolph Hearst (*San Francisco Examiner* and *New York Journal*). Pulitzer reserved more space for advertisers and sold his paper based on circulation. He used illustrations and simple writing, aggressively promoted his papers on their very pages, and reintroduced sensationalistic stories. Scripps' papers focused on concisely edited news, human-interest stories, editorial independence, and frequent crusades for the working class; he also created the first newspaper chain and expanded into other cities. Hearst was a crusading champion of the people and did his share of cleaning up corruption through exposure. He focused on sensationalistic stories and had a nationalistic style; he also engaged Pulitzer's papers in bitter circulation battles.

According to Doug Arthur, Morgan Stanley's publishing analyst, 54 million newspapers circulate daily in the U.S., and 78% of Americans read papers each day. For 1996, domestic revenue for the industry is estimated at $46 billion, of which 79% came from advertisements and 21% from subscriptions. Advertising revenue can be broken down as follows: 50% retail, 38% classifieds, and 12% national. While national advertisers, such as Procter & Gamble, split advertising spending among various media, local advertisers (such as retailers) direct about 70% of advertising dollars to newspapers, with the exception of national newspapers like *The Wall Street Journal, The New York Times, The Washington Post*, and *USA Today*. Most newspapers serve local markets.

Even though newspapers are indispensable tools for advertisers, some surveys indicate that this medium is having trouble holding onto some key groups: younger readers and women. A number of newspapers — including *The Wall Street Journal, The New York Times, The Washington Post,* *and USA Today* — have responded by offering not only more news that's focused on these demographics but also fairly extensive Web versions of their publications.

Evolution of a Medium: U.S. Magazines

About 50 years after the debut of American newspapers, in the mid-1770s, the first magazines, *American Magazine* and *General Magazine,* were introduced by Andrew Bradford and Benjamin Franklin, respectively. However, neither of these political publications lasted long, as they were costly, lacked advertising, and had small circulations.

However, magazine supporters persisted. While newspapers covered daily issues for local readers, magazines reached beyond local concerns and focused on the cultural, political, and social issues for an emerging nation. Magazines quickly became America's only national medium, and often became the country's teachers. The most successful early magazine was *The Saturday Evening Post,* launched in 1821 at 5 cents per issue. Early issues were a total of four pages, had no illustrations, and devoted one-fourth of the magazine to advertising. *The Post* featured news, fiction, poetry, essays, theater reviews, and a column called "The Lady's Friend." Early contributors included Edgar Allan Poe, Harriet Beecher Stowe, and Nathaniel Hawthorne.

Finally, in the 1800s, magazine circulation began growing, by focusing on women and social issues (*The Ladies' Home Journal* was launched in 1887); becoming literacy showcases for American writers (*Harper's* and *The Atlantic Monthly* were launched in 1850 and 1857, respectively, and featured writers such as Mark Twain, Stephen Crane, and Henry David Thoreau); and encouraging political debate (*The Nation* and *The New Republic* were launched in 1865 and 1914, respectively).

Magazines got a further boost in 1879 with passage of the Postal Act, which created second-class mailing privileges. Prior to the act, magazine publishers paid high postage rates. With lower distribution costs, publishers were able to not only run more ads but also create new magazines — in the last 40 years of the 19th Century, the number of monthlies jumped from less than 200 to about 1,800.

In 1923, Henry Luce, with the launch of *Time* magazine, helped broaden the magazine business from a focus on targeted audiences to an increased focus on broad, general audiences. Luce and his empire, Time, Inc., went on to publish *Fortune, Life, Sports Illustrated, Money,* and *People.*

Women's magazines also appeared early, in part because advertisers want to reach their readers. One need only pick up a copy of *Vogue* or *Cosmopolitan* to get an idea of the overwhelming amount of ads. Up until the mid-1930s, though, such magazines were essentially trade papers for home-makers. This trend helped establish many new magazines in the first half of this century, including: *Better Homes & Gardens* (1922), *Family Circle* (1932), *Women's Day* (1937), *Better Living* (1951), and *Seventeen* (1944).

Eventually, though, competition from radio and television appeared, and in response publishers sought to expand their audiences (for both broad and narrow market segments). This targeting helps magazine publishers provide relevant demographic data for advertisers. And specialized magazines can deliver narrowly defined audiences to advertisers, with very little wasted circulation.

According to our colleague Doug Arthur, 10,387 magazines are currently published in the U.S. The 1995 per-issue circulation was 363 million, for 583 magazines under audit by the Audit Bureau of Circulation. About 166 million American adults (or 87% of the over-18 population) read magazines. Estimated 1996 domestic revenue for the industry was $23 billion (55% from advertising and 45% from subscriptions). On average, 671 new magazines were launched per year from 1988 through 1995, but, according to the Magazine Publishers Association, only 3 out of 10 survive for four years or more.

It's important to note average magazine production costs. According to the MPA, the average breakdown of cost as a percentage of revenue is as follows: circulation, 33%; manufacturing and distribution, 29%; editorial, 10%; advertising and promotion, 10%; administrative and other expenses, 8%; and pretax profit comprises about 9%.

Evolution of a Medium: U.S. Radio

Radio is an inexpensive media option and is often used as a supplemental medium to television and movies. Radio's greatest strengths are its ubiquity, diversity of programming (music, news, sports, talk), and low cost. According to Frank Bodenchak, Morgan Stanley's broadcasting analyst, there are currently 11,550 U.S. radio stations (versus 1,200

TV stations), comprising about 6,500 FM stations and more than 5,000 AM stations. On average, Americans listen to radio for 3.1 hours per day. Estimated 1996 domestic advertising revenue for the radio industry is $12 billion.

Radio was an innovative technology/product that brought together millions of people, who gathered to listen to live news (the Great Depression, the New Deal, Pearl Harbor) and entertainment (The Shadow, the big bands, Jack Benny).

Radio had its beginnings with the invention of the telegraph (by Samuel Morse in 1835) and the telephone (Alexander Graham Bell, 1876), as well as the first description of radio waves (Heinrich Hertz, 1887) and the promotion of wireless radio transmission using Morse code (Guglielmo Marconi, 1897). Then, in 1899, Marconi transmitted the results of an America's Cup Race via radio; he soon received venture money and founded American Marconi. Amateur radio operators created radio clubs and began to experiment with Marconi's products. Between 1906 and 1910, Reginald Fessenden and Lee de Forest used continuous waves to carry voice and music over the radio waves. But it was David Sarnoff who made radio broadcasting a viable business in the U.S. — he was an early amateur radio operator and an employee of American Marconi.

In 1916, Sarnoff, at the age of 25, wrote the following memo:

I have in mind a plan of development which would make radio a household utility. The idea is to bring music into the home by wireless. The receiver can be designed in the form of a simple "radio music box," and arranged for several different wave lengths which should be changeable with the throwing of a single switch or the pressing of a single button. The same principle can be extended to numerous other fields, as for example, receiving lectures at home which would be perfectly audible. Also, events of national importance can be simultaneously announced and received. Baseball scores can be transmitted in the air. This proposition would be especially interesting to farmers and others living in outlying districts.

In the early 1920s, General Electric subsidiary RCA acquired American Marconi and, subsequently, nabbed David Sarnoff. RCA soon garnered key radio patent rights from

Westinghouse, General Electric, and AT&T and became partially owned by all three companies. Sarnoff went on to become the radio industry's champion and chairman of RCA, a key beneficiary of the growth in radio.

The first commercial radio station started up in 1920, in Pittsburgh. And by the end of 1921, 28 radio stations had been granted licenses, and nine were on the air. By July 1922, 430 more licenses had been issued, all on the single frequency of 833 kHz.

The demand for radio receivers in 1922 was impressive. In only the second year of radio broadcasting, industry radio receiver sales were approximately $60 million; by the end of 1926, more than 5 million homes had radios, and industry sales had reached $506 million for the year.

Radio industry growth was rapid, and lots of radio frequency and station chaos ensued. In response, in 1927 Congress created the Federal Radio Commission (precursor to the FCC) to regulate the industry.

Initially, radio stations played phonograph records; later, artists were invited to perform live in radio station studios. In 1923, the American Society of Composers, Authors, and Publishers (ASCAP) sued several stations for playing recorded music. Subsequently, stations agreed to pay ASCAP royalties. In turn, station owners began selling time to advertisers to finance operations — despite opposition from early industry leaders, including David Sarnoff, who thought that advertising on radio was "too unseemly."

The first radio commercial — from a local real estate firm — was broadcast in New York in 1922. Within six months, 25 advertisers were using the New York radio station, including Macy's, MetLife, and Colgate. From this modest beginning, the use of radio as an advertising medium grew exponentially.

Early on, advertisers like Citgo, Schraffts, and Wanamaker began creating sponsored programing, such as Citgo's Band of America. In 1929, the first known national jingle was produced for Wheaties. Radio and print also learned to work together: *True Detective Mysteries* increased its circulation from 190,000 to 690,000 in six months by dramatizing some of its stories as "thriller" radio shows. One of the classic early radio advertising efforts was the launch of Johnson's Wax sponsorship of Fibber McGee and Molly in

1935 — this 15-minute daytime serial, which targeted housewives, was the precursor to the soap opera.

Evolution of a Medium: U.S. Broadcast Television

Like radio, television was developed rather than invented. Much of its development is owed to the many technical innovations that came out of wireless, radio, photography, motion pictures, and wire transmission.

Of the legions of engineers that worked on television, one of the most notable participants in its evolution was Westinghouse's Dr. Vladimir Zworykin, who in 1923 invented the electric iconoscope. Further development led to the kinescope in 1926, an electronic picture tube in a television set that translates electrical impulses into visual images.

By 1935, most of the essential technologies for monochrome TV had been developed, with a great deal of innovation occurring at RCA under the guidance of David Sarnoff. It was at this time that Sarnoff, eager to get television off the ground, announced that RCA was prepared to spend $1 million (a sizable sum during the Depression) for the development of a complete television system.

Sarnoff attempted RCA's first major experiment in TV, broadcasting from the Empire State Building in New York City to receivers in the homes of VIPs and employees of RCA and NBC — the experiment was a success, and by 1937, there were 17 other experimental stations. Sarnoff moved aggressively to create a commercial television market, with RCA as its leader. However, RCA quickly encountered regulatory issues, transmission standard issues, channel allocation difficulties, and bickering from competitors, which slowed RCA's progress as it sought commercialization approval from the FCC.

For some time, the FCC heard arguments from the industry and committees that had been assembled to make recommendations to the FCC. Sarnoff became increasingly impatient with the progress of the hearings. In October 1938, he made a bold but calculated risk, stating that "television in the home is now technically feasible. The difficulties confronting this difficult and complicated art can only be solved from operating experience, actually serving the public in their homes." He gambled that public awareness would stimulate desire for the rollout of television, thereby causing intense political pressure — and he was right. In early 1940, the FCC, under public pressure, issued a compromise that satisfied no one. It essentially allowed what was called "limited" commercial broadcasting. Loosely translated, advertising sponsors would foot the bill for the cost of programming, and the stations would have to pay the operating cost. Fortunately for Sarnoff, this approval turned out to be all that RCA needed to forge ahead with commercial broadcasting.

Within six months of Sarnoff's pledge, RCA debuted a telecast of the opening ceremonies of the 1939 World's Fair and continued with a daily television schedule. The FCC, though, had left the rest of the industry in a state of chaos. Rival manufacturers mounted huge publicity campaigns urging the public not to buy RCA receivers because higher-performance sets would soon be available.

In May 1940, the FCC rescinded its earlier compromise, effectively putting TV back in the laboratory until the industry could reach a new agreement on standards. The industry formed an ad hoc committee, the National Television System Committee (NTSC), which studied key broadcasting issues and submitted a set of recommendations to the FCC. In April 1941, the FCC adopted the NTSC recommendations in issuing the Standards of Good Engineering Practice Concerning Television Broadcasting Stations.

The FCC authorized commercial TV operations to start in July 1941. By May 1942, there were six operational stations that broadcast throughout the war. In effect, WWII postponed television's broadcasting growth, but the war effort stimulated enormous advances in television technology. As the end of the war approached, major manufacturers, such as RCA, GE, and Dumont, geared up for production of transmitting studio equipment, and radio manufacturers began converting plants to make television receivers. However, because of the high costs associated with the construction and operation of news stations, there was a general reluctance on the part of broadcasters to move forward quickly.

For example, in 1949, there were 98 television stations reporting total operating expenses of $57 million, with an average of $608,000 in operating expenses per station. On the other hand, 1,824 radio stations in the same year reported total operating expenses of $342 million, with average operating expenses of $108,000 per station. Radio's revenue capture from advertising was compelling, and it

appeared that television broadcast economics simply did not make sense.

Adding to the confusion was the lack of television programming and poor, unsophisticated programming techniques. Finally, there was "the chicken-and-egg problem" for new broadcast services — there was no incentive to broadcast programs without receivers and no incentive to buy receivers without programs.

In 1947, at the National Association of Broadcasters (NAB) convention, David Sarnoff gave a rousing motivational speech to the NBC radio affiliates, encouraging them to build stations for the NBC broadcast television network and to provide programs so that the public would buy TV sets. Excerpts of his "defining moment" speech follow:

I have lived through several periods of development in the fields of communication and entertainment. I remember the day when wireless as a service of transoceanic communication was regarded by some as a joke. Those who owned cables could not see wireless as a competitor of cables. Who would entrust important messages to a medium that was filled with static?

I lived through the day when the Victor Talking Machine Company could not understand how people would sit at home and listen to music that someone else decided they should hear. And so they felt that the "radio music box" and radio broadcasting were a toy and would be a fancy.

I saw the same thing happen in the field of talking motion pictures. It was urged by many that people would not go to a movie that made a lot of noise and bellowed through an amplifier and disturbed the slumber of those who enjoyed the silent movie...and then — in 1927 — came Warner Brothers with "The Jazz Singer" and Al Jolson. Almost overnight a new industry was born. Today, who goes to a silent movie?

Let me assure you, my friends, after more than forty years of experience in this field of communications and entertainment, I have never seen any protection in merely standing still. There is no protection except through progress.

Therefore, may I leave you with this final thought: I would suggest that you reflect carefully and thoughtfully upon the possible ultimate effects of television upon your established business if you do nothing, and of the great opportunities for your present and future businesses if you do the right thing!

The growth of the television industry had been slow. By 1947 there were only 16 stations. In part, because of Sarnoff's urging, growth began to ramp — in 1948 there were 51 stations and in 1950 there were 107. As the commission had foreseen, it became increasingly evident that there weren't enough available channels for nation-wide service. In September 1948 the FCC stopped granting new station licenses to study the problem. This became known as the so-called "freeze" order.

In July 1949, comprehensive changes were proposed to improve and extend TV service. These included new engineering systems, reservation of channels for noncommercial educational use, and a national assignment plan for all channels.

The big initial television networks were old competitors from radio (Sarnoff's NBC and William Paley's CBS). Initial television programming was well, stiff — like radio anchors behind a camera. In the early years, news dominated, and desk-bound anchors like Edward R. Murrow, David Brinkley, and Chet Huntley set the tone. Then along came the variety shows (*The Ed Sullivan Show* and *The Mickey Mouse Club)*, sitcoms (*I Love Lucy)*, dramas (*The Loretta Young Show)*, Westerns (*Cheyenne)*, soap operas (*The Search for Tomorrow)*, quiz shows (*$64,000 Question)*, and talk shows (*Tonight Show)*.

At the outset, television was an advertising medium — viewers think of television product as the programming, while advertisers and television executives think of the product as the audience. Industry pioneers borrowed the highly successful business model from radio and utilized direct sponsorship. Early examples of these sponsorships included the *Texaco Star Theater,* which starred Milton Berle in a variety-show format, and *The Hallmark Hall of Fame* dramas, which continue today. Sponsorship began to fade in the 1960s following the quiz-show scandals of the late 1950s, when several advertisers/sponsors were accused of rigging programs. Commercials, as we know them, first debuted around 1948; early memorable commercials included those for Lucky Strike cigarettes, SOS soap pads, Mr. Clean, and Pepsodent toothpaste. One of our favorite

examples of the power of TV advertising occurred in 1970, when Coca-Cola debuted a multinational ad campaign that featured children from many different countries singing the song, "I'd Like to Teach the World to Sing." Coca-Cola saturated the radio and television airwaves with the song, which became a hit. Coca-Cola went on to sell a million records featuring a noncommercial version of the popular jingle.

According to our colleague Frank Bodenchak, Morgan Stanley's broadcasting analyst, there are currently 1,200 broadcast television stations in the U.S., approximately 75% are commercial stations and 25% are noncommercial, with more than half affiliated with a network. American households watch an average of 50 hours of TV per week, or 7 hours per day (up from 33 hours per week in 1950, or 4.6 hours per day). Average adult usage is currently 4.4 hours per day. Estimated 1996 domestic advertising revenue for the industry was $35 billion, including $12.5 billion in network ad spending.

At prime time, there are approximately 10 minutes and 30 seconds of commercials shown per hour (CBS is low at 10 minutes and Fox is high at 10 minutes, 41 seconds). The cost per 1,000 homes for a 30-second major network prime-time commercial spot is $11.00. The average prime-time 30-second commercial has a reach of 9 million, putting the cost of an average 30-second spot at about $100,000. However, certain prime-time spots can cost more than $500,000 to air (some advertisers admit to paying $600,000 this season for ER and Seinfeld). The cost for a 30-second Super-bowl spot can be over $1 million.

Evolution of a Medium: U.S. Cable Television

Cable TV first appeared around 1948 in the form of community antenna television, or CATV. Soon, CATV was used to help sell television receivers in remote or hilly areas, where broadcast television signals were difficult, if not impossible, to receive.

In 1949, E.L. Parsons, the owner of radio station DAST in Astoria, Ore., erected an antenna system to receive station KING-TV in Seattle, 125 miles away. He then distributed its signal by cable to 25 "subscribing neighbors."

It was soon discovered that CATV could present consumers with better reception and could, via microwave relay stations, be used to import television signals from distant television stations. Thus, in addition to growth in rural areas, CATV systems began sprouting up in areas that already were served by local broadcast stations.

Attempts to wire the major urban areas in the early 1970s largely failed, as companies discovered that laying coaxial cable in cities was far more expensive than expected and that demand was light in areas that were already well served by standard broadcast stations. Generally, costs for deploying cable in the 1970s were prohibitive, capital was tough to come by, and customer/subscriber churn rates were high.

In the mid-1970s, when FCC restrictions on cable's distant-signal-importation and programming options began to ease, demand for cable increased sharply. At the same time, Time Inc.'s Home Box Office (HBO) began distributing its pay-TV movie service via satellite. Other entrepreneurs followed HBO's lead, distributing programming of their own, via satellite, and cable increased its appeal to consumers in suburban and urban areas.

The Multiple Systems Operators (MSOs), such as TCI, which were well-funded organizations that owned cable systems in more than one city, began to build momentum and help expand the cable industry. By the early 1980s, most cities were either wired or in the midst of franchising battles for the right to wire them.

On a different front, Ted Turner, a well known station owner and entrepreneur, began working on a concept called the Superstation. His idea was to transmit the signal from his Atlanta studio via satellite and relay the signal to cable systems across the country. However, it was actually illegal for a station owner to use this tactic. Turner found a legal loophole that allowed him to use a third party to retransmit the signal.

Turner's accomplishment with the superstation concept laid the groundwork for the launch of CNN (Cable News Network). It was a daring and risky move — the annual expenses of the news departments at the major broadcast networks for one hour's worth of daily programming were near $200 million. Turner gambled that he could obtain enough revenue from subscriber fees collected from cable systems, plus advertising, to support a news service that would equal those of the networks in quality and exceed them in quantity. In a monumental moment for Turner,

Procter & Gamble and General signed on as CNN sponsors in 1980.

Advertisers were slow to adopt cable, though, because the cable audience was so fragmented that it was difficult for advertisers to reach the mass audiences they needed. But as the reach of networks grew, cable proved that its ability to target specific audiences, such as MTV's youth market and ESPN's sport fans, was indeed attractive to advertisers.

Growth in the cable business was affected by a host of regulatory issues, which we discuss only in part here. On that front, the FCC started regulating cable TV in April 1965, adopting rules for CATV systems served by microwave. The commission required CATV operators to carry the signals of local stations and to refrain from duplicating the programs of local stations (by carrying other stations broadcasting the same programs) within 15 days of the local broadcast.

In 1966, the FCC adopted must-carry rules which required that the signals from most local stations be carried on cable systems, and to protect their programs from duplications. The rule was challenged in court, and subsequently the 15-day protection was modified to protection only on the day of the broadcast. In 1969, the broadcast requirements of fairness and sponsor identification were extended to cable.

In 1972, the commission began deregulating cable, dropping most of its cable regulations over the next 10 years. In 1980, the FCC eliminated its distant-signal and syndicated exclusivity rules.

In 1984, Congress basically deregulated cable with passage of the Cable Communications Policy Act of 1984. The law removed local franchising authorities' rights to regulate cable rates. It also banned cross-ownership of cable television systems and cable programing networks with telephone companies in their local telephone service areas.

In July 1985, the Court of Appeals in Washington repealed the must-carry rules. In August 1986, the FCC issued new rules that were much less burdensome on cable operators, but they too failed to pass judicial muster.

The evolution of cable TV advertising has followed its home penetration and its ratings gains. More subscribers meant more ratings, so these increases also gave the added benefit of increased ad revenue per subscriber and increased ad revenue per rating point. This increased revenue base gave the programmers greater programming budgets, which also boosted ratings. As a result, cable television advertising's share of total TV advertising grew from 0.5% in 1980 to 11% in 1996.

Interestingly, this successs made cable TV advertising more local, as the share of national-to-local advertising moved from 85/15 in 1980 to 74/26 in 1996. Cable TV competes not only with the broadcast networks but also with the local broadcast affiliates which sell spot advertising. As cable increased its number of subscribers, its share of local advertising also increased, rising from 1% in 1980 to 11% in 1996.

As cable TV advertising has evolved, so has the revenue mix for the industry. In 1986, about 70% of cable TV revenues was derived from net advertising sales. By 1996, the mix changed to about 50/50, as affiliate revenue growth outperformed net advertising growth during 1986–92. This growth tracked the period of increased cable penetration during these six years, meaning a compounded four-year growth rate of 33% in subscribers and 2–3% increases in fees per subscriber.

According to Rich Bilotti, Morgan Stanley's cable analyst, in 1995 there were 64 million cable subscribers in the U.S., with cable accounting for 11% of television advertising spending. Estimated 1996 domestic advertising and subscription revenue for the industry is $3.5 billion.

Cable TV Channel Descriptions

Cable evolved in time to have a leading channel in each major information category (ESPN in sports, USA Network in entertainment, CNN in news, Turner in movies, and MTV in popular music). Since we believe the Internet may evolve in a similar fashion, with a leading brand in each category, below we list the top 27 cable channels (ranked in order of 1996 estimated gross advertising revenue).

1) **ESPN (Sports),** launched in 1979, focuses on a broad spectrum of sports-related programing, 24-hours-a-day, with more than 4,000 live or original hours of sports content covering more than 65 sports. ESPN says it reaches in excess of 157 million households in the U.S. and abroad. ESPN launched its sister station, ESPN2, on October 1, 1993, to extend its event programming on a variety of sport-specific events.

2) **USA Network (USA, Entertainment)** is a joint venture between Viacom and MCA. Programming focuses on targeting specific demographics throughout the day. Original programs are complemented by popular syndicated series, off-network successes, family specials, and top box-office theatricals. Launched in 1980, USA is one of the highest-rated prime-time networks, with more than 67 million subscribers and over 12,000 affiliates.

3) **Cable News Network (CNN, News),** launched in June 1980 as Ted Turner's vision of the future for news delivery, is today one of the largest news broadcasting services in the world. Its 24-hour format is now a staple for close to 70 million viewers, with stations such as MSNBC now vying for a piece of its market. CNN targets a broad demographic range, aiming to keep viewers continuously updated on late-breaking news at home and abroad.

4) **Turner Broadcasting System (TBS, Entertainment),** launched in 1970, was the original superstation. It now has an audience of more than 63 million subscribers and features a large mix of movies from such studio libraries as MGM, RKO, and pre-1950 Warner Bros. Additionally, TBS offers original programming, multi-part documentaries, and selected sporting events.

5) **Music Television (MTV, Music)** was launched on August 1, 1981. It targets a young, Generation X-type audience with a variety of music, music news, and game shows, such as the popular *Singled Out*. MTV is owned by Viacom, which also owns VH-1 and Nickelodeon and can boast more than 60 million viewers. MTV is aggressively pursuing international growth.

6) **The Nashville Network (TNN, Music)** is the No. 1 source of country music entertainment, offering original concert specials and series, music videos, high-quality entertainment news, interviews with top country artists, and live variety shows. Weekends on TNN are dedicated to the activities country fans love: motor sports and outdoors. TNN televises more live motor sports and outdoors programming than all major networks combined. It has 63 million subscribers.

7) **Turner Network Television (TNT, Entertainment)** has more than 63 million viewers. Launched in 1988, it owes its success to high-profile events, such as cable rights to the 1994 Winter Olympic Games. In addition to sports, it features original movies, such as *Gettysburg*, which drew more than 37 million viewers over a four-week period.

8) **Nickelodeon, Nick at Nite (NICK, NAN, Children)** was launched in 1979 and has built a reputation for offering a unique variety of children's programming, which was inspired by the network's efforts to seek out what kids want to watch and to take a risk on unconventional programming (such as *The Ren and Stimpy Show* and *Are You Afraid of the Dark?*). The station's reach is worldwide, with an estimated audience of more than 60 million.

9) **Lifetime Television (LIFE, Women),** launched in 1984, targets women as its primary audience. It has a substantial market of 61 million viewers, with approximately 5,800 cable systems on board. In 1985, LIFE debuted Lifetime Original Movies, bringing to its audience a mix of original programming with an emphasis on quality and thought-provoking themes.

10) **The Discovery Channel (Education)** specializes in delivering high-quality, reality-based entertainment to approximately 65 million cable viewers in the United States. It is operated by Discovery Networks, which includes The Learning Channel. Parent company DCI (Discovery Communication, Inc.) is a privately held media company with a diverse business operation that includes international distribution and syndication.

11) **Arts & Entertainment Network (A&E, Arts and Entertainment),** originally Alpha Repertory Television Service (ARTS) and the Entertainment Channel, launched in 1984. Its goal: to provide quality programming to an upscale audience looking for quality, alternative programming.

12) **The Family Channel (FAM, Family),** launched in 1977, offers families a variety of programming, including classic television series, children's programming, and original made-for-TV movies. The channel also offers a mix of shows focused on health and fitness.

13) **Cable News Business Channel (CNBC, Business News)** was launched by NBC in 1989; it provides up-to-the-minute business information as well as entertainment. Its format includes business trends and market news throughout the day; night programming offers talk show talent covering a variety of lively and entertaining conversations.

14) **Video Hits One (VH-1, Music),** launched in 1985, targets the 25- to 49-year-old baby boomer. Featuring music videos, VH-1 complements its programming with music/interview shows, fashion programs, and movie news and reviews.

15) **Black Entertainment Television (BET, African-American)** provides viewers with an African-American programming alternative. The station was launched in 1980 with an emphasis on featuring black entertainment productions in education, sports, public affairs, and music. BET's goal is to reflect the African-American culture and serve as a link to other cultural groups. In 1993, BET International was formed as a subsidiary of BET, helping the station to penetrate numerous foreign markets.

16) **Comedy Central (COM, Comedy)** caters to a primarily male, college-educated audience. About 33% of its viewers live in households with average incomes of more than $60,000. The network highlights stand-up comedians and comedy shows. Complementing its comedic highlights are original programming and classic movies, such as *Saturday Night Fever*.

17) **E! Entertainment Television (Entertainment)** delivers the only all-entertainment programming station to approximately 32 million subscribers on more than 2,105 cable systems and direct-satellite providers. E!'s content includes celebrity interviews, talk shows, news, movies, behind-the-scenes features, comedy, classic variety shows, movie previews, and comprehensive coverage of the entertainment industry's award shows.

18) **The Weather Channel (TWC, Weather)** was launched in 1982 and has more than 62 million subscribers. In a weather-related emergency, many communities use TWC as a central part of their disaster planning and response efforts.

19) **The Learning Channel (Education),** launched in 1980, targets all age groups with a diverse blend of educational topics. The channel seeks to program high-quality

content that allows viewers to explore and learn about the world.

20) **Sci-Fi Network (SCI-FI, Science Fiction)** strives to tap into all age groups of viewers, searching for the very best of the science fiction genre. Launched in 1992, the station reaches 22 million cable TV screens and has approximately 3,000 affiliates.

21) **The Cartoon Network (Cartoons, Children)** is the first 24-hour, all-animated network, featuring many stars of the cartoon world. It has the world's largest library of cartoons — with more than 8,500 titles, including favorites from Hanna-Barbera, Warner Bros., MGM, and Paramount.

22) **The Prevue Channel (Search/Information)** is a satellite-delivered, system-specific video promotion network. It highlights basic, premium, and pay-per-view services, incorporates video clips, and scrolls to update program listings, 24 hours a day. It has 42 million subscribers.

23) **Courtroom Television Network (Court TV, Human Interest)** is a 24-hour cable access service covering live and taped judicial proceedings and offering regular legal news briefs from across the United States. Since its launch in 1991, Court TV has covered more than 360 trials and hearings, and it now reaches a viewership of approximately 20 million U.S. households.

24) **Country Music Channel (CMT, Music)** is a 24-hour country music video channel that carries a mix of country music videos by chart-topping and cutting-edge country music artists. It has 30 million subscribers.

25) **The Travel Channel (TRAV, Travel),** launched in 1987, is a superstation devoted to those viewers looking for up-to-the-minute travel and related information. Culture, customs, history, how-to, and recreational information are explored in depth by a variety of hosts, including celebrities, authors, and travel experts.

26) **Fox Sports Net (FSXN, Sports),** formerly the Prime SportsChannel Network (PSCN), brings to the viewer network-caliber production and promotion delivered through local regional cable outlets, and focusing predominantly on local teams. As the cornerstone to the more than 1,200 live events televised by Fox Sports Net affiliates each year, FSXN uses an innovative, multimedia design to take viewers directly to the heart of the action, as it happens.

27) **Nostalgia Television (NOS, Lifestyle),** launched in 1986, targets the active adult audience with a variety of entertainment, information, and lifestyle programming. The station was recently overhauled, with 75% of its programming changed to better represent what viewers want.

Chapter 10: Emerging Companies in the Internet Ad Space

Summary

◆ There are **many existing and emerging companies, both public and private, capitalizing on the rapid growth of advertising on the Web.**

◆ We have identified four unique Internet market subsegments, comprising four major categories (besides the companies that create and operate Internet sites that are funded, in whole or in part, by advertising dollars):

1. **Advertising Agencies and Web Site Developers** — Companies involved in the generation of Internet advertising campaigns, from campaign planning to media buying, as well as developers of sites that allow companies to promote their brands and develop an online consumer presence. Since advertising is essentially the promotion of the company and its products and services, on the Web this is achieved either through buying advertising space at other sites or through simply designing a site that serves the same purpose.

2. **Market Research Providers** — In such a new field, advertisers, publishers, investors, and other interested parties are all looking for real data about what's happening, how big it is, and where it's going. These are companies that are tracking the evolution of Internet technology with a focus on its impact on business and certain industries, including the Web advertising arena.

3. **Traffic Measurement and Analysis Companies** — To validate advertising media buys on the Internet, advertisers need to be able to justify and verify the investments they make. These companies fill that need by offering software and services to aid publishers in tracking traffic and executing advertising delivery on their Web sites.

4. **Networks/Rep Firms** — These companies provide value-added services for Web advertisers and publishers alike, by brokering the distribution of advertisements and overseeing their delivery.

5. **Order Processing and Support** — Companies that provide outsourcing services to Internet publishers and service providers.

In this section, we detail a number of the companies that are affecting, or should be affected by, the increase in Internet advertising spending. Our discussion breaks the space into distinct categories, including advertising agencies and Web site design and management, market research, traffic measurement and analysis, and network/rep firms (companies are listed in the table below).

Many of the companies in this section are only a year old, or even less. While our list and descriptions could not possibly be comprehensive (the field is extremely young, and new companies are constantly emerging, merging, and evolving), we have attempted to list the companies that have caught our attention to date. As we have stated before, the one thing that seems certain about companies in the Internet space today is that most will likely have a very different look one year from now. We also list the URLs (Internet addresses) for all companies, and stock tickers are given for those that are publicly traded.

Advertising Agencies and Web Site Developers

Agency.com	*Internet Media Services*	*Razorfish*
Avalanche	*i-traffic*	*<siteline>*
CKS Group	*The Leap Group*	*SiteSpecific, Inc.*
DimensionX	*Margeotes, Fertitta, Donaher, and Weiss*	*Streams Online Media*
Group Cortex	*Messener Vetere Berger McNamee Schmetterer*	*TBWA Chiat / Day*
ICon	*Organic Online*	*Vivid studios*

Market Research

Forrester	*Jupiter Communications*
Find/SVP	*PC-Meter*

Traffic Measurement and Analysis

Accipiter	*Firefly Network*	*NetCount*
Accrue	*Focalink*	*net.Genesis*
Bellcare	*I/PRO*	*Net Gravity*
BroadVision	*Intersé*	

Network/Rep Firms

BURST! Media	*DoubleClick*	*Softbank Interactive Marketing*
Commonwealth Network	*Internet Link Exchange*	

Order Processing and Support

TeleTech Holdings

Advertising Design and Delivery

Agency.com (New York; www.agency.com) is a full-service electronic/online marketing firm that creates strategies for Fortune 50 companies with an emphasis on content-driven sales. The company focuses on translating complex corporate services and diverse product offerings into graphically appealing, easy-to-use interactive environments. Based in New York, Agency.com's client list includes such notables as British Airways, American Express, Claris, GTE, Hitachi, Lucent Technologies, MetLife, Sun Microsystems, and Time Inc.

The company, founded in February 1995, has since grown to a staff of 54 employees, created over 42 Web sites in the past year, and is expected to earn $5.4 million in 1996. It recently opened a London office after landing the sizable British Airways account, and expects to expand to other cities in the near future. Earlier this year, Omnicom Group made a minority equity investment in the company, which Agency.com expects will help it continue its aggressive growth, stabilize its finances, expand its operations, and compete in the rapidly growing interactive marketing industry.

Avalanche (New York; www.avsi.com) is an electronic design and production company for interactive media for the Web, CD-ROM, and Cdi. Just two years old, Avalanche's products have grown to include online publications, digital press kits, interactive kiosks, corporate media, and complete Internet environments. The company's approach integrates concept design with programming and technology to create new ideas for its clients in electronic marketing, publishing, and communication.

Avalanche divides its services into three categories: design, technology, and marketing. Design includes multimedia interface design, Web site design and publication, logos, package design and corporate identity, CD-ROM titles, point-of-purchase kiosks, and laptop presentations. Technology services include Web site development, interactive multimedia programming, automated e-mail services, and Internet forums, and databases and customer tracking on the Internet. Market position analysis, Internet research, and complete communications strategies are among Avalanche's marketing services.

The agency has grown to 45 employees and has worked on such major sites as Super Bowl XXX, the Olympics (via client NBC), VF Corp. (maker of Lee and Girbaud jeans), and Carnegie Hall. Other clients include BMG Entertainment, Sony Theatres, F.A.O. Schwarz, Con Edison, and Elektra.

CKS Group (CKSG; Cupertino, Ca.; www.cks.com) specializes in a wide range of integrated marketing communications services that help companies market their products, services, and messages. These services include strategic corporate and product positioning, corporate identity and product branding, new media, packaging, collateral systems, advertising, direct mail, consumer promotions, trade promotions, and media placement services.

The company believes that it is a leading provider of integrated marketing programs that utilize advanced technology solutions and new media, which it defines as media that deliver content to end-users in digital form, including the Web, the Internet, proprietary online services, CD-ROMs, laptop PC presentations, and interactive kiosks.

Since the first CKS company, CKS Partners (the more traditional advertising arm), was founded in 1987, the CKS Group has grown from two employees in a single office to 328 employees in seven offices and has generated $39 million in revenue in the first three quarters of 1996. On August 1, 1996, CKS Group acquired Schell Mullaney, a seven-year-old high-technology advertising and marketing firm based in New York. Aside from the Cupertino headquarters, CKS Group has offices in: Campbell and San Francisco, Ca.; Portland, Ore.; New York City; Washington, D.C.; and London. CKS customers include General Motors, Citibank, Clinique, McDonald's, Apple Computer, America Online, NASDAQ, Fujitsu Computer, MCI, Microsoft, Prudential, Visa International, and Mitsubishi Motors.

Dimension X (San Francisco; www.dimensionx.com), founded in 1995, is an interactive studio that produces Web sites from concept development to graphical design to implementation of custom tools; it also handles day-to-day operational challenges. Through products like Liquid Reality (a 3-D VRML toolkit) and Liquid Motion (a drag-and-drop Java animator), Dimension X's mission is to blend the best in technology with the latest in entertainment to deliver compelling content to users. Its client list includes Fox, AT&T, Grey Advertising, MCA Records, Sega, Sun Microsystems, and Intel.

Group Cortex (Philadelphia; www.cortex.net) focuses on developing products and services that help businesses use the Internet to target customers and conduct business more efficiently. Group Cortex provides consulting services and turn-key solutions that include security, legal, design, marketing, custom software programming, internal and external corporate services, system administration and technical services, and marketing expertise and training. Its client list includes: Campbell Soup, US Healthcare, Flip Chip Technologies, VWR Scientific Products, Rohm and Haas, Rhone-Poulenc Rorer, and Philadelphia AIDS Walk.

ICon (New York; www.iconnet.com), founded in 1991, publishes and distributes content over high-performance networks. Through its IConWorks high-performance content distribution platform, the company publishes, produces, manages, and distributes new-media content over its 45-Mbps ATM digital backbone. This digital backbone provides high-speed ATM network access to all major metropolitan business centers in the United States and is supported by Icon's Network Operation Center with round-the-clock service. ICon's hosting services include management, maintenance, and support of Internet/intranet servers and Web sites. Its Backup and Business Recovery services include proprietary software that allows transport and mirroring of data over WANs and LANs.

Word, ICon's first publication, launched in July 1995, is a sponsor-driven publication targeted at an 18- to 34-year-old audience and featuring articles on social issues, travel, sex, and personal finance. *Charged,* the company's second publication, is targeted at action-sports/extreme-leisure enthusiasts. Articles cover topics such as snowboarding, mountain biking, and surfing.

Internet Media Services (Palo Alto, Ca.; www.netmedia.com) builds interactive hi-tech Web sites. IMS produces its own software for use in designing and implementing clients' Web sites. Its products and services include: 1) Wander, a Web server enhancement that allows for advanced interactivity between the site visitor and the

online service; 2) Open Forum Messaging System, a technology that allows Web users to join in both moderated and unmoderated discussion groups specific to the client's Web site; 3) Web Development tools, including WebBuilder and Sweep, which assist in the rapid development and modification of Web sites; 4) InterCat Online Ordering System, a virtual online store that caters to any market of customers and enables merchants to convert traditional print catalogs into online catalogs; and 5) IMS Consulting Services, which assists in the entire Web site development process.

IMS has designed Web sites for such companies as Hewlett-Packard, Adobe Systems, Sun Microsystems, UB Networks, and Harvard University. In addition, the company has formed strategic partnerships with UB Networks and Tandem Computers to strengthen its ability to provide companies with solutions to Web problems.

i-traffic (New York; www.i-traffic.com) is an online media planning agency that helps clients create and strategically place inbound links from other sites to the client's home site. It terms itself "the Internet traffic-driving agency." The company's approach stems from its belief that traffic, the major force behind revenue for advertising-based sites, has two main drivers: 1) people typing in addresses they have seen in traditional media or heard by word-of-mouth and 2) people clicking online links in the form of banners, icons, buttons, listings, and the like. Therefore, it works to increase traffic for its clients through the strategic placement of creative, accountable inbound links. i-traffic has four main services: paid links (media planning and buying), non-paid links (online publicity and promotions), traded links (crosslinking campaigns referral networks) and creative (banner development and production). Founded in April 1995, i-traffic has a staff of 17; its clients include: Duracell, Hearst New Media, BigBook, Cox Enterprises, Disney, and SI Online.

The Leap Group (LEAP; Chicago; www.leapnet.com) is a communications, marketing and advertising company that develops both traditional and new media marketing campaigns for clients. Traditional marketing services include: television, print, radio, outdoor advertising, promotions, direct mail, and logo design. New media services include digital interactive publications, CD-ROMs, and interactive presentations. The company seeks to build brand equity for clients by leveraging strategic brand marketing, creative talent, traditional production capabilities, and technological expertise.

Leap targets Fortune 500 clients and has successfully competed for and managed such accounts as Nike and Miller Brewing Co. The company has been the agency of record for Niketown and Nike Factory Stores, Tommy Armour Golf Co., U.S. Robotics, and Ameritech. In addition, Nike, Tommy Armour, and the Chicago Tribune Co. have retained Leap for Web site development.

Margeotes, Fertitta, Donaher and Weiss (New York; www.margeotes.com) founded their new media arm in 1994, M/F+P Digital Media. Notable clients include: Godiva Choclatier, Inc., The Hearst Corporation, The McGraw-Hill Companies, NFL Enterprises, Putnam Investments, 3DO, and Carillon Importers (Stolichnaya and Royalty Vodka).

Messner Vetere Berger McNamee Schmetterer EuroRSCG (New York; www.mvbms.com) is a full-service advertising agency. MVBMS conceives, produces, serves, and maintains brand Web sites — more than 40 since 1994 — and, more recently, CD-ROMs and interactive kiosks. It also plans and buys online media, maintains active relationships with interactive television projects, and designs intranet applications for enterprise marketing functions.

The agency's interactive staff numbers approximately 30; a third are account managers and the balance are interactive designers and software programmers. Art directors and copywriters are drawn from the larger agency's creative talent pool. Its interactive teams work in partnership with the traditional account teams to create seamless, reinforcing branded communications and marketing applications for clients. Its interactive credits include works for MCI, Philips Electronics, International Paper, New Balance, Hiram Walker, and Dunkin' Donuts.

Organic Online (San Francisco; www.organic.com), founded in 1993, is one of the more notable Web development companies, with a staff of 53 and estimated 1996 revenues in the neighborhood of $10 million. Organic creates innovative and effective sites by utilizing technology to meet client needs while building valuable informational databases. The company focuses on educating clients to use the interactive medium to bridge the gap between

company and consumer. The stated philosophy is to: 1) design sites where form follows function; 2) use the medium and its inherent capabilities to interact with the target audience; 3) develop navigational tools that are intuitive; 4) design sites to be scalable to allow for future growth; and 5) develop content that will be accessible and attractive through different platforms.

Organic's relative experience (in a very young field) in interface design, programming, security, and online marketing has gained it a client list that includes Saturn motorcars, Apple Computer, Nike, McDonald's, Microsoft, Harley-Davidson, Kinko's, Colgate-Palmolive, Levi Strauss & Co., and *Advertising Age.*

Razorfish (New York; www.razorfish.com) is a digital media design, marketing, and development company offering a wide range of products and services for Fortune 100 companies, media and entertainment companies, and online services. The company is composed of three divisions: 1) Razorfish Integrated Services, which provides digital design, production, and marketing services (for Web sites, commercial online services, CD-ROMs, broadband networks, broadcast graphics, movie titles, kiosks, and corporate intranets); 2) Razorfish Studios, which creates and distributes original content for digital and analog media; and 3) Razorfish Technologies, which provides administration and development tools for digital media that are developed in a variety of languages and environments to provide effective solutions.

Razorfish's clients include IBM, Simon & Schuster, Ralph Lauren, Pepsi-Cola International, Microsoft, America Online, Sony, Bankers Trust, AT&T, CMP Publications, and Lycos.

<siteline> (New York; www.siteline.com) provides Web production services to clients that want to establish a presence on the Internet. Services include the creative direction and implementation of Web site architecture, navigational streamlining, HTML coding and graphic design, customized database programming, Intranet constructions, and systems integration services.

<siteline> has created a number of sites, including: Brouillard Communications, Duracell, Snapple, L'Oreal, Olympus America, Atlantic Records, Champion Records, Cigar

World, and Warner Bros. Many of <siteline>'s clients are major advertising agencies.

SiteSpecific, Inc. (New York; www.sitespecific.com), founded in September 1995, is a "direct response" Internet media company that syndicates transactional marketing programs on the Internet, connecting consumers and advertisers in innovative and intimate ways. SiteSpecific is creating a network of highly targeted, direct-response programs that leverages historical transactional program data.

Instead of targeting a large audience with a broadcast-type campaign, Site Specific's marketing process is based upon delivering the specific targeting capability of the Internet advertising infrastructure. The process, which it calls "Smart Syndication," takes full advantage of the "narrowcast" strengths of the medium to deliver targeted ads to the appropriate audience. Rather than bringing more shoppers to the store, Smart Syndication takes the store directly to the shoppers by tying in with a distributor or network to target banner placement, then loading the banner with a "Commercial Vignette." The Commercial Vignette contains programming that binds, adds value to, and supports the advertiser's message, increasing the likelihood of generating a transaction.

The company, which employs a staff of 30, has generated $2 million in revenues in the year since its founding in November 1995. SiteSpecific's client list includes: Duracell, 3M, AT&T, BMG, CUC, IBM, Intuit, Microsoft, and Sony. In February 1996, SiteSpecific received a minority investment from direct-marketing giant Harte-Hanks Communications.

Streams Online Media Development Corp. (Chicago; www.streams.com), founded in 1994, uses a concept called "interactive branding" to develop an Internet brand personality for its clients. Through creative development and design, Streams integrates traditional marketing and design know-how with creative applications of Internet technology. Streams is a full-service agency offering site production and programming that includes Shockwave games, Java applets, RealAudio multimedia shows integrated with Web page layouts, and functional publishing systems.

Additionally, Streams has developed a proprietary suite of response measurement tools. Instead of measuring the dynamics from within one's Web site, "Lilypad" reports the path by which the user arrived at a client's site. The software-based system can measure whether a user clicked on a commercial or non-commercial hyperlink at another Web site, a search tool, a newsgroup, or a local file on a hard drive — via a bookmark or a directly typed address. This enables the Lilypad user to identify which links are providing the best response and adjust the marketing expenses appropriately.

TBWA Chiat/Day, Inc. (New York; www.chiatday.com) is a full-service interactive/traditional ad agency, with a number of offices throughout the U.S. Its interactive efforts are divided among its New York, Los Angeles, and Toronto offices. TBWA Chiat/Day is part of TBWA International, an Omnicom company, with offices in 47 countries around the world. The company's interactive services include 1) marketing, research, and strategy; 2) design and implementation; 3) ongoing evaluation and maintenance; 4) media planning; 5) media buying; and 6) tracking and analysis. The agency's capabilities extend to Web sites, web advertising ("banners" and beyond), online service content areas, CD-ROMSs, diskettes, and kiosks.

TBWA Chiat/Day's interactive projects have included Web work for Nissan Pathfinder, Sony Playstation, America Online, Infiniti, Absolut, NYNEX, Chase Manhattan Bank, and Metro Toronto Zoo. The agency has created content areas on AOL for Nissan, Infiniti, and NYNEX, as well as CD-ROM projects for Nissan.

Vivid Studios (San Francisco; www.vivid.com), founded in 1990, focuses on creating a compelling "Internet experience" for global networks and online communities. The company has developed proprietary technologies, automated production tools, Web site management methodologies, and original programming to create experiences like Net hunts, live product launches (e.g., Windows 95), and large turnkey systems for its clients. As a full-service online developer and creator of Vivid's proprietary technology, Vivid's team incorporates a wide scope of skills, including interaction design and network architecture.

Recently, Vivid completed development of the global Web site architecture for Bell Atlantic Internet Solutions, including the framework and tools for creating, building, and managing dynamically generated Web pages. For J. Walter Thompson, Vivid built a forms-oriented remote publishing engine that gives each of the 200 JWT offices worldwide the ability to create their own Web pages within the framework of the master JWT Web site. Vivid worked with Microsoft on the Windows 95 launch to develop, implement, and maintain one of the largest Web site endeavors to date (the site received 20 million hits in its first 24 hours). Vivid has also produced Web sites for a number of other high-profile companies, including: IDG, Sony, Silicon Graphics, and Simon & Schuster.

Major Agency Efforts

Many of the major traditional advertising agencies, including Ogilvy & Mather, Leo Burnett Co., DDB Needham, Grey Advertising, and Saatchi & Saatchi, have ramped up interactive efforts within their own organizations (through acquisitions or by building divisions of their own that are dedicated to digital/Internet media). In addition, a number of these agencies work with, or subcontract to, many of the above companies as an alternative to building internally the talent and expertise for Internet advertising.

Market Research

Forrester Research (Cambridge, Mass.; www.forrester.com) provides research services tracking the evolution of technology and its impact on consumers and businesses. The company breaks its offerings into nine strategic research services in three categories: Strategic Management Research, Corporate IT Research, and New Media Research. Strategic Management Research has one component, Leadership Strategies, that focuses on how management can maximize the business benefits of technology.

Corporate IT Research is broken into five services: 1) Computer Strategy, concerned with IT structure; 2) Network Strategy, an analysis of high-performance network services in the Internet era; 3) Packaged Application Strategies, analyzing purchased business applications; 4) Software Strategy, which covers overall corporate software architecture; and 5) Telecom Strategies, which discusses the use of communications services. New Media Research is composed of four strategy services: Interactive Technology, Media & Technology, People & Technology, and Money & Technology, each of which addresses a particular aspect of online/interactive media. In addition to its written research, Forrester also offers consulting services to its clients, helping them define technology strategy and understand how market developments affect their business.

Find/SVP (FSVP; New York; www.findsvp.com) provides a number of consulting and research services that address the multitude of needs and questions for business intelligence. Such services range from the "American

Home Financial Services Survey" to the "American User Survey."

Find/SVP's primary business is its Quick Consulting & Research Service, which, through its base of consultants, offers fast, confidential, and cost-effective answers to questions posed by individual "Cardholders" (about 18,000 individuals in over 2,250 firms). Typically, requests through this division take no more than a few hours of research. For longer requests, the company's Strategic Research Division performs custom assignments, such as market analyses, surveys, extensive and complex information collection, and benchmarking and customer satisfaction studies. Find/SVP's Customer Satisfaction Strategies Division works with clients to determine customer needs and expectations.

Additionally, the Emerging Technologies Research Group performs primary research on new technologies available in the marketplace. Dedicated to analyzing consumer and small-business demand for digital products and services, this group serves more than 500 leading corporations that are capitalizing on the Internet marketplace. Since 1994, more than 65,000 interviews have been conducted to develop in-depth profiles of 8,000 households regarding current behaviors, unmet needs, and interest in using new interactive products and services. The primary research is available through a continuous advisory service, multi-client studies, custom consulting and research assignments, market reports, and a monthly primary research report.

Other FIND/SVP businesses include FINDOUT, an Internet-based question-answering service for consumers (www.findout.com), and seminars and conferences in conjunction with Strategic Research Institute, or SRI.

Jupiter Communications, LLC (New York; www.jup.com) is a New York City-based research, consulting, and publishing firm with a focus on emerging consumer online and interactive technologies. Its products and services include newsletters, research reports, white papers, conferences, packages services, consulting, and multi-client studies. Newsletters include *Interactive Content,* covering the consumer online services industry; *Interactive Home,* on emerging access devices for the home; *The Digital Kids Report,* an "edutainment" monthly; *Online Marketplace,* on home electronic commerce; and *Internet Business Report,* which looks at commercial development of the Internet and Worldwide Web. Some recent reports and white papers include "Web Development Strategies," "World Online Report," "Women Online," "Search Engines and Internet Directory Report," "The Home Banking Report," and "The Internet Security White Paper."

Jupiter also provides several services for clients, including: Strategic Planning Services (SPS), which packages relevant research and information for development teams; Custom Research and Work Consulting, which prepares customized market and industry analysis; and Multi-Client Studies, where several companies participate in long-term market research.

WebTrack, a subsidiary that Jupiter acquired from Caddis International, Inc., in May 1996, is an information service that tracks advertising, publishing, and usage on the Internet and other online services. WebTrack addresses the role of advertising as it relates to the Internet, and AdSpend tracks advertising on over 100 Web sites. Jupiter also offers the "Online Advertising Report" and "Consumer Experience Probe on Web Advertising."

PC Meter (a service of The NPD Group; Port Washington, N.Y.; www.pcmeter.com) is a subsidiary of The NPD Group, the seventh-largest market research firm in the U.S. (based on 1994 revenue, according to the American Marketing Association). PC Meter is an industry market research information and analysis service providing demographic data on home PC usage patterns, including time spent on specific Web pages, in departments of online services, and in desktop applications. The company serves advertising agencies, advertisers, online content providers, computer product developers, and related groups. Demographic information tracked includes each PC user's age, gender, income, number of children, and geographic location. The data tracked per PC are title and type of active software programs; the name of, and active features and departments for, online service connections; the date, time, and length of usage/connection; the frequency of connection; and the share of computer use.

PC Meter's sample size has grown from 1,000 households in January 1996 to 10,000 in July 1996. To collect data, PC Meter's proprietary software is installed on PCs and automatically tracks activities of individual users by intercepting, monitoring, and logging selected events at the operating-system level. PC Meter only collects data for PCs running Windows 3.x or Windows 95. Clients include CKS, Grey Advertising, Leo Burnett Co., Excite!, Universal, Intuit, Ogilvy and Mather, Modem Media, AT&T, Infoseek, Time-Warner, Microsoft, and Yahoo!

Traffic Measurement and Analysis

Accipiter (Raleigh, N.C.; www.accipiter.com), founded in April 1996, provides solutions for site publishers to track individual visitors and their activity at publishers' sites, with the intention of generating data on the quality and focus of a site's audience to advertisers. The company's main product is AdManager, which automatically schedules, places, and rotates ads. AdManager can generate real-time reports for each ad, which can be viewed by advertisers as well as site managers. Accipiter's system allows advertisers to schedule an exact number of ad impressions based on a visitor's site registration information, as well as by page groupings and other criteria.

Accrue Software (Mountain View, Ca.; www.accrue.com), founded in February 1996 (and formerly known as Gauge Technologies), provides online user-response analysis software, which gives Web site managers the information they need to modify site offerings, improve site performance, and more fully leverage the Web for direct marketing. Released in October, the company's debut product, Accrue Insight, is a scalable visual measurement and analysis system that, in addition to providing the usual site performance data (hits, bytes, pages served, browser types, domain breakdowns, etc.), emphasizes accuracy, detail, and flexibility in data querying and visualization. Through Java-based visualization tools, Web site data can be viewed in aggregate or broken down by area within the site, either "live" or historically. The tool can also generate reports of these data.

The company's approach is to create a more accurate and complete record of site usage by sitting "on-the-wire" and viewing the network protocol to get more accurate network data. In the case of high-level processing, by the time a Web server receives a transaction, it is possible that much of the underlying data can be lost or modified (e.g., when a Web server logs that it has sent a report to a client, it cannot tell if the client actually receives the report). Accrue Insight can then, by nature of its design, observe and report on the entire transaction and provide data about the user experience at the site (time required for delivery of a page, pages stopped in transit, and effective line speeds).

Beta sites for Accrue Insight include Yahoo!, BigBook, Organic Online, General Motors/Mediaworks, Perot Systems, HotWired, and CKS Group. Since its formation, Accrue Software has raised over $2.5 million in financing from such sources as Organic Online, CKS Group, an investor group led by Sterling Payot Co., and Eos Partners.

Bellcore (Morristown, N.J.; www.bellcore.com), founded in 1984, is a business-to-business enterprise that offers software solutions, training, education, consulting, and engineering services. Software products include the Adapt/X TM suite of Internet products for the Web; Intelligent Networking and Advanced Intelligent Networking solutions; the AirBoss family of voice, integrated messaging, wireless web access, and personalized information service applications for wireless and wireline networks; and the MediaVantage suite of operations software and services. Consulting services include training services, systems integration; Local Number Portability; unbundling and interconnection; network integrity and reliability; fraud management; and pricing and costing analyses.

Adapt/X Internet Solutions is a package of technologies, products, services, and training that provides businesses with competitive solutions for harnessing the power of the Web. Adapt/X solutions can be used by any business in any industry for targeted ad placement, personalized Web sites, product recommendations, legacy data access, and network security. The Adapt/X suite of products includes Adapt/X Advertiser — an ad server software product designed for management and configuration of advertisement rotation and inventory allotment; Adapt/X Profiler — a personalization software tool designed to develop user-specific profiles that help Web sites tailor ad delivery to each user; and Adapt/X Recommender — an interactive software tool that provides Web site visitors with recommendations that are tailored to individual preferences.

Recently, Bellcore was named Netscape's education partner, in an effort to train system administrators to install, maintain, and work with a range of Netscape server products for the UNIX and NT systems platforms.

Major U.S. telecommunications clients include AT&T, Cincinnati Bell, GTE, Southern New England Telephone Co., Rochester Telephone, Sprint, Stentor, and numerous government entities. Bellcore currently has over 5,800 employees serving more than 800 customers worldwide in 55 countries.

BroadVision (BVSN; Los Altos, Ca.; www.broadvision.com) provides a software application system to conduct full-scale marketing and selling on the Web and interactive broadband networks. The system, called BroadVision One-to-One, enables companies to tailor interactive Internet marketing and selling services to the interests of the Web site user, thus personalizing the visit on a real-time basis. It has three key parts: 1) application programming interfaces (APIs) for programming One-to-One applications. These enable the creation of integration objects, called "object adapters," which allow external data and software to be integrated into the flow of the application. 2) The ability for One-to-One applications to be installed on application servers for large-scale Web site production operations. The system manages Web site content and interactions by gathering and organizing profile information of Web site visitors. 3) The Dynamic Command Center, which allows marketing, advertising, and editorial managers to exercise real-time control over their online applications.

BroadVision customers include Prodigy Services, Ameritech, Thompson-Sun Interactive, Olivetti Telemedia in Italy, the Virgin Entertainment Group in the U.K., Itochu Internet in Japan, and Hong Kong Telecom. BroadVision's One-to-One Partner's program includes Andersen Consulting, AVP, CyberCash, Ikonik Interactive, KPMG, Microsoft, Novo Media Group, Oracle, Organic Online, RSA Data Security, Sybase, and VeriFone. The company had revenues of $2.3 million in the second quarter of 1996, against operating expenses of $4.1 million.

Firefly Network (formerly Agents, Inc.; Cambridge, Mass.; www.firefly.com) was founded in 1995 and provides software that uses advanced algorithms based on certain collaborative filtering technologies to make recommendations to users based on their preferences. In January 1996, the company (then called Agents, Inc.) launched this intelligent agent technology on the Web in the form of Firefly. As a user continues to visit the network, Firefly's technology "learns" his or her likes and dislikes, can compare and contrast these with other users' patterns, and is able to offer members personalized recommendations for music, movies, and so forth. This technology therefore offers marketers the ability to target messages and advertisements based on an individual's preferences and interests. As a result, marketers can maximize efforts on a prequalified audience and offer a more relevant experience for consumers. The company currently has 95 employees and more than 500,000 registered members.

Firefly Network's customers and partners include: Yahoo!, Ziff Davis's ZD Net, Reuters, Rolling Stone, Newbury Comics, The All Music Guide, Hits World, and Muzak's Enso Audio Imaging Division. They have raised in excess of $18 million from investors, including: Atlas Ventures, Dun & Bradstreet Enterprises, Merrill Lynch, PAFET, Softbank, Trident Capital, Goldman Sachs, and Reuters New Media.

Focalink Communications (Palo Alto, Ca.; www.focalink.com) provides software and services designed for advertising agencies and their clients, to improve the process of media planning, ad placement, and post-buy analysis. Its products include MarketMatch, a media planning tool, and SmartBanner, a software product for online advertising campaign management and execution. MarketMatch, currently in beta test at over 60 agencies, is soon to be released in version 1.0. The software helps design targeted advertising plans by combining a large database of ad-seeking Web sites with a search engine that utilizes artificial intelligence to analyze advertising opportunities according to audience criteria.

Focalink recently announced an agreement with SRI Consulting to allow MarketMatch users to leverage SRI's VALS2 (Values and Lifestyles) psychographic typology. Using VALS2 to type sites and their audiences, MarketMatch would provide advertisers with a proven tool for the measurement of consumer choice and behavior.

I/PRO (San Francisco; www.ipro.com), or Internet Profiles Corp., is a provider of services and software for independent measurement and analysis of Web site usage. I/PRO's offerings include: I/CODE, I/COUNT, I/AUDIT, and I/RESEARCH. I/CODE simplifies user registration and provides site owners with demographic information and visit patterns; I/COUNT monitors and analyzes aspects of Web site usage, allowing access to customized reports through any Web browser; I/AUDIT compiles a third-party report of Web site activity, which can be provided to advertisers; and I/RESEARCH is a value-added consulting group that pools census-based usage data collected from I/PRO's 150-plus customers to build a normative database and generate cross-site comparison reports. This system fills a marketplace need for an accurate assessment of Web site audiences, which in turn has helped organizations determine the value of their Web sites as a marketing medium. I/PRO's success in meeting this demand has made the company a leader in providing measurement standards on the Internet.

I/PRO has formed a strategic partnership with Nielsen Media Research, an established leader in television audience measurement. The company is also working with Double-Click (a Web advertising network) to create more accountable ad targeting, NetGravity to provide seamless tracking and auditing technology and service to clients, and Enterprise Integration Technologies (EIT) (a developer and marketer of electronic commerce initiatives that was recently acquired by VeriFone). I/PRO customers include AMERICAN EXPRESS, AT&T WorldNet, Big Book, CompuServe, CMP Publications, CyberCash, Intuit, Individual Inc., Internet Shopping Network, Microsoft, Netscape Communications, Pathfinder, Visa, Yahoo!, and Ziff-Davis Publishing.

Intersé (Sunnyvale, Ca.; www.interse.com) develops products and services that help customers analyze site usage. Rather than counting hits, Intersé's market focus software provides users with a precise tally of Web site users. The software also translates Internet addresses into actual organization names and filenames into document titles, making it easier to understand site traffic. Market focus includes the Intersé Internet database, which contains most U.S. Internet domains, indexed by city, state, and zip code, combined with other Internet demographic information. The product integrates this information with a company's or organization's files to develop detailed, professional-looking reports.

Intersé has more than 1,000 customers worldwide, including BASF, Federal Express, Hasbro International, Knight-Ridder, Microsoft, and Toshiba. The company also has formed a strategic alliance with Arbitron New Media, which selected Intersé to provide Web analysis technology that enables aggregation of data across industries.

NetCount (Los Angeles; www.netcount.com) is a third-party Web-site measurement service that has gained more than 200 customers since its commercial launch in October 1995, including NBC, Conde Net, Times Mirror, United Media (Dilbert Zone), and Nando Net. NetCount's mission is to provide accurate measurement of the Web, including user counts and demographic collection, without violating user privacy. NetCount is a technology leader in Web measurement using census-based tracking techniques, auditable systems, and timely reporting practices. Net-Count provides a suite of products and services designed to meet the measurement requirements of Web sites, media research professionals, advertisers, and media buyers.

Through its AdCount service, advertisers and media buyers can accurately determine and compare the effectiveness of their online advertisements. Combined with NetCount's user-counting service HeadCount, AdCount facilitates the tracking of users from an advertisement on one Web site to a purchase on another site. This enables a new form of electronic commerce advertising rates based on online sales commissions.

In June, NetCount announced that Price Waterhouse was licensing its name and taking an equity stake in the company. NetCount recently announced its Marketing Alliance Partner (MAP) program, which provides channel distribution of its products and services through major Web-site development agencies and Internet service providers. Potomac Interactive, Media Circus, Digital Planet, and Whirlwind Interactive join BBN Planet as the first companies to sign on. BBN Planet has bundled NetCount's services into its Web Advantage hosting services since November 1995.

net.Genesis (Cambridge, Mass.; www.netgen.com), founded in January 1994, provides Web-site performance and usage analysis tools. Its net.Analysis product suite allows user to create and view customized reports of site traffic. net.Sweep is an Internet service offering measurement of server performance, which tracks and reports on site access and retrieval times at different times of the day and week, aiding customers in diagnosing any performance problems. net.Sweep results can be integrated with net.Analysis to provide a comprehensive solution for understanding the relationship between traffic and performance.

In August, net.Genesis announced a partnership with Net-Carta Corp., a CMGI company that provides Web-site content management and navigation tools, to bundle the two companies' software products together and to develop new products and services for customers. Additionally, the company formed a partnership with Wiley Computing, a division of technology publisher John Wiley & Sons, to produce a series of Web-related books. net.Genesis also produces a monthly column in *Internet World* magazine called "Web Watch." net.Genesis' customers include large commercial Web sites, ISPs, Fortune 500 companies, and small businesses.

NetGravity (San Mateo, Ca.; www.netgravity.com), founded in September 1995, develops software solutions for managing advertising delivery on Web sites. Its AdServer software has several functions: ad inventory management, dynamic targeting, and rotation of advertisements; real-time copy testing; sales process automation; reliable real-time reporting; and extensible APIs. The company also offers its AdService support program for NetGravity customers, which provides a flexible system of service plans for the varying needs of Web publishers. Plans range from round-the-clock support to simple access to knowledge databases and e-mail service.

In June, NetGravity formed an alliance with I/PRO to develop complementary technologies and integrate their products and services, allowing NetGravity customers to easily include I/PRO's services on their Web sites. I/PRO will support NetGravity AdServer APIs and log formats, allowing for more customized reporting and audit information for advertisers. NetGravity customers include Time Inc.'s Pathfinder, Netscape, Open Market, CyberCash, and The Internet Shopping Network (ISN).

Network/Rep Firms

BURST! Media LLC (Katonah, N.Y., www.burstmedia.com) Formed in the fall of 1995, BURST! is an advertising sales representative that sells national advertising on its affiliated Web sites in exchange for a percentage of the gross revenue. The company currently represents over 850 Web sites, adding roughly five per day, or about 150 per month.

BURST! sold its first advertising in June 1996 and maintains a mixture of exclusive and non-exclusive agreements with its constituent Web sites. According to the company, it typically controls 100% of its customers' revenue base and maintains long-term (up to three years) exclusive agreements with many of them, resulting in a fairly stable revenue base. Some of BURST!'s more notable exclusive contracts are with US West Interactive, Rosenbluth International, and Chatterbox. Advertisers that have used the BURST! network include: TravelWeb, Microsoft, Procter & Gamble, Hewlett-Packard, America Online, LifeSavers, Firefly Network, Fujitsu, and Ford Motor Co.

Commonwealth Network (Interactive Imaginations) (New York; www.riddler.com), founded in June 1996 by Interactive Imaginations, Inc. (developer of the Riddler entertainment site), is a network designed to bring ad revenues to small, emerging Web sites created by independent Web developers (affiliates). Affiliates receive monthly payments for ad banners that are sold and loaded onto the sites by Commonwealth. As of October 1996, Commonwealth has grown to over 5,300 affiliates, which have registered over 90,000 individual Web pages currently generating 35 million impressions per month.

The Commonwealth Network allows advertisers and direct marketers to reach a broad-based audience with a single media buy, but it also allows advertisers to target particular consumers by choosing only certain Commonwealth site content categories. In addition, advertisers can use the Commonwealth Network as a broadcast model, promoting specific events in real time across the network, such as celebrity chat sessions, breaking news stories, price changes, or time-limited offers. NBC utilized Commonwealth in this way as a "mass notification platform" during the 1996 Summer Olympics to announce which athlete would participate in the daily chat session on NBC's own site. Other advertisers and Web sites (including Riddler) have used Commonwealth as a sweepstakes model, leveraging the broad reach of Commonwealth to promote instant prizes or special deals ("click here to win").

SoftBank Interactive Media Sales represents the Commonwealth Network for advertising sales under an alliance with Interactive Imaginations. Current Commonwealth Network advertisers include Yahoo!, ZD Net, NBC, Starwave, *Sports Illustrated,* Firefly, and Prodigy.

DoubleClick (New York; www.doubleclick.com), formed in February 1996, has a proprietary technology that pinpoints targets, controls reach, determines frequency, and provides verifiable measures with which advertisers can craft online campaigns. The company describes its service as marrying "the reach and cost of advertising with the targeting and the statistical projectability of direct marketing."

DoubleClick is essentially an advertising network service that enables advertisers to target ads by leveraging a large database of Internet users and organization information that the company maintains for this purpose. Web sites looking to generate revenue through advertising join the network, which provides them with access to DoubleClick's advertiser base. Advertisers have the advantage of a wide number of sites to choose from when crafting ad campaigns, for which they can specify things like a maximum number of impressions and particular characteristics of the users to which their ads are delivered.

DoubleClick offers a number of criteria for advertisers in creating value-added, targeted ad campaigns, including operating system, browser type, geographical location, domain type, organization type (SIC Code), organization size and revenue, days and hours of distribution, distribution frequency, user exposure frequency, and the order (series) in which a set of ads are delivered.

Advertisers such as Intel, Microsoft, IBM, 20th Century Fox Film Corp., Bank of America, Nissan, Tri-Star Pictures, United Parcel Service, and QuarterDeck have joined the network. DoubleClick projects there will be more than 200 sites affiliated with the network by the end of its first year. Participating sites include Excite!, Sportsline USA, USA Today Online, Quicken Financial Network, NETworth, EDGAR ONLINE, and Travelocity.

Internet Link Exchange (San Mateo, Ca.; www.linkexchange.com) is currently one of the largest advertising networks, linking together approximately 50,000 member Web sites, with an average of 2.3 million ad impressions served daily. The ILE reports that, as of this writing, more than 700 new Web sites are joining its network every day through an automated membership system. The ILE's growth is fueled entirely by advertising itself with banner ads on its own network.

The ILE has applied a business model that offers members free advertising for their sites in exchange for giving up a piece of the their own "online real estate" — essentially members are required to display two banners for each one of their own advertisements displayed elsewhere on the network. This creates a huge surplus in ad inventory available to ILE, which ILE can then resell to paying advertisers (at low CPMs due to the near-zero cost of the inventory). The company also has the ability to offer these advertisers a more targeted product, by grouping member sites into various categories (e.g., sports, health, business, politics, etc.). The result is that ILE-displayed ads are seen by 0.9 unique visitors every day, there are no complicated transactions or collection required among its member sites, and the company has an inventory, both in size and diversity, to sell.

Softbank Interactive Marketing (San Francisco; www.simweb.com), a division of Softbank, specializes in the representation of leading advertising-supported Web sites to major advertisers in sales, marketing, and planning capacities. SIM's Media Sales Group is organized by industry specialization to ensure the highest degree of customer responsiveness. The Foundation Buy Program, the benchmark service of the Media Sales Group, is designed to maximize an advertiser's reach. The program strategically places an advertiser's messages on multiple Web sites in a prescribed manner, thus pinpointing the advertiser's target market in multiple market segments with a single media buy.

Web sites represented by Softbank Interactive Marketing include: AT&T Business Networks, The Commonwealth Network, iGuide, MSNBC Weather by Intellicast, NBC.com, Net Radio, Netscape, Playboy Enterprises, The Site, Yahoo!, Yahooligans!, Who Where?, and ZD Net.

Order Processing and Support

TeleTech Holdings (Denver; www.teletechusa.com) has emerged as the customer support company for the Internet. TeleTech provides call-center outsourcing services and can point to a solid list of Internet-related clients for which it is handling incoming support calls, including AT&T Worldnet, America Online, Compuserve, and, to a lesser degree, Microsoft and Novell. TeleTech's strategy is to aim for customer support contracts that involve products of high complexity because the company believes it can add more value with upscale services. TeleTech prefers to use highly skilled agents working on complex incoming customer support calls, so it sees technical support for the Internet as a large opportunity. As electronic commerce on the Web starts to gel, the company's services could evolve to include processing orders, implementing customer retention programs, providing order tracking services, and other commerce-related services.

Chapter 11: Glossary of Internet Advertising Terms

Summary

◆ As this new medium emerges, and as new business models and payment methods evolve, new sets of terminology are required to describe them. We have included this short glossary as an aid in understanding Internet ad jargon. Hope it helps. :-)

ad clicks The number of times a user "clicks" on an online ad, often measured as a function of time ("ad clicks per day").

ad click rate The number of ad clicks as a percentage of ad views, or, the number of times an ad is clicked on by users as a percentage of the number of times an ad was downloaded and viewed by users.

advertorial A print advertisement styled to resemble the editorial format and type face of the publication in which it runs.

ad views On the Internet, the number of times an online ad was downloaded by users, often measured as a function of time ("ad views per day"). The actual number of times the ad was seen by users may differ because of "caching" (which increases the real number of ad views) and browsers that view documents as text-only (which decreases the number of ad views).

affiliate A broadcast station bound to a contractual relationship with one or more networks to carry network-originated programs and commercial announcements.

affinity group People with a common interest. On the Internet, typically a subject-oriented mailing list, a newsgroup, or a conference on a Web site.

audience accumulation The net number of people (or homes) exposed to a medium during its duration; e.g., a half-hour broadcast program, or a magazine issue.

audience composition The demographic profile of a media audience.

audience turnover The average ratio of cumulative audience listening/viewing to the average audience listening/viewing.

average audience (AA) In broadcast, the average number of homes (or individuals) tuned to a given time segment of a program. In print media, the number of individuals who looked into an average issue of a publication and are considered "readers."

barter The exchange of goods and services without the use of cash. Usually the acquisition of media time or space by a media company in exchange for similar time/space in return.

basic cable A "basic" service agreement in which a subscriber pays a cable TV operator or system a monthly fee. Does not include "pay" services that might be offered by the cable operator.

cable TV Reception of TV signals via cable (wires) rather than over the air (i.e., via a TV antenna).

caching This phenomenon occurs when access providers or browsers store or buffer Web page data in a temporary location on their networks or in their disk space to speed access and reduce traffic. Reduces the number of measured page views at the original content site.

circulation In print media, the number of copies sold or distributed by a publication. In broadcast, the number of homes owning a TV/radio set within a station's coverage area. Or, in cable TV, the number of households that subscribe to cable services for a given network. In out-of-home media, the number of people passing a advertisement who have an opportunity to see it.

click-throughs same as **ad clicks**.

cost-per-rating-point (CPP) The cost of an advertising unit (e.g., a 30-second commercial) divided by the average rating of a specific demographic group (e.g., women, 18–49).

cost per thousand (CPM) The cost to deliver 1,000 impressions (associated with delivery of ad views on the Internet, and delivery to people or homes in traditional media).

cookie A persistent piece of information, stored on the user's local hard drive, that is keyed to a specific server (and even a file pathway or directory location at the server) and is passed back to the server as part of the transaction that takes place when the user's browser again crosses the specific server/path combination.

coverage The percentage of a population group covered by a medium. Commonly used with print media to describe an average issue's audience within defined demographic or purchasing groups. Akin to *rating*.

creative The name given the art/design within an advertisement.

cume (cumulative) Rating the reach of a radio or TV program or station, as opposed to the "average."

demography The study of the characteristics of population groups in terms of size, distribution, and vital statistics.

domain name The unique name that identifies an Internet site, such as "microsoft.com." A domain name always has two or more parts, separated by periods. A given server may have more than one domain name, but a given domain name points to only one machine.

duration time The length of time between two events, such as successive requests to one or more Web pages (page duration) or visits to a given Web site (inter-visit duration).

effective frequency The level of exposure frequency at which reach is deemed "effectively" delivered.

effective reach The percentage of a population group reached by a media schedule at a given level of frequency.

efficiency Generally refers to the relative costs of delivering media audiences. See *Cost-per-rating-point* and *Cost-per-thousand*.

frequency The number of times people (or homes) are exposed to an advertising message, an advertising campaign, or a specific media vehicle. Also, the period of issuance of a publication, e.g., daily, monthly.

frequency discount A rate discount allowed an advertiser that purchases a specific schedule within a specific period of time, e.g., six ads within one year.

frequency distribution The array of reach according to the level of frequency delivered to each group.

gross rating points (GRPs) The sum of all ratings delivered by a given list of media vehicles. Although synonymous with TRPs, GRPs generally refer to a "household" base. In out-of-home media, GRPs are synonymous with a *showing*.

hit Web-speak for any request for data from a Web page or file. Often used to compare popularity/traffic of a site in the context of getting so many "hits" during a given period. A common mistake is to equate hits with visits or page views. A single visit or page view is usually recorded as several hits, and depending on the browser, the page size, and other factors, the number of hits per page can vary widely.

homes using TV (HUT) The percentage of homes using (tuned in to) TV at a particular time.

HTML (hypertext markup language) A simple coding system used to format documents for viewing by Web clients. Web pages are written in this standard specification.

hyperlink See **link**.

hypertext Generally, any text on a Web page that contains "links" to other documents — words or phrases in a document that can be chosen by a user and which cause another document to be retrieved or displayed.

impressions The gross sum of all media exposures (number of people or homes) without regard to duplication.

inventory Normally defined as the quantity of goods or materials on hand. On the Internet, a site's inventory is the number of page views it will deliver in a given period of time, and is thus the amount of product that can be sold to advertisers.

link The path between two documents, which associates an object, such as a button or hypertext, on a Web page with another Web address. The hyperlink allows a user to point and click on an object and thereby "move" to the location associated with that object by loading the Web page at that address.

network A broadcast entity that provides programming and sells commercial time in programs aired nationally via affiliated or licensed local stations — e.g., ABC television network, ESPN cable network. On the Internet, an aggregator/broker of advertising inventory from many sites.

out-of-home media Those media meant to be consumed only outside of one's home, e.g., outdoor, transit, in-store media.

page An HTML (hypertext markup language) document that may contain text, images, and other online elements, such as Java applets and multimedia files. It may be statically or dynamically generated.

page view The number of times a page was downloaded by users, often measured as a function of time ("page views per day"). The actual number of times the page was seen by users may be higher because of "caching."

paid circulation Reported by the Audit Bureau of Circulation, a classification of subscriptions or purchases of a magazine or newspaper, based upon payment in accordance with standards set by the ABC.

penetration The percentage of people (or homes) within a defined universe that are physically able to be exposed to a medium.

psychographics Pertains to the identification of personality characteristics and attitudes that affect a person's lifestyle and purchasing behavior.

rating The percentage of a given population group consuming a medium at a particular moment. Generally used for broadcast media but can by applied to any medium. One rating point equals one percent of the potential viewing population.

reach The number of different homes/people exposed at least once to an impression (ad view, program, commercial, print page, etc.) across a stated period of time. Also called the cumulative or unduplicated audience.

session A series of consecutive visits made by a visitor to a series of Web sites.

share "Share of audience" is the percentage of HUT tuned to a particular program or station. "Share of market" is the percentage of total category volume (dollars, unit, etc.) accounted for by a brand. "Share of voice" is the percentage of advertising impressions generated by all brands in a category accounted for by a particular brand, but often also refers to share of media spending.

sponsorship The purchase of more than one commercial within a program, allowing advertisers to receive bonus time via billboards, or exclusivity of advertising within the brand's product category, or both.

spot Refers to the purchase of TV or radio commercial time on a market-by-market basis, as opposed to network (national) purchases. Also commonly used in lieu of "commercial announcement."

superstation An independent TV station whose signal is transmitted throughout the United States via satellite. Technically refers only to WTBS, but is also used for other stations.

syndication In broadcasting, when a program is carried on selected stations which may or may not air at the same time in all markets. In newspapers, when an independently written column or feature is carried by many newspapers (e.g., "Dear Abby"). In magazines, a centrally written or published section carried by newspapers, generally in the Sunday edition (e.g., *Parade)*.

unique users The number of unique individuals who visit a site within a specific period of time. With today's technology, this number can only be calculated with some form of user registration or identification.

universe The total population within a defined demographic, psychographic, or product consumption segment against which media audiences are calculated to determine ratings, coverage, reach, etc.

URL (uniform [or universal] resource locator) The URL provides information on the protocol, the system, and the file name, so that the user's system can find a particular document on the Internet. An example of a URL is http://www.sholink.com/, which indicates that "hypertext transfer protocol" is the protocol and that the information is located on a system named "www.sholink.com," which is the Sholink Corporation's Web server. This example does not show a particular file name (such as index.htm), since most Web servers are set up to point to a home page if no file name is used.

viewers per 1,000 households The number of people within a specific population group tuned to a TV program in each 1,000 viewing households.

visit A sequence of hits made by one user at a site. It is important to understand that Internet technology does not maintain a continuous "connection" (like a radio signal) to a site. The data is sent in packets. If a user makes no request for data from the site during a predetermined (and discretionary) period of time, the user's next hit would constitute a new visit. This length of time is known as the "time-out" period. While this interval is different for each site, I/PRO currently uses 30 minutes for all sites for purposes of comparability.

volume discount The price discount offered advertisers who purchase a certain amount of volume from the medium — e.g., pages or dollar amount in magazines.

wearout A level of frequency, or a point in time, when an advertising message loses its ability to effectively communicate.

Web page An HTML (hypertext markup language) document on the Web, usually one of many that together make up a Web site.

Web server A system capable of continuous access to the Internet (or an internal network) through retrieving and displaying documents and files via hypertext transfer protocol (http).

Web site The virtual location for an organization's presence on the Worldwide Web, usually made up of several Web pages and a single home page designated by a unique URL.

Worldwide Web The mechanism originally developed by Tim Berners-Lee for CERN physicists to be able to share documents via the Internet. The Web allows computer users to access information across systems around the world using URLs (uniform resource locators) to identify files and systems and hypertext links to move between files on the same or different systems.

Chapter 12: A Time Line of Internet Advertising 1993–96*

Summary

◆ On the second anniversary of the first Web advertisement on *HotWired* (Halloween 1994), *Advertising Age* printed a time line of the history of Internet Advertising. It is reproduced here, with permission, along with some early Internet advertising/marketing events.

* *All data from October 1994 forward is reprinted with permission from the October 21, 1996, issue of Advertising Age. Copyright, Crain Communications Inc. 1996.*

November 1993

- **GNN** introduces advertising to the Internet at its launch. Some early advertisers included: Lonely Planet, Mountain Travel Sobek, The Company Corporation, Lens Crafters, and Nordic Track.

September 1994

- **GNN** introduced GNN Direct, offering the sale of merchandise via the Internet. Initial merchants included Nolo Press, Thanksgiving Coffee, American Youth Hostels, and O'Reilly Books.

October 1994

- **HotWired** site launches with ads from AT&T, Sprint, MCI, Volvo and others.

- Mecklermedia launches, then pulls, **MecklerWeb** service.

- Time Warner opens **Pathfinder** service with test ads from AT&T; Ziff Davis launches **ZD Net** on the Web.

- **Hotel chains** Hampton Inn, Embassy Suites and Hyatt Hotels Corp. open on the Web.

November 1994

- Only 3 million U.S. households have access to the **Internet**, Find/SVP reports.

- The **NCSA Mosaic** What's New Page on the Net says it's seeking sponsors.

- CMP Publications launches **TechWeb** with ads from AT&T, MCI and Tandem Computers.

- Mosaic Communications Corp. changes its name to **Netscape Communications Corp**.

January 1995

- Prodigy becomes the first online service to offer Internet access to its subscribers.

- Five advertisers — MCI, Saturn, Timex, Jim Beam and AirWalk — join Vibe Online in deals ranging in price from $40,000 for 6 months.

February 1995

- Procter & Gamble names **Grey Interactive** its interactive agency of record.

- **CBS** launches its Web site.

- **ESPN** Starts pitching advertisers on $1 million charter sponsorship of its upcoming Web site and other online properties.

March 1995

- **Yahoo!**, a Web directory created by two Stanford grad students, goes commercial.

- **Ragu** becomes one of the first package-good marketers to open a Web site

- AT&T picks **Modem Media** to be its interactive agency of record.

April 1995

- Time Warner's **Pathfinder** signs first advertisers, AT&T and Saturn. Ads cost $30,000 per quarter. **ZD Net** also starts taking ads.

- **Internet Profiles Corp.** and NetCount launch competing Web tracking services.

- ESPN launches **ESPNET SportsZone** via Starwave Corp.

- **Interactive Traffic** opens to help marketers with online media planning.

- Interactive Imaginations launches **Riddler**, a gaming site that incorporates marketer sites as clues.

May 1995

- Conde Nast forms **CondeNet** new-media unit.

- Sun introduces **Java** programming language.

July 1995

- **Forrester Research** reports that online ad spending will total $37 million for the year.

- InfoSeek and Netscape shift to a **CPM model** to sell Web Ads. HotWired, Pathfinder, and ZD Net resist the change.

- **Agency Poppe Tyson** starts selling ad space for Netscape, *Playboy,* and others.

August 1995

- Microsoft launches **MSN** online service.

- Kraft and P&G register a combined **184 domain names** on the Net, ranging from hotdogconstructionco.com to luvs.com.

September 1995

- CNN launches a Web site; **Hachette** opens Web versions of *Elle* and *Car and Driver*.

- ESPNET SportsZone, one of the Web's most expensive sites at $100,000 per quarter, signs **eight advertisers** to contracts totaling more than $1 million.

October 1995

- **Audit Bureau of Circulations** starts testing audits of Web sites.

- **Conde Net** nabs eight charter advertisers for Epicurious and *Conde Nast Traveler* Web sites, including AT&T, American Airlines, and Westin.

- Intel unveils **Intercast** technology to deliver Web content and TV programming simultaneously.

- Poppe Tyson spins off its Web ad sales unit as **DoubleClick.**

- Some **24 million** adults in the U.S. and Canada have access to the Internet, according to a report from CommerceNet and Nielsen Media Research.

January 1996

- Microsoft pays **$200,000** to sponsor the Super Bowl Web site.

- **The New York Times** launches on the Web with ads from $120,0000-per-year "partners" Toyota and Chemical Bank.

- NetGravity introduces the **AdServer** ad management system for web sites.

February 1996

- **Focalink** Communications introduces SmartBanner media planning services.

- **PointCast** launches an offline news and information network featuring animated ads.

March 1996

- Sony Corp. of America says it's seeking partners for its upcoming **Sony Station** Web site. Price: $500,000 to $1 million.

April 1996

- **Juno** Online Services launches a free, ad-supported e-mail service. **Freemark** Communications follows with a similar product.

May 1996

- Content developer **iVillage** nets $800,000 in ad commitments on an ad model that intermingles editorial with marketing.

- FocalLink Communications introduces **Market Match** Web media planning tool.

June 1996

- Microsoft zine *Slate* debuts on the Web.

- HotWired taps Levi's Dockers for one-year sponsorship of the Dream Jobs channel.

July 1996

- AT&T breaks its "intermercial" ad campaign featuring animated banners.

- Intelliquest reports that 35 million U.S. residents 16 and over accessed the Internet or online services in the past three months.

August 1996

- Poppe Tyson, boosted by Internet work, files for an **IPO.**

- Major sites agree to provide free content to users of **Microsoft's Web browser.**

- @Home Corp. starts to pitch marketers on the **@Home** high-speed online network.

September 1996

- **GM** doubles its Web site content to more than 38,000 pages, making it one of the largest marketer sites.

- **BackWeb Technologies** introduces a private online broadcast system, with GM as one of the first users.

October 1996

- CASIE issues proposed Web ad banner **guidelines.**

Chapter 13: Advertising Data

Table 13-1
U.S. Advertising Expenditures, 1935–95

	1935	1940	1945	1950	1955	1960	1965	1970	1975	1980	1985	1990	1995
Television										(Network Big Three)		9,383	10,263
Network*	–	–	–	85	550	820	1,237	1,658	2,306	5,130	8,060	9,863	11,600
Syndication	–	–	–	–	–	–	–	–	–	50	520	1,589	2,016
Spot (National)	–	–	–	31	260	527	892	1,234	1,623	3,269	6,004	7,788	9,119
Spot (Local)	–	–	–	55	225	280	386	704	1,334	2,967	5,714	7,856	9,985
Cable (National)	–	–	–	–	–	–	–	–	–	50	634	1,802	3,685
Cable (Local)	–	–	–	–	–	–	–	–	–	8	181	737	1,657
Total	–	–	–	171	1,035	1,627	2,515	3,569	5,263	11,474	21,113	29,635	38,062
Annual Growth Rate	--	--	--	--	27.9%	6.4%	9.9%	-0.4%	8.4%	13.0%	6.1%	8.2%	6.5%
Radio													
Network	63	113	198	196	84	43	60	56	83	183	365	482	480
Spot	15	42	92	136	134	222	275	371	436	779	1,335	1,635	1,959
Local	35	60	134	273	327	428	582	881	1,461	2,740	4,790	6,609	8,899
Total	113	215	424	605	545	693	917	1,308	1,980	3,702	6,490	8,726	11,338
Annual Growth Rate	--	16.8%	7.9%	6.0%	-2.5%	5.6%	8.4%	3.5%	7.8%	11.8%	11.6%	4.8%	7.7%
Newspapers													
National	148	161	203	518	712	778	784	891	1,109	1,963	3,352	3,867	3,996
Local	613	654	716	1,552	2,365	2,903	3,642	4,183	7,125	12,831	21,818	28,414	32,321
Total	761	815	919	2,070	3,077	3,681	4,426	5,704	8,234	14,794	25,170	32,281	36,317
Annual Growth Rate	--	2.8%	3.7%	8.3%	14.6%	4.4%	7.4%	-0.2%	5.0%	6.7%	7.0%	-0.3%	5.7%
Magazines													
Weeklies	54	103	188	261	397	525	610	617	612	1,418	2,297	2,864	3,347
Women's	51	49	97	129	161	184	269	301	368	782	1,294	1,713	2,236
Monthlies	25	34	59	88	133	200	282	374	485	949	1,564	2,226	2,997
Total	130	186	344	478	691	909	1,161	1,292	1,465	3,149	5,155	6,803	8,580
Annual Growth Rate	--	10.1%	12.8%	4.4%	9.9%	9.3%	8.1%	-3.9%	-2.6%	7.4%	4.5%	1.3%	8.4%
Farm Publications	10	19	32	58	72	66	71	62	74	130	186	215	283
Annual Growth Rate	--	11.8%	10.3%	5.5%	1.4%	-7.0%	7.6%	-3.1%	2.8%	8.3%	2.8%	1.4%	8.0%
Direct Mail	282	334	290	803	1,299	1,830	2,324	2,776	4,124	7,596	15,500	23,370	32,866
Annual Growth Rate	--	0.3%	-11.0%	6.2%	8.1%	8.4%	6.4%	4.0%	1.7%	14.2%	12.3%	6.5%	10.9%
Business Publications	51	76	204	251	446	609	671	740	919	1,674	2,375	2,875	3,559
Annual Growth Rate	--	10.1%	15.3%	1.2%	9.3%	7.0%	7.7%	-1.6%	2.1%	6.3%	4.6%	4.1%	6.0%
Outdoor													
National	23	34	50	96	130	137	120	154	220	364	610	640	701
Local	8	11	22	46	62	66	60	80	115	214	335	444	562
Total	31	45	72	142	192	203	180	234	335	578	945	1,084	1,263
Annual Growth Rate	--	2.3%	28.6%	8.4%	2.7%	5.2%	2.9%	9.9%	8.4%	7.0%	8.4%	-2.4%	8.2%
Yellow Pages													
National	–	–	–	–	–	–	–	–	–	–	695	1,132	1,410
Local	–	–	–	–	–	–	–	–	–	–	5,105	7,794	8,826
Total	–	–	–	–	–	–	–	–	–	–	5,800	8,926	10,236
Annual Growth Rate	--	--	--	--	--	--	--	--	--	--	18.4%	7.2%	4.2%
Miscellaneous													
National	168	225	327	608	1,002	1,364	1,745	2,126	2,841	5,483	8,604	11,608	15,041
Local	174	195	228	514	791	978	1,240	1,722	2,665	4,975	3,503	4,347	5,191
Total	342	420	555	1,122	1,793	2,342	2,985	3,848	5,506	10,458	12,107	15,955	20,232
Annual Growth Rate	--	4.7%	5.1%	9.8%	12.1%	6.2%	7.6%	0.9%	4.9%	50.8%	3.7%	4.5%	7.5%
National Total	890	1,190	1,740	3,260	5,380	7,305	9,340	11,350	15,200	29,820	53,395	73,669	95,295
Annual Growth Rate	--	6.3%	5.1%	9.0%	11.6%	20.6%	7.1%	-0.4%	3.4%	11.7%	7.4%	6.4%	8.0%
Local Total	830	920	1,100	2,440	3,770	4,655	4,910	8,200	12,700	23,735	41,446	56,201	67,441
Annual Growth Rate	--	3.4%	5.3%	9.9%	13.2%	5.4%	8.4%	2.2%	6.5%	7.5%	8.6%	1.9%	6.4%
Grand Total	1,720	2,110	2,840	5,700	9,150	11,960	15,250	19,550	27,900	53,555	94,841	129,870	162,736
Annual Growth Rate	--	5.0%	5.2%	9.4%	12.3%	6.1%	7.8%	0.7%	4.8%	9.8%	7.9%	4.4%	7.4%
Nominal GDP	–	–	–	–	–	527	719	1,036	1,631	2,784	4,181	5,744	7,254
Annual Growth Rate	--	--	--	--	--	3.8%	8.5%	5.4%	8.9%	8.9%	7.1%	5.6%	4.6%

Sources: McCann-Erickson Inc., Paul Kagan Associates, Morgan Stanley Technology Research.
*Note: Fox reported as Syndication 1986-91; effective 1990 reported as Network.
Note: These figures represent advertising expenditures; they include production costs, agencies fees, talent costs, etc.

Table 13-2

U.S. Advertising Expenditures, 1985–95

	1985	1986	1987	1988	1989	1990	1991	1992	1993	1994	1995
Television			(Network Big Three)			9,383	8,933	9,549	9,369	9,959	10,263
Network*	8,060	8,342	8,500	9,172	9,110	9,863	9,533	10,249	10,209	10,942	11,600
Syndication	520	600	762	901	1,288	1,589	1,853	1,370	1,576	1,734	2,016
Spot (National)	6,004	6,570	6,846	7,147	7,354	7,788	7,110	7,551	7,800	8,993	9,119
Spot (Local)	5,714	6,514	6,833	7,270	7,612	7,856	7,565	8,079	8,435	9,464	9,985
Cable (National)	634	748	891	1,135	1,461	1,802	2,046	2,339	2,726	3,221	3,685
Cable (Local)	181	217	301	426	570	737	828	958	1,142	1,373	1,657
Total	21,113	22,991	24,133	26,051	27,395	29,635	28,935	30,546	31,888	35,727	38,062
Annual Growth Rate	*6.1%*	*8.9%*	*5.0%*	*7.9%*	*5.2%*	*8.2%*	*-2.4%*	*5.6%*	*4.4%*	*12.0%*	*6.5%*
Radio											
Network	365	423	413	425	476	482	490	424	458	463	480
Spot	1,335	1,348	1,330	1,418	1,547	1,635	1,575	1,505	1,657	1,902	1,959
Local	4,790	5,178	5,463	5,955	6,300	6,609	6,411	6,725	7,342	8,164	8,899
Total	6,490	6,949	7,206	7,798	8,323	8,726	8,476	8,654	9,457	10,529	11,338
Annual Growth Rate	*11.6%*	*7.1%*	*3.7%*	*8.2%*	*6.7%*	*4.8%*	*-2.9%*	*2.1%*	*9.3%*	*11.3%*	*7.7%*
Newspapers											
National	3,352	3,376	3,494	3,586	3,720	3,867	3,685	3,602	3,620	3,906	3,996
Local	21,818	23,614	25,918	27,611	28,648	28,414	26,724	27,135	28,405	30,450	32,321
Total	25,170	26,990	29,412	31,197	32,368	32,281	30,409	30,737	32,025	34,356	36,317
Annual Growth Rate	*7.0%*	*7.2%*	*9.0%*	*6.1%*	*3.8%*	*-0.3%*	*-5.8%*	*1.1%*	*4.2%*	*7.3%*	*5.7%*
Magazines											
Weeklies	2,297	2,327	2,445	2,646	2,813	2,864	2,670	2,739	2,850	3,140	3,347
Women's	1,294	1,376	1,417	1,504	1,710	1,713	1,671	1,853	2,009	2,106	2,236
Monthlies	1,564	1,614	1,745	1,922	2,193	2,226	2,183	2,408	2,498	2,670	2,997
Total	5,155	5,317	5,607	6,072	6,716	6,803	6,524	7,000	7,357	7,916	8,580
Annual Growth Rate	*4.5%*	*3.1%*	*5.5%*	*8.3%*	*10.6%*	*1.3%*	*-4.1%*	*7.3%*	*5.1%*	*7.6%*	*8.4%*
Farm Publications	186	192	196	196	212	215	215	231	243	262	283
Annual Growth Rate	*2.8%*	*3.2%*	*2.1%*	*0.0%*	*8.2%*	*1.4%*	*0.0%*	*7.4%*	*5.2%*	*7.8%*	*8.0%*
Direct Mail	15,500	17,145	19,111	21,215	21,945	23,370	24,460	25,931	27,266	29,638	32,866
Annual Growth Rate	*12.3%*	*10.6%*	*11.5%*	*11.0%*	*3.4%*	*6.5%*	*4.7%*	*6.0%*	*5.1%*	*8.7%*	*10.9%*
Business Publications	2,375	2,382	2,458	2,610	2,763	2,875	2,882	3,090	3,260	3,358	3,559
Annual Growth Rate	*4.6%*	*0.3%*	*3.2%*	*6.2%*	*5.9%*	*4.1%*	*0.2%*	*7.2%*	*5.5%*	*3.0%*	*6.0%*
Outdoor											
National	610	600	615	628	653	640	637	610	605	648	701
Local	335	385	410	436	458	444	440	421	485	519	562
Total	945	985	1,025	1,064	1,111	1,084	1,077	1,031	1,090	1,167	1,263
Annual Growth Rate	*8.4%*	*4.2%*	*4.1%*	*3.8%*	*4.4%*	*-2.4%*	*-0.6%*	*-4.3%*	*5.7%*	*7.1%*	*8.2%*
Yellow Pages											
National	695	759	830	944	1,011	1,132	1,162	1,188	1,230	1,314	1,410
Local	5,105	5,741	6,470	6,837	7,319	7,794	8,020	8,132	8,287	8,511	8,826
Total	5,800	6,500	7,300	7,781	8,330	8,926	9,182	9,320	9,517	9,825	10,236
Annual Growth Rate	*18.4%*	*12.1%*	*12.3%*	*6.6%*	*7.1%*	*7.2%*	*2.9%*	*1.5%*	*2.1%*	*3.2%*	*4.2%*
Miscellaneous											
National	8,604	9,120	9,703	10,454	10,998	11,608	11,588	12,124	12,759	13,928	15,041
Local	3,503	3,679	3,728	4,077	4,273	4,347	4,185	4,303	4,522	4,884	5,191
Total	12,107	12,799	13,431	14,531	15,271	15,955	15,773	16,427	17,281	18,812	20,232
Annual Growth Rate	*3.7%*	*5.7%*	*4.9%*	*8.2%*	*5.1%*	*4.5%*	*-1.1%*	*4.1%*	*5.2%*	*8.9%*	*7.5%*
National Total	53,395	56,922	60,756	65,903	69,254	73,669	73,760	77,214	80,766	88,225	95,295
Annual Growth Rate	*7.4%*	*6.6%*	*6.7%*	*8.5%*	*5.1%*	*6.4%*	*0.1%*	*4.7%*	*4.6%*	*9.2%*	*8.0%*
Local Total	41,446	45,328	49,123	52,612	55,180	56,201	54,173	55,753	58,618	63,365	67,441
Annual Growth Rate	*8.6%*	*9.4%*	*8.4%*	*7.1%*	*4.9%*	*1.9%*	*-3.6%*	*2.9%*	*5.1%*	*8.1%*	*6.4%*
Grand Total	94,841	102,250	109,879	118,515	124,434	129,870	127,933	132,967	139,384	151,590	162,736
Annual Growth Rate	*7.9%*	*7.8%*	*7.5%*	*7.9%*	*5.0%*	*4.4%*	*-1.5%*	*3.9%*	*4.8%*	*8.8%*	*7.4%*
Nominal GDP	4,181	4,422	4,692	5,050	5,439	5,744	5,917	6,244	6,553	6,936	7,254
Annual Growth Rate	*7.1%*	*5.8%*	*6.1%*	*7.6%*	*7.7%*	*5.6%*	*3.0%*	*5.5%*	*4.9%*	*5.8%*	*4.6%*

Sources: McCann-Erickson Inc., Paul Kagan Associates, Morgan Stanley Technology Research.
*Note: Fox reported as Syndication 1986-91; effective 1990 reported as Network.
Note: These figures represent advertising expenditures; they include production costs, agencies fees, talent costs, etc.

Table 13-3
20 Largest Advertising Organizations in the World

1995 Rank	Company	Headquarters	Revenue ($MM)
1	WPP Group	London	$3,130
2	Omnicom Group	New York	2,577
3	Interpublic Group of Companies	New York	2,337
4	Dentsu	Tokyo	1,999
5	Cordiant	London	1,378
6	Young & Rubicam	New York	1,198
7	Hakuhodo	Tokyo	959
8	Havas Advertising	Levallois-Perret, France	909
9	Grey Advertising	New York	897
10	Leo Burnett Co.	Chicago	804
11	True North Communications	Chicago	759
12	D'Arcy Masius Benton & Bowles	New York	646
13	Publicis Communication	Paris	606
14	Bozell, Jacobs, Kenyon & Eckhardt	New York	405
15	BDDP Group	Paris	279
16	Asatsu Inc.	Tokyo	254
17	Tokyu Agency	Tokyo	239
18	Daiko Advertising	Tokyo	211
19	Dai-Ichi Kikaku Co.	Tokyo	168
20	Dentsu, Young & Rubicam Partnerships	Tokyo/Singapore	161

Source: Advertising Age; January 22, 1996.

Table 13-4

Top 50 Megabrands in U.S. by 1995 Ad Spending

Rank	Brand, Product, or Service	Company	Total ($000s)
1	AT&T telephone services	AT&T Corp.	$673,387
2	Ford cars & trucks	Ford Motor Co.	564,866
3	Sears stores	Sears, Roebuck & Co.	540,053
4	McDonald's restaurants	McDonalds Corp.	490,550
5	Kellogg breakfast foods	Kellogg Co.	488,205
6	Chevrolet cars & trucks	General Motors Corp.	477,600
7	Dodge cars & trucks	Chrysler Corp.	414,531
8	Toyota cars & trucks	Toyota Motor Co.	384,074
9	MCI telephone services	MCI Communications Corp.	320,956
10	Warner Bros. movies	Time Warner	294,004
11	Circuit City electronic stores	Circuit City Stores	291,558
12	Columbia entertainment	Sony Corp.	289,666
13	Nissan cars & trucks	Nissan Motor Co.	281,968
14	Honda cars & trucks	Honda Motor Co.	278,827
15	Disney entertainment	Walt Disney Co.	269,495
16	J.C. Penney stores	J.C. Penney Co.	268,749
17	**IBM computers**	**IBM Corp.**	**257,912**
18	General Mills cereals	General Mills	253,071
19	Burger King restaurants	Grand Metropolitan	251,933
20	Mazda cars & trucks	Mazda Motor Corp.	241,283
21	Chrysler cars & trucks	Chrysler Corp.	240,129
22	Paramount entertainment	Viacom	221,327
23	Tylenol remedies	Johnson & Johnson	213,730
24	Sprint telephone services.	Sprint Corp.	212,903
25	American Express financial services.	American Express Co.	207,380
26	Universal Studios movies	Seagram Co.	206,861
27	Budweiser beers	Anheuser-Busch Cos.	201,017
28	Buick cars	General Motors Corp.	193,323
29	Kraft foods	Phillip Morris Cos.	192,192
30	Post cereals	Phillip Morris Cos.	173,072
31	Buena Vista movies	Walt Disney Co.	172,073
32	Taco Bell restaurants	PepsiCo	172,029
33	Saturn cars	General Motors Corp.	169,812
34	Kmart stores	Kmart Corp	167,573
35	Pizza Hut restaurants	PepsiCo	164,359
36	Miller beers	Phillip Morris Cos.	161,544
37	Wendy's restaurants	Wendys International	161,185
38	Visa credit cards	Visa International	154,596
39	KFC restaurants	PepsiCo	149,397
40	Mercury cars & trucks	Ford Motor Co.	149,386
41	**Microsoft software**	**Microsoft Corp.**	**147,733**
42	Macy's stores	Federated Department Stores	144,445
43	Nike footwear & apparel	Nike Inc.	142,648
44	Wal-Mart stores	Wal-Mart Stores	141,412
45	Jeep vehicles	Chrysler Corp.	141,385
46	L'Oreal cosmetics	L'Oreal	137,362
47	20th Century Fox movies	News Corp.	137,246
48	Cadillac cars	General Motors Corp.	135,595
49	Pontiac cars & trucks	General Motors Corp.	134,278
50	Mitsubishi cars & trucks	Mitsubishi Motor Corp.	130,723

Note: Sources for ad spending include consumer magazines; local and national papers; outdoor; network, spot, syndicated, and cable TV; and national spot and network radio.

Source: Advertising Age, May 6, 1996.

Table 13-5

Top Online Services by Subscriptions

Service	Parent Company	Subscribers (as of 6/30/96)
Consumer		
America Online	America Online	6,000,000
CompuServe Information Service	CompuServe Inc.	5,000,000
Prodigy	Prodigy Services Co.	*1,400,000
Microsoft Network	Microsoft Corp.	1,200,000
ZD Net	Ziff-Davis Interactive	275,000
TIP, Billboard, CSN, AIA, Schwab	Telescan Inc.	200,000
CRIS, BBS Direct	Concentric Network Corp.	120,000
Wow! (1)	CompuServe Inc.	70,000
The ImagiNation Network (2)	AT&T	65,000
Delphi	Delphi Internet Services Corp.	50,000
Business/Professional		
LEXIS-NEXIS	Reed Elsevier	762,000
Dow Jones News/Retrieval	Dow Jones Information Services	240,000
TRW Information Services	Bain Capital and Thomas H. Lee	205,000
Dialog Worldwide	Knight-Ridder Information	200,000
First!, Heads Up, iNews	Individual Inc.	**175,000
D & B Information Services N.A.	Dun & Bradstreet Corp.	143,000
MEDLARS	National Library of Medicine	125,043
DowVision	Dow Jones & Co.	115,000
Physicians' Online	Physicians' Online Inc.	110,000
NewsEDGE	Desktop Data	98,000
		Terminals
Financial		
Reuters real-time data services	Reuters Holdings plc	345,000
DJ News Services (Broadtape)	Dow Jones Information Services	205,000
Telerate	Telerate Inc.	99,000
Brokerage Services	Automatic Data Processing	96,000
DTN AgDaily, DTNiron, DTNStant, DTN Produce, DTN Weather Center	Data Transmission Network Corp.	79,000
S & P MarketScope	McGraw-Hill/Standard & Poor's	74,800
The Bloomberg	Bloomberg Financial	62,000
ILX	Thomson Financial Services	60,000
Knight-Ridder Financial	Global Financial Information Corp.	50,000
Signal, QuoTrek, SporTRAX	Data Broadcasting Corp.	35,000

*Figure is for households.
**Figure includes lower-priced, ad-supported services.
Source: Electronic Information Report; July 12, 1996, SIMBA Information Inc., Stamford, CT (203-358-9900).
(1) CompuServe announced in November that it will discontinue Wow! on January 31, 1997.
(2) Now owned by America Online.

Table 13-6
Top 20 Cable Operators in the U.S. by Subscription

Rank	Company	Headquarters	Basic Subscriptions
1	Tele-Communications Inc.	Englewood, CO	12,494,000
2	Time-Warner Cable	Stamford, CT	11,700,000
3	Continental Cablevision	Boston	4,200,000
4	Comcast	Philadelphia	3,600,000
5	Cox Communications Inc.	Atlanta	3,282,080
6	Cablevision Systems Corp.	Woodbury, NY	1,915,000
7	Adelphia Communications	Coudersport, PA	1,651,850
8	Jones Intercable	Englewood, CO	1,476,000
9	Marcus Cable	Dallas	1,245,259
10	Viacom Cable	Pleasanton, CA	1,157,600
11	Century Communications	New Canaan, CT	1,100,000
12	Falcon Cable	Los Angeles	1,085,513
13	Charter Communications	St. Louis	900,000
14	Scripps-Howard Cable	Cincinnati	804,464
15	TKR Cable	Warren, NJ	750,121
16	Prime Cable	Austin	657,508
17	InterMedia Partners	San Francisco	571,000
18	Lenfest Group	Pottstown, PA	563,909
19	TCA Cable TV	Tyler, TX	549,000
20	Post-Newsweek Cable	Phoenix	542,000

Source: Cablevision; April 29, 1996.

Table 13-7
Top 25 Television Groups in the U.S. by Market Coverage

Rank	Group	Headquarters	% Coverage of 95MM U.S. TV Homes	No. of Stations
1	Westinghouse/CBS	New York	31	14
2	Tribune (including Renaissance*)	Chicago	25	16
3	NBC	New York	25	11
4	Disney/ABC	New York	24	10
5	Fox	Los Angeles	22	12
6	Silver King	St. Petersburg, FL	20	16
7	Paxson Communications	West Palm Beach, FL	18	16
8	Chris Craft/BHC/United Television	New York	18	8
9	Gannett	Arlington, VA	14	15
10	Univision	New York	13	11
11	New World	Atlanta	13	11
12	Telemundo	Hialeah, FL	10	8
13	Viacom (Paramount)	Los Angeles	10	12
14	Young Broadcasting	New York	9	13
15	Sinclair Broadcasting	Baltimore	9	22
16	Scripps-Howard	Cincinnati	8	9
17	A.H. Belo	Dallas	8	7
18	Cox Broadcasting	Atlanta	8	7
19	Hearst	New York	7	7
20	Post-Newsweek	Hartford, CT	7	6
21	LIN Television	Providence, RI	6	9
22	Providence Journal	Providence, RI	5	11
23	Pulitzer	St. Louis	5	10
24	Ellis Acquisitions/Raycom Media	Atlanta	4	22
25	Allbritton Communications	Washington	4	8

* Acquisition pending FCC and shareholders' approval.
Source: Broadcasting & Cable; July 8, 1996.

Table 13-8
Top 20 Radio Groups in the U.S. by Audience

Rank	Company	City	Listeners	No. of Stations
1	CBS/Group W/Infinity	New York	2,568,050	82
2	Clear Channel Communications Inc./ Radio Equity Partners/US Radio/Heftel	San Antonio	1,011,400	102
3	Evergreen Media Corp.	Irving, TX	815,500	35
4	Disney/ABC	New York	734,400	21
5	Chancellor Broadcasting Co.	Dallas	618,000	39
6	Jacor/Noble/Citicasters	Cincinnati	556,300	51
7	American Radio Systems Corp.	Boston	546,700	57
8	Emmis Broadcasting Corp.	Indianapolis	527,400	8
9	Cox Communications Inc.	Atlanta	519,500	38
10	SFX Broadcasting Inc./Multi-Market Radio	Austin	480,000	59
11	Viacom	New York	423,400	13
12	EZ Communications Inc.	Fairfax, VA	340,000	23
13	Bonneville International Corp.	Salt Lake City	339,500	20
14	Spanish Broadcasting System Inc.	New York	316,600	9
15	Gannett Co. Inc.	Arlington, VA	274,800	11
16	Secret Communications LP	Cincinnati	248,900	13
17	Susquehanna Radio Corp.	York, PA	247,600	17
18	Nationwide Communications Inc.	Columbus, OH	239,300	15
19	Greater Media Inc.	East Brunswick, NJ	206,200	13
20	Sinclair Broadcasting Group Inc./River City	Baltimore	201,800	33

Source: Broadcasting & Cable; July 8, 1996.

Table 13-9
10 Magazine Ad Page Leaders in the U.S.

Rank	Magazine	Parent Company	Pages
1	*PC Magazine*	Ziff-Davis Publishing Company	6,633
2	*Forbes*	Forbes, Inc.	4,542
3	*Business Week*	The McGraw-Hill Companies, Inc.	3,816
4	*People*	Time Inc.	3,328
5	*TV Guide*	NewsCorp. (The News Corporation Limited)	3,229
6	*Fortune*	Time, Inc.	3,328
7	*PC Computing*	Ziff-Davis Publishing Company	2,994
8	*Bride's & Your New Home*	Advance Publications, Inc.	2,931
9	*The Economist*	The Economist Group	2,851
10	*Modern Bride*	K-III Communications Corporation	2,734

Source: Advertising Age; January 22, 1996.

Chapter 14: Rate Card Data

◆ We have collected rate-card data from several sites to show how different publishers go about packaging and pricing their product.

CNET   (www.cnet.com)

The computer network on-air and online interactive showcase for computers, multimedia, and digital technologies

CNET online serves 12MM pages of original content each month
830,000+ members
Average response rates across all advertising banners range between 3% and 4%.
Well-developed and executed banner campaigns have generated response rates of over 25%
All rates are gross and are based on a three-month minimum contract
Premium ad rates include, but are not limited to the following technologies: Java, Shockwave, server-push, Real Audio
Premium ad rates for SHAREWARE.COM, DOWNLOAD.COM, and NEWS.COM are calculated using a 15% markup

CNET online
$15,000/month per 200K impressions
$28,500/month per 400K impressions
$38,475/month per 600Kimpressions
$57,873/month per 1MM impressions

Premium Program for CNET online
$17,250/month per 200K impressions
$32,775/month per 400K impressions
$44,246/month per 600K impressions
$56,045/month per 800K impressions
$66,554/month per 1MM impressions

SHAREWARE.COM/DOWNLOAD.COM
$15,000/month per 500K impressions
$28,500/month per 1MM impressions
$38,475/month per 1.5 MM impressions

NEWS.COM
$15,000/month per 150K impressions
$28,500/month per 300K impressions
$38,475/month per 450K impressions

ESPNET SportsZone   (espnet.sportszone.com)

A full sponsorship package on ESPNET has three components:

1) A sponsorship rotation across a minimum of 1,000 non-franchise pages
2) A targeted sport rotation
3) A listing in the Sponsor Index

Traffic:
110MM qualified pages views/week
19MM HTML pages/week
An average of 2.5 MM visits/week
An average of 11.75 MM visits/month

Sponsorship (Rates) of One Sport Rotation:
One Month: $25K per 1MM guaranteed impressions
Three Months: $72K per 1MM guaranteed impressions each month

Full Sponsorship General Rotation:
One Month: $15K per 500K impressions
Three Months: $43K per 500K impressions each month

GeoCities   (www.geocities.com)

A builder and operator for themed, virtual communities on the Web where individuals, businesses, and advertisers interact.

Average CPM $30

Traffic:
15 MM+ visits per/month
70 MM page views/month

Rates:	**Cost per month:**
Platinum	$15,000/month per 500K impressions
Gold	$10,500/month per 350K impressions
Silver	$8,750/month per 250K impressions
Targeted	$3,500/month per 100K impressions
Custom activities and events	$1MM plus

Happy Puppy (happypuppy.com)

Traffic:
1.7 MM visits/month
An average of 70K visits/day

Open CPM rate is $30
Inventory sold from 100K to 1.5MM per month, in increments of 100K impressions

Customized advertising programs are offered

HotWired   (www.hotwired.com)

Online cyberstation whose editorial content is developed entirely for this medium

400K+ registered subscribers
18% of readers request information from advertisers
34% bookmark advertiser's home page

HotWired guarantees 100K page views
with a combination of banners in top
level and content level areas.

Rates:
$15,000/month per 100K impressions

International Data Group (IDG)   (www.idg.com)

Information specified is for PC World Online

Sites include:
*Computerworld, Infoworld,
Macworld, PC World, NetworkWorld*

Traffic:
4MM page views/month

CPM Range $40-70

Volume Sponsor Blocks:
$18,240/Quarter for 2MM impressions
$14,535/Quarter for 1.5MM impressions
$10,260/Quarter for 1MM impressions
$5,700/Quarter for < 500K impressions

Gross Rates:
$58,800/Quarter for 1MM impressions
$43,890/Quarter for 750K impressions
$30,590/Quarter for 500K impressions
$15,960/Quarter for 250K impressions
$6,650/Quarter for < 100K impressions

Lycos   (www.lycos.com)

Navigational tool and search engine

Traffic:
5MM page views/day

Rates:
$6K/month for 200K impressions
$12K/month for 500K impressions
$20K/month for 1MM impressions
$1,750 for Quick-start 60K impressions

Home Page Sponsored Button:
$128K/month per 14MM impressions
Targeted Domain: $32-40 CPM

Target Country or Company:
$8K/month for 200K impressions
$18K/month for 500K impressions
$32K/month for 1MM impression

CPM Range $20-30

Nando Times   (www.4nando.net)

News & Observer of Raleigh, N.C.

Traffic:
Approximately 7MM hits/week

Rates:

General (Run of Server)	$26-29 CPM
Nando Times (ROS)	$30-38 CPM
Sports Server (ROS)	$27-34 CPM
Entertainment (Special Section)	$34-42 CPM
Travel (Special Section)	$36-45 CPM
Business (Section)	$34-42 CPM

Netscape   (www.netscape.com)

Millions of Internet users begin each session on Netscape's home page
CPM Range $17-25

Total Coverage:
$46,000/month per 2.25MM impressions for
all pages in Platinum, Gold, or Silver

Fixed Pages $12,750/month

Platinum: $20,400/month for 1MM impressions
Gold: $17,000/month for 750K impressions
Silver: $12,750/month for 500K impressions
Banner Ads on Destinations: $8,500/month for 500K impressions

Pages included with each program

Platinum	**Silver**
Net Search	Net Search, What's Cool?
Company & Products	Helper, Applications
Assistance, Netscape Products	Destinations
Windows Helper, Applications	Home Page, People

Gold	**Banner Ads on Destinations**
Net Search	Hardware/Software
What's New?	General & Technology News
About the Internet	Finance, Marketplace
Table of Contents	Sports, Travel
Yellow Pages	Entertainment

Pathfinder   (www.pathfinder.com)

Time Warner home page includes:

People Online,
Sports Illustrated SI online,
Money & Personal Finance,
CNNfn, Fortune Business & Investing
Entertainment Weekly Online,
Techwatch with The Netly News,
Fitness & thrive@

Traffic:
40MM hits/week
9MM page views/week

Rates:
$19 CPM — 1 month
$22 CPM — 2 months
$25 CPM — 3 months

CPM Range $19-25

Catalog Select — Promote a retail catalog
$0.50 per qualified lead

$1,000/months buys an ad directory link

United Media   (The Dilbert Zone)   (www.unitedmedia.com/comics/dilbert/)

An electronic comic strip featuring the trials and tribulations of a beleaguered corporate employee and his canine companion

Average CPM $70

Traffic:
778K+ unique visitors in October
3MM+ ad exposures delivered in October

Rates:
Masthead — $15,500/week for 310K impressions
Archive — $6,000/week for 120K impressions
Sunday Strips — $1,750/week for 35K impressions

USA Today Online   (www.usatoday.com)

Graphically oriented online paper

Eight-week minimum ad run
Headlines — ad located in front lead story on main section and next to lead story on special section front (section and special section fronts)
Ribbons — ad located in title of contents page (content pages)
Floating strips — ad located on bottom of middle of pages (all)
Sponsor units — button logo on chart of map (section fronts)

Traffic:
53 MM page views/month
8MM+ visitors/month
Average pages accessed per visit 6.5

Rates:
$30 CPM for any type and placement ad
Free overdeliveries ($0.03 per exposure)

Sampling of Ad buys

Fixed Graphics Space	8/96 Estimated Exposures
General Life Headline	534K exposures/month — $16K
Money Headline	900K exposures/month — $27

Floating Graphic Space	7/96 Estimated Exposures
General USA TODAY Index Page	734K exposures — $22K
Life Front Page	549K exposures — $16
Crossword Puzzle Page	86K exposures — $2.5K

Yahoo!   (www.yahoo.com)

Contains organized information on tens of thousands of computers linked to the Web

CPM Range $20-50

Rates:
$10-15K/month per 500K impressions
$5K/month per 100K impressions
$20 CPM — Run of Yahoo!
$20 CPM — Run of category
$30+ CPM Fixed category

Traffic:
1MM individual visitors/day

Search Keywords Rates:
Top 100 keywords are $60 CPM
10,000+ impressions/month $50 CPM
Up to 10,000/month $500 flat fee

"Weblaunch" rate for new Web sites:
$1,000/week to share rotation on 60-80K impressions
(All keywords are single words)

interactive promotions with giveaways — $50-75K

ZD Net   (www.zdnet.com)

Ziff Davis Publications — from the publisher of several computing publications and newspapers, including:

PC Magazine
PC Week
PC Computing
Computer Shopper
Windows Sources
MacUser & MacWeek
Inter@ctive Week
Computer Life
FamilyPC
Internet Life

CPM Range $40-74

Rates:

Full Coverage Package (quarterly)	$40,500/quarter for 750K impressions
Full Coverage Package	$13,750/month for 250K impressions
Business Package, Internet Package	$12,475/month for 167K impressions
PC Direct Package	$6,000/month for 100K impressions
WWW Consumer Package	$4,800/month for 50K impressions
Classifieds	$600/month for 40K text impressions

List of Companies, Sites, and Products Mentioned in this Report

<siteline>
@Home Networks
1-800-Flowers
20th Century Film
3Com
3DO Company
3M
Abbott Laboratories
Absolut Vodka
Accipiter
Accrue Software
Adobe Systems
Adolph Coors
Advertising Age
Aetna Health Plans
Agency.com
AltaVista
Amazon.com
America Online
American Airlines
American Express
American Marconi
Ameritech
Andersen Consulting
Anheuser-Busch
Apple Computer
Arbitron New Media
Arts & Entertainment Network
Ascend
Associated Press
Astra Merck
AT&T
Atlantic Records
Atlas Ventures
Audit Bureau of Circulation
Auto-by-Tel
Avalanche
BackWeb Technologies
Bank of America
Bankers Trust
BASF
Bay Networks
Bayer
BBC
BBN Planet
Bellcore
Berkeley Systems
Bertelsmann AG
BigBook
Black Entertainment Television
BMG
BMW
British Airways
BroadVision
BURST! Media
Cable News Business Channel
Cabletron Systems
Caddis International
Campbell Soup Company
Carillon Importers
Carnegie Hall
Cartoon Network
Cascade
CBS

Champion Records
Charles Schwab
Chatterbox
Chemical Bank
Chicago Cubs
Chicago Tribune Company
Cigar World
Cigna Healthcare
Cincinnati Bell, Inc.
Cisco
Citgo
CKS Group
Clear Channel Communications
Cleveland Press
Clinique
CMG Information
CMP Group
CNET
CNN
Coca-Cola
Colgate-Palmolive
Comedy Central
Commonwealth Network
CompuServe
Con Edison
Conde Net
Coopers & Lybrand
Cosmopolitan
Country Music Channel
Courtroom Television Network
Cox
CUC
CyberAtlas
CyberCash
CyberGold
Digital Planet
Dimension X
Direct Marketing Association
Discovery Channel
Dockers
DoubleClick
Dow Jones
Dreyfus
Dun & Bradstreet Enterprises
Dunkin' Donuts
Duracell
E! Entertainment Television
E-Trade
Electronic Media Research Council
Elektra
Eli Lilly
ESPN
Evergreen Media
Excite
F.A.O. Schwarz
Family Channel
Federal Express
Fidelity
Find/SVP
Firefly Network
Flip Chip Technologies
Focalink Communications
Ford Motor Co.
Forrester Research

Fox Film Corp.
Fox Network
Franklin Mint
Freeloader
Freemark Communications
Fujitsu
Gartner Group
General Electric
General Motors
Glaxo Wellcome
Godiva Chocolatier
GolfWeb
Grey Advertising
Group Cortex
GTE
GTG Entertainment
Harley-Davidson
Harvard Pilgrim Health Care
Hasbro International
HBO
Hearst Corporation
Hearst New Media
Hewlett-Packard
Hiram Walker
Hitachi
Hoechst Marion Roussel
Home Shopping Network
HotWired
Humana
i-traffic
I/PRO
IBM
ICon
IDC
IDG
IFusion Com
iGuide
Ikonik Interactive
Industry.Net
Infiniti
Infoseek
Intel
Intellicast
International Paper
Internet Link Exchange
Internet Media Services
Internet Shopping Network (ISN)
Internet.org
Interse
Intuit
io360
J. Walter Thompson
Juno Online
Jupiter Communications
Kaufmann
Kinko's
KMPG
Knight-Ridder
L'Oreal
Leap Group
Learning Channel
Leo Burnett
Levi Strauss
LifeSavers

List of Companies, Sites, and Products Mentioned in this Report *(continued)*

Lifetime Television
LLBean
Los Angeles Times
Lotus
Lucent Technologies
Lucky Strike
Lycos
Macromedia
Macy's
Magazine Publishers of America
Magellan
Margeotes, Fertitta, Donaher and Weiss
Marion Roussel
Matsushita
McCann-Erikson
McDonald's Corp.
McGraw-Hill Companies
MCI
Media Circus
Meredith
Merrill Lynch
Messner Vetere Berger McNamee
MetLife
Microsoft
Miller Genuine Draft
Montgomery Ward
Motley Fool
MSNBC
Music Television
Mutual Fund Center
Muzak's Enso Audio Imaging Division
Nashville Network
National Geographic
NBC
Net Carta Corporation
Net Radio
net.Genesis
NetCount
NetGravity
NetGuide
Netscape
Network Wizards
New Balance
New York Times
Newbury Comics
News Corp.
NFL Enterprises
Nickelodeon & Nick at Nite
Nielsen Media Research
Nike
Nissan
Northern Telecom
Nostalgia Television
Novo Media Group
NYNEX
Ogilvy & Mather
Olivetti Telemedia
Olympus America
ONSALE
Oracle
Organic Online
Oxford Health Plans
PAFET

Pathfinder
PC Financial Network
PC Meter
PC Week
Penthouse
Pepsi-Cola International
Pepsodent
Pfizer
Philip Morris
Philips Electronics
Physicians' Online
PointCast
Poppe Tyson
Potomac Interactive
Prevue Network
PrivNet, Inc.
Procter & Gamble
Prodigy
Prudential
PSINet
Putnam Investments
Quality Value Control
Quarterdeck
Quicken Financial Network (QFN)
Ralph Lauren
Razorfish
RCA
Reuters News
Rhone-Poulenc Rorer
Riddler
Rochester Telephone
Rohm and Haas
Rosenbluth International
RSA DATA Security
Saatchi & Saatchi
San Jose Mercury News
Saturn Motor Cars
Schraffts
Sci-Fi Network
Scudder
Sears Roebuck
Sega
SI Online
Simon & Schuster
SiteSpecific
Slate
Snapple
SOFTBANK
Sony Corp. of America
Sotheby's
Southern New England Telephone Co.
Sports Illustrated
SportsLine USA
Sprint
Star Magazine
Starwave
Stentor
Streams Online Media Development
Strong
Sun Microsystems
Sybase
T. Rowe Price
Tandem Computers

TBWA Chiat/Day
TCI
TeleTech Holdings
Teva Marion
Thompson-Sun Interactive
Time Inc.
Time Warner
Times Mirror Magazines
Toshiba
Toyota
Travel Channel
Travelocity
Tri-Star Pictures
Trident Capital
Tripod
Turner Broadcasting System
Turner Network Television
Twentieth Century
U.S. News and World Report
U.S. Robotics
UB Networks
United Media
United Parcel Service (UPS)
United Press
Universal
US Healthcare
US West Interactive
USA Network
USA Today
UUNet
Vanguard
VeriFone
Veronis, Suhler & Associates
VF Corp.
Viacom
Victor Talking Machine Co.
Video Hits One
Virgin Entertainment Group
Visa
Vivid Studios
Volvo
VWR Scientific Products
Wall Street Journal
Walt Disney Co.
Wanamaker
Warner Bros.
Washington Post
Weather Channel
WebCrawler
WebTrack Information Services
Westin
Westinghouse
WGN-TV
Whirlwind Interactive
Wiley Computing
Wired
Wired Magazine
Xylan
Yahoo!
ZD Net
Ziff-Davis Publishing

About the Author

Mary Meeker
Managing Director, Morgan Stanley
Internet/New Media & PC Software/Hardware
Equity Research Analyst

Mary Meeker joined Morgan Stanley in 1991 as the firm's PC Software/Hardware & Internet/New Media analyst. Earlier, she was a technology research analyst at Cowen and at Salomon Brothers. She received an MBA in finance from Cornell University in Ithaca, New York, and a B.A. from DePauw University in Greencastle, Indiana.

Mary's work has been recognized in various Wall Street analyst polls, including those conducted by *Institutional Investor*, *The Wall Street Journal*, *Forbes*, and *The Red Herring*. Her research coverage includes Internet/New Media companies such America Online, Broderbund, CNET, CUC, Electronic Arts, Maxis, Netscape, and TMP Worldwide. PC Software companies include Adobe, Intuit, Macromedia and Microsoft. In PC Hardware, she co-covers companies that include Apple, Compaq, Dell and SeaChange. Mary is coauthor of *The Internet Report* (HarperBusiness, 1996).